Advance praise for
AMERICAN DREAMER

"'I know what poverty looks like on the faces and in the eyes of someone who is starving; having seen this for the first time on that fateful family trip to Brazil when I was 17,' writes David T. Ives. There are life events and experiences that transform our views of the world, reshape our life trajectory, and cause us to re-examine the values of our parents and culture to find the values and beliefs that are our own. *American Dreamer* reveals the man of peace and advocate for the world's poor that Ives has become."
—*Lois Wright Morton, PhD Professor of Sociology, Iowa State University*

"David Ives not only provides us with a compelling, riveting story; he sketches a model of personal conduct and perspective that provides our species with a way forward. As David so clearly recognizes and this work so vividly articulates, we need love 'not just for some, but for everyone.'"
—*John Thomas, Professor of Law at the Quinnipiac University School of Law, Author of* Child Refugees: Exploring Public Health, Mental Health, Epigenetic, Neurological and Legal Needs

"David's memoirs are a heartwarming story of his journey to becoming a global citizen who has worked consistently and tirelessly for peace at home and around the world. His writing is authentic, unassuming, refreshing, optimistic, and humorous. He makes you laugh, cry, think, and, most importantly, feel. After reading his story, you will be moved to ask yourself with enthusiasm: 'How can I serve?'" —*Brian J. McAree, Vice President for Student Affairs at Ithaca College, Retired*

"A nomination for a Nobel Peace Prize is a huge worldwide honor. It indicates that the nominee has dedicated a lifetime to bringing about more peace and harmony to humankind. Professor David Ives has been nominated for this award four times! His recently published book, *American Dreamer*, does a wonderful job of laying out the groundwork for how this can happen to the son of a small town Presbyterian minister from Ohio!" —*Dave H. McKay, Historical Artisan*

AMERICAN DREAMER

Memoirs of a Peace Corps Volunteer
in Central America and Beyond

David Taylor Ives

Foreword by *Leymah Gbowee*
Introduction by *Muhammad Yunus, PhD*
Afterword by *Jose Zaglul, PhD*

EPIGRAPH BOOKS
RHINEBECK, NEW YORK

American Dreamer: Memoirs of a Peace Corps Volunteer in Central America and Beyond © 2020 by David Taylor Ives

Paperback ISBN 978-1-951937-07-2
Hardcover ISBN 978-1-951937-08-9

Library of Congress Control Number 2020901324

Cover photo by Maureen Gates: Sharper Image Photographic, Rhinebeck, NY
Book design by Colin Rolfe

Epigraph Books
22 East Market Street, Suite 304
Rhinebeck, NY 12572
(845) 876-4861
epigraphps.com

Dedicated to my mom, Dorothy Bowman Taylor Ives,
who motivated me to want to see what was around the bend and to
celebrate other cultures and countries—and helped me conquer polio;

to my brothers Don and Peter and my sister Carol, all of whom have
dedicated their lives to helping others. I appreciated more than words can
express their love and support throughout my life;

to my family—Barb, Taylor, Giana, Kelsey, and Heiner—
who accompanied me on many of my journeys
and are now having their own adventures;

to Dr. Jose Zaglul,
the visionary founding president of EARTH University,
who has worked to inspire literally thousands of students
to make this world a better place;

to Nobel Peace Prize Laureate Dr. Muhammad Yunus,
for his visionary leadership in founding the Grameen Bank,
which awards microloans to women to help them support
their families by starting small businesses;

to Nobel Peace Prize Laureate Leymah Gbowee,
founder and president of the Gbowee Peace Foundation Africa
and leader of Women of Liberia Mass Action for Peace,
for her courage in confronting and removing a dictator
to instill democracy in her home country of Liberia;

and

to the Rotary Club of Rhinebeck, New York,
for their imaginative and original leadership in their local community, our
Rotary District—and for their immensely creative work
serving others on a global basis.

In Memory of Betty Williams, the 1977 Nobel Peace Prize Laureate who passed on recently. She was known for her courage in fighting for peace in Northern Ireland and for her work with children and refugees from the Middle East and Africa. I loved her and admired her with all my heart!

The significance of a man is not in what he attains
but rather what he longs to attain.
—Kahlil Gibran

CONTENTS

Foreword by Leymah Gbowee   xi

Introduction by Muhammad Yunus, PhD   xv

Prologue   xix

I. PIERPONT, OHIO: DREAMS OF A YOUNG BOY   1

Chapter 1—Round One: Polio   3

Chapter 2—Growing Up in Pierpont   6

II. SOUTH OF THE BORDER: DREAMS OF A YOUNG MAN   13

Chapter 3—The Richness of Difference   15

Chapter 4—OSU vs. Vietnam   20

Chapter 5—My World Falls Apart   25

Chapter 6—Ohio State: A Great University   30

III. THE PEACE CORPS/COSTA RICA:
DREAMING THE IMPOSSIBLE   37

Chapter 7—In Pursuit of the Dream: Costa Rica-Bound   39

Chapter 8—Letters Home   41

Chapter 9—Los Chiles at Last:
Cucarachas and the Jue-Puta Daiquiri   52

Chapter 10—The CIA Nightmare   66

Chapter 11—Liberty Lost?   81

Chapter 12—Return to Los Chiles   89

Chapter 13—*Mucho Gusto!* 94

Chapter 14—Starting Over 109

Chapter 15— Democracy with Enthusiasm 113

Chapter 16— Puerto Jimenez 118

Chapter 17—Ugly Americans 127

Chapter 18—Ricardo 134

Chapter 19— Four "Thats" 137

Chapter 20—Machiavelli and Eight Pigs on a Leash 144

Chapter 21—Sandinistas in Los Chiles 150

Chapter 22—Raining Cats and Dogs and Snakes 153

Chapter 23—David and the Skiing Horse 158

Chapter 24— Patriotism vs. Communism 161

Chapter 25—Chico's News and Jerry's Dilemma 170

Chapter 26—Dad's Questions 181

Chapter 27—A Day in the Life of Puerto Jimenez 188

Chapter 28—A Painful Story on a Joyful Day 192

Chapter 29—The CIA Delusion 196

Chapter 30—Pondering the Last Two Years 205

III. BEYOND COSTA RICA: DREAMS OF STATESMEN 209

Chapter 31—Becoming a Global Citizen 211

Chapter 32—United in Service and Dedicated to Peace 215

Chapter 33—Teens Take On Conflict 219

Chapter 34—Round Two: Guillain-Barré Syndrome 225

Chapter 35—The Best Medicine: Laughter *and Children* 230

Chapter 36—Reverence for Life 234

Chapter 37—Round Three:
Parkinson's Disease—Chumbawamba! 243

Afterword by Jose Zaglul, PhD 245

Appendix 1: A Day of Unity, Peace and Prayer 249

Appendix 2: Suggested Reading 263

Acknowledgments 265

FOREWORD

When you win a significant prize, like a Nobel Peace Prize, you get to meet all kinds of interesting people: from activists in parts of the world that you have never visited before, to kings and queens, presidents and prime ministers, top-level CEOs, and people living in refugee camps. You might meet people on the worst day of their lives, the best day of their lives, or just an average day. The golden thread that links all of these experiences and people together across nationality, economic status, gender, race, and ability is our common humanity.

In the years that I have known David Ives, I am always impressed by how effortlessly he sees and centers the humanity of other people. As a global community we are fighting many vices, and it is easy to allow our negative experiences to influence how we see people and issues. Yet David wrestles with many challenges without his negative experiences coloring his world view. He maintains a deep faith that there is good in humanity and he brings that into his interactions with every person, regardless of who they are or what status they hold. You can't fake authenticity. David is David, through and through. He is optimistic, he believes we can create change, and he has an unshakable sense of justice.

David and I share a passion, which is mentoring young people and ensuring that the next generation has the skills, knowledge, and outlook required to be peacebuilders and democratic leaders. I have seen David's eyes light up when he talks with young people. We both share a deep sense that we haven't yet done enough and that we must keep pushing to make sure that young people have the tools and training necessary to exercise their leadership skills today and into the future.

I remember spending time with David in Bogota, Colombia during the World Summit of Nobel Peace Laureates. His face was white like he was about to faint, but he was concerned about taking care of the youth delegates to the summit, when he really needed someone to take care of him. As David shares in his book, he is now dealing with the daily reality of his Parkinson's diagnosis, but it has only made him more determined to connect and inspire young people with every opportunity he has. This is something that I've taken from the playbook of David's life: be as passionate today about the change that you want to see as when it first lit a fire within you when you were younger. David has a zeal for mentoring young people regardless of their social status, nationality, or language. He refused to allow these things to be a barrier to connection.

Readers can look forward to learning from his wisdom and deliberate reflection. David has spent his life working across cultures and learning from others. For those who are wondering how to best use their privileges in the service of making significant change, David provides a wonderful example of someone who has used his privileges (such as being a white man from one of the most powerful countries in the world) with humility. I am inspired by David's constant desire to reach out to people and understand their lives. He embodies resilience, overcoming multiple challenges. David lives his life to the fullest. He understands our collective humanity and that the fate of every single person on the face of this planet is linked. He seizes every opportunity to enjoy light and laughter. May each and every one of us find inspiration in David's stories and be moved to see the world with as much compassion and good faith as David does.

Leymah Gbowee
2011 *Nobel Peace Prize Laureate and Founder/President of the Gbowee Peace Foundation Africa*

INTRODUCTION

I *have known Professor* David T. Ives for over ten years, mostly
through his work at the summits of Nobel Peace Prize
Laureates, where he has taken hundreds of students from
around the world. Often working as a panelist and/or speaker in
these summits, Professor Ives always emphasized and promoted
the ideals of the 1952 Nobel Peace Prize Laureate, Dr. Albert
Schweitzer, known as the "Reverence for Life," and his staunch
opposition to nuclear weapons. Dr. Schweitzer's philosophy that
every life—be it a plant, animal, or human—is precious was a
refreshingly new idea for the Western World. Professor Ives did a
marvelous job in nurturing this ideal and promoting it on a worldwide basis.

In my view, Dr. Schweitzer was one of the greatest thinkers and
change-makers of the twentieth century. He took an unusual path
to fame, becoming world-renowned for his humanity—by caring
for and about others. Dr. Schweitzer was one of the first Europeans
to go to Africa with the intent of alleviating the pain and suffering
of the people of that historically beleaguered continent, rather than
exploiting its vast resources and its people. Although he initially
went to Africa under the auspices of a Christian mission, he did
not go with the intent of proselytizing or converting Africans to a

Christian belief. Rather, he went to Africa to mitigate the pain and sufferings by improving the health of all people, and especially that of women who came to the hospital in Gabon, West Africa that he established. Indeed, the goals of the Grameen Bank that I founded mesh very well with the ideas of Dr. Schweitzer. In the course of my work at Grameen Bank, and later in developing various social business enterprises, I realized that things are never as complicated as we imagine them to be. It is only our arrogance that seeks to find complicated answers to simple problems. Dr. Schweitzer was one of those philosophers who preferred to look for simple solutions and do the work himself, rather than philosophizing. I am glad that Professor Ives, through his work, has kept Dr. Schweitzer's dream alive. As a torch bearer of Schweitzerian Philosophy, David Ives has been working around the world and especially in Central America. Professor Ives' success in various educational, humanitarian, and peace-building work show that changes are products of intensive efforts. I also commend David for his peace-related work, whether it be organizing an international conference on peace or reconciliation, or working directly with a leadership training program for young people, or building a classroom for children in a poor community, or looking for physically disabled persons to teach them physical therapy. Just as Dr. Schweitzer wanted to have a world in which there is respect for nature and peace and a spontaneity in fostering the values of human relationships with the whole of creation—similarly, David too has been working to build peace and harmony and empower people to achieve their true potentials.

What made Dr. Schweitzer unique among his peers was that, in proving his point, he was not prepared to rely on statements or pronouncements or arguments; he simply made his life his argument and turned himself into an example to others. Following the path of Dr. Schweitzer, Professor Ives too has turned his life into an argument for philosophy of reverence for life that is hard to refute. His autobiography vividly captures and illuminates that argument.

I often lament that we prepare our students for jobs and careers, but we don't teach them how to think as individuals about what kind of world they would create. I have no doubt that the powerful stories in David's autobiography would make the readers ponder how they can contribute to make the world a better place for posterity. I also believe that David's autobiography would inspire a legion of future leaders to work toward making possible what today seems impossible. Reading David's autobiography is akin to taking a journey that is well worth the time. I wish David and the readers taking this journey all the best.

Muhammad Yunus, PhD
2006 Nobel Peace Prize Laureate
and Founder of the Grameen Bank

PROLOGUE

Peninsula de Osa, Costa Rica—November 1982

Ella no puede respirar—no puede respirar!
She cannot breathe, she cannot breathe, she cannot breathe!

A little girl about eleven months old lay dying in her hovel when I ran into her father, or I should say he was looking for me because he had heard that I was in the area. Indeed, I was nearby looking for families with young children or babies who were malnourished.

Finding families with malnourished babies, whom I diagnosed by measuring their height and weight, was an essential part of my job. If I judged that a child needed to see a doctor or was the least bit malnourished, I would encourage the family to work with me to find food and, when necessary, would help them get to a doctor. Unfortunately, there was only one boat that left Puerto Jimenez for Golfito, where the nearest doctor was located, and it left at around 4:00 or 5:00 a.m.

As it happened, that afternoon the above-mentioned father took me into his home, where they lived in squalor. I saw that they had a daughter who looked to be just under a year old or so. I had previously helped this family plant some vegetable seeds and build a makeshift fence to keep wandering pigs from eating everything we put in the ground.

Inside the house, the baby girl was having trouble breathing. She would take these long sighs and not quite catch her breath. Then she would try several times more until she finally did catch a breath. Then the whole process would start over. I checked on whether or not her mother could breast feed, but she couldn't because she too was malnourished. I arranged to meet them at the boat for Golfito the next morning, offering to pay the fare for the whole family, including another child, a son of about three. It turned out that the mother of the family had gotten some formula from somewhere and was trying to feed this to her two kids, often diluting it with polluted water from their well. The next morning I arrived at the rendezvous point on the beach and waited for them to get there. When the boat captain threatened to leave, I said to wait or I would throw him overboard. Finally, the little girl's family came running down the embankment, her parents yelling *she cannot breathe, she cannot breathe—ella no puede respirar!* They pushed her into my arms, and we shoved off. I tried to revive her with artificial resuscitation, but it was to no avail. I could not get air into her lungs. And then, with one last gasp I felt her die in my arms, and I am sure that I felt her soul leave her body. There in the middle of the bay, I cried. We took her to the clinic and the doctor there pronounced her dead, probably from the worms that had filled up her lungs from drinking polluted water. I will never get over this and, even now, I feel her presence with me, sitting on my shoulder.

After hearing one of my stories, several of my family members, friends, and students have said to me that I should write a book. I laughed and said thank you and didn't think much about it. But as I am now on the downhill side of my life, I began to think that my experiences may be interesting to a wider circle of listeners and readers. So with the encouragement of family and friends, and with the hope that George Clooney will play me in the movie version, I gradually began to put my stories down on paper, and with my retirement I have had more time to write. I hope that my adventures provide some inspiration and smiles for those who choose to read these lines and share my thoughts with others. Throughout my life I have had a lot of dreams to accomplish and obstacles to overcome for my family and friends and for the people I met and worked with around the world. I have shared them in any way that I could, and each one was an adventure. Sometimes I didn't accomplish my dreams and sometimes I did. But more important, I think I helped a lot of people to accomplish their dreams in the fifty-six countries around the world I have visited.

In the course of my work, I learned that too many people in this world do not give enough of a damn about poverty to make it even the smallest campaign issue. There is no excuse for the lack of political will to change what causes the poverty I saw. I still feel that I did not do enough. I think that United States citizens often do not seem to recognize that people who are our southern neighbors are humans with the same rights we have. Our southern borders have fluctuated over the years and it is through an accident of war or a treaty or something like the Gadsden Purchase and/or the Louisiana Purchase that says nowadays who is a Latin and who is not, and who is a US citizen and who is not.

All persons on this earth are, or should be, equal in the eyes of God. I firmly believe that the moral conscience of the Declaration of Independence should be upheld on a *global* basis to any member of the human race, despite their skin color, ethnicity, and religious beliefs. The Declaration does not say that the United States is the only place in the world where it applies. Rather, it can go far beyond our boundaries to ensure that *all men are created equal, that they are endowed by their*

Creator with certain inalienable Rights, that among these are Life, Liberty, *and the pursuit of Happiness.* All men, not just a few. And I must insist that women be included. As our indigenous friends say, women hold up half the sky.

In a letter written in 1859, Abraham Lincoln (a distinguished writer, himself) praised Jefferson's wisdom and literary brilliance in creating the immortal document: "All honor to Jefferson—to the man who, in the concrete pressure of a struggle for national independence by a single people, had the coolness, forecast, and capacity to introduce into a merely revolutionary document, *an abstract truth, applicable to* *all men and all times,* and so to embalm there, that to-day, and in all coming days, it shall be a rebuke and a stumbling-block to the very harbingers of re-appearing tyranny and oppression."[1] I also like to think of the moral code woven into the Declaration of Independence as the foundation for all law and governance. Clearly, it ensures that mankind must govern not only its nations, but the hearts and minds of its people as well.

I am probably one of the few people on earth who has done something for peace on every continent except Antarctica, with some programs requiring action and some requiring thoughtful analysis—and many requiring both. I have met, worked, and supped with world leaders, and have also lived and worked among the poorest of the poor, with whom I have supped as well. I have been to where the rich and famous live and also encountered people living in garbage dumps around the world. However, when it comes down to it, human beings have many more similarities than differences. And there is a profound richness in difference which, if we let it, can bring us closer to each other.

I often dreamed about doing something which was thought impossible. I have done the impossible! And I have also failed miserably. But

---

[1] Lincoln was responding to "Messrs. Henry L. Pierce & others" to respectfully decline an invitation to attend a birthday celebration honoring Thomas Jefferson (Springfield, Illinois, April 6, 1859),

I have always gotten back up. My mother had to teach me to walk twice in her lifetime, and when I had to learn one more time by myself, it was her determination that drove me onward.

Professor David Taylor Ives

Executive Director Emeritus

The Albert Schweitzer Institute/Quinnipiac University

| I |

PIERPONT, OHIO: DREAMS OF A YOUNG BOY

*I look back upon my youth and realize how so many peo-
ple gave me help, understanding, courage…they entered
into my life and became powers within me.*
—Albert Schweitzer

Chapter One

ROUND ONE: POLIO

I woke up screaming. I couldn't feel or see my body below my neck. There seemed to be a loud breathing sound which future generations would recognize as Darth Vader. There was something stiff and white encircling my neck which future generations would identify as plastic.

My mother was right there and tried to comfort me as best she could. Nevertheless, it took me a while to calm down, especially when it seemed I was continuously urinating on myself. I vaguely remembered (and sometimes I was not sure if it was my memory or what I had been told) going to the bathroom and collapsing in front of the toilet—and that I couldn't control my urine flow, and urine was all over the place. I was embarrassed because I had been potty-trained for a couple years, and I did not want to get scolded. I don't remember anything else, except I thought someone had taken my body and left only my head.

I was in an iron lung. It looked like a big white cigar and it was used often in the forties or fifties to help victims of polio breathe. It was 1955, and I was four-to-five years old at the time and had contracted polio literally weeks before the polio vaccine was widely available.

It colored the rest of my life and was the first adventure I would remember—and walking unaided was the first dream I wanted to accomplish.

I was in that iron lung for about a week until the doctors were sure I could breathe on my own. I was sent home with the advice of the physician ringing in my mother's ears that I would never walk again without crutches or leg braces of some sort. I didn't find out about the doctors' prognosis until some years later—when I was an active, normal, pain-in-the-ass teenager and my mother told me about the struggles she and I had gone through. It was not the first time my mother demonstrated the power of a woman determined to get things done. She didn't like being called a feminist, but heaven help anyone who told her or even hinted that she could not do something because she was a woman. I remember telling her that cleaning toilets was women's work, and I was promptly sentenced to cleaning our family toilet on a weekly basis for at least three months.

We didn't know much about occupational or physical therapy at the time, but my mother, whose name was Dorothy (nicknamed Dot) did some serious research as to the efficacy of exercise for victims of polio. She knew how determinedly FDR had fought polio and that exercise seemed to help him. So my mother decided to fight fire with fire.

For the next year, we did exercises twice a day six days a week almost without fail. I learned to use crutches and a set of heavy leg braces. But my mother's dream was that I would learn to walk unaided once again.

Finally, after a year of hard work and coming close to taking a few unaided steps several times, I finally took *four or five steps* without support. No crutches! No braces! My mother burst into tears and couldn't wait to tell my father. Finally, she rushed across the campus of Gordon Divinity School, where my father was studying to become a minister, and ran into his classroom and exclaimed—our son is walking! There wasn't a dry eye in the house—and there was a big party that night—and it seemed like many prayers had been answered.

It turns out that polio comes in degrees, and my case of polio was not that serious, comparatively speaking. I had some weakness in my right arm and my left leg, but no one could really tell that I had a physical problem unless they looked closely when I was wearing shorts or swim trunks. When they did, I was taunted and called names like "crip" for cripple and "pencil leg." I therefore avoided wearing shorts unless I had to for swimming. By first grade I was a fairly active little boy, and by second grade my legs and arms were near normal size and symmetrical. So my first dream was to walk and play again, especially baseball. I often fell asleep at night listening through my crystal radio headphones to my beloved Cleveland Indians and dreamed of hitting the World Series winning walkoff solo home run á la the Pittsburg Pirates' second baseman Bill Mazoraski—who did exactly that in the 1960 World Series to beat the Yankees in the bottom of the ninth.

However, I soon learned that, in the US, disabled people were often ignored and made to feel like second-class citizens. In the developing world it was much, much worse.

| *Chapter Two* |

GROWING UP IN PIERPONT

*I*n 1955, *my father* accepted a position as a pastor in the little town of Pierpont, Ohio—home to around three hundred people and three thousand cows—located in the northeast corner of the county of Ashtabula (a guesstimate). Nowadays, I occasionally visit this little town that has seen better days, and I am forever grateful for the life lessons I learned from the farmers I worked for and the many people there whom I still love. In many ways, Pierpont was an idyllic place to live in, being much like a Norman Rockwell painting. We left our doors unlocked, and the ladies of the church would clean our house before we returned from vacation and leave us a spaghetti and meatballs supper to come home to. We spent hours playing in and around a creek (pronounced *crick*) about half a mile from my house catching frogs and climbing trees. We played baseball in a cow pasture behind my house, and I remember vividly sliding head first into what I thought was third base but was instead a recently deposited, crusted-over cow pie. We had a huge vegetable garden, and my Dad would often come home for lunch and pick a tomato from our garden and some lettuce and would make himself the best sandwich, using homemade bread and mayonnaise. We (my best friend growing up, Jack Hudson, and I) would take our .22 rifles to the town dump on our bicycles and shoot rats or cans or bottles without a care in the world. The best roasted corn on the cob came from that garden, as did our Halloween pumpkin and the most wonderful string beans. When I was about fourteen, I was big enough to throw bales of hay around weighing about forty pounds or so. I spent many summers grabbing bales of hay off the baler and stacking them on the wagon—taking them to the barn, throwing the bales up above my head and stacking them up in the hayloft when the temperature was sometimes over 100 degrees. After the day's work was done, we often went swimming in the farmer's pond to cool off. I made about a dollar an hour but made up for this by eating huge amounts of the downhome country food that the farmer's wife had prepared (especially babyback ribs).

Pierpont had nine streetlights, a general store, a gas station, three stop signs, a volunteer fire station, and the Pierpont Presbyterian Church, where my Dad was pastor and I spent a lot of time. On Sundays, we had: Sunday School at 9:30 a.m., the main church service at 11:00 a.m., lunch around 12:30 p.m., services at the county home for the elderly at 2:00 p.m., youth group at 6:00 p.m., and evening service at 8:00 p.m.. It was a full day, one with which I had a love/hate relationship because I wanted to play football and baseball on Sundays with my friends. I had become an avid fan of the Cleveland Indians (wish they would change their name) and the Cleveland Browns. Many a night I fell asleep with my crystal radio headphones on, listening to my beloved Indians and dreaming of playing major league baseball. I tried playing basketball, but found that I had trouble with the concept of a foul—and committed many of them, often fouling out after a short time in a game, if I got into a game at all!

In Little League, when I came to bat I would imitate the mannerisms of my baseball hero, Rocky Colavito, as he prepared to step into the batter's box. Rocky had a certain way he put his bat behind his head and stretched. I did that stretch to perfection. Anytime I got a hit, it was because I did the stretch correctly. If I didn't get a hit, it was because I didn't stretch correctly a la Rocky!

In eighth grade I had an opportunity to play tackle football, but my parents were worried about my getting injured, given my history of polio. So, I played flag football instead until they eventually relented and let me play center on the offensive line in ninth, tenth, eleventh, and twelvth grade. I was the first-string center my senior year, and I made the first team/All-City Team for Ashtabula, Ohio and honorable mention in the All-County team. I was very proud of the fact that, as a former victim of polio and having been told that I would never walk again unaided, I made these teams. This has been an enormous confidence booster in my life. Football has had its share of problems in recent years in terms of concussions, but for me it was life-changing, and I learned the importance of teamwork and rising above the fray to meet any challenge. My speed was pretty slow, so after practice—when we all had to do a series of wind sprints and a hundred-yard sprint—I was given a fifteen-yard head start. I still lost, but I was quick for about ten yards, which was enough to do most blocking assignments. When it was cold outside, my right hand refused to grip the ball correctly, so I sometimes snapped the ball, using two hands. And when the offense was on the sideline, I made sure I held a hot cup of anything in that hand, so I could grip the ball. When I snapped the ball for a punt and my hands were cold, my snaps went end over end instead of a nice spiral. No one really noticed because if my snap was not spiraling correctly, I blamed it on a wet ball or mud on the ball. But I was scared I would cost my team the game with a bad snap on my part. Over the years, probably as a result of post-polio syndrome and Guillain-Barré syndrome and now Parkinson's, my grip on my right hand has weakened, and now it is hard to grip the zipper on my pants and pull it down or button up my dress shirts or tie my ties.

It is not something I discuss very much and it won't kill me, but it is somewhat of a pain in my life.

The real world did, from time to time, intrude into little Pierpont. When I was twelve, there was a car accident outside my home. I ran out of the house and saw four black people with minor bumps and bruises in a car that was up against a tree with steam coming from the engine. They seemed nervous and apprehensive but had no other choice but to accompany me into our house. My mom was home and had heard the crash. She immediately washed and dressed their minor wounds and made sandwiches for all. My Dad came home from writing his sermon, and it turned out that one of the passengers was also a minister. We got along fine after that and pushed the car to our local gas station owned by Bob Richcreek, who was willing to help anyone regardless of skin color. My father and Bob consulted, and soon the broken hose and belt were replaced, the gas tank was filled, and the black family was on their way with more sandwiches from my mother. I didn't understand the tension I had heard about in other towns because every Sunday we sang, *Jesus loves the little children, all the children of the world—red and yellow, black and white, they are precious in his sight. Jesus loves the little children of the world.* I did not understand why that song was not always true until I began paying attention to the civil rights movement when I was older. I began hearing the N word upon occasion and knew that it was derogatory, but I just didn't how pejorative it was.

At about age twelve or so, I went to a bigger school in the town of Kingsville—bigger than Pierpont, at least. I began to hear words that I had not heard before, like bastard, which I didn't really understand. Around the same time, we studied Australia where they have a big bird also known as a bustard. One night at supper, my dad corrected my table manners and I said back to him something like, "Aw—you old bastard." My mom dropped her fork on the floor and Dad's face got red and I, recognizing the danger signs, quickly said,

"Yes, Dad—I meant this bird called a *bustard* in Australia that we just studied in Geography class." Dad calmed down and, wanting to be an open dad, said "Well, son, what other words have you heard?" I said, "I have heard the word Fuck." My mom dropped her glass this time and my dad's face got red again, and he said it's time to have *the talk*. So Mom called another Dorothy, the mother of my best friend Jack Hudson, and we got the birds and the bees talk that night. Later on, it became one of our favorite stories.

My dad, as is often the case in rural pastorates, not only got a salary in real money, but parishioners would also sometimes pay in-kind—with a pound of homemade butter or a jar of jam, and often with an animal or a bird that I had to chase down. One parishioner said that he had a goose that my Dad could have if I could catch it. When I arrived at this person's home I was directed to the kitchen and then outside, where I encountered the biggest goose I have ever seen. I think it knew that its demise could be imminent, so it launched a preemptive attack at me. Geese are very fast and can peck very hard, and it soon had me running around trying to escape. I decided to commute the death sentence of this goose and beat a hasty retreat and have never tried to kill a goose since then. To make matters worse, I jumped off the porch with that honking goose right behind me and fell in a mud puddle. Eventually, I arrived back at my father's office covered with mud. It took an hour to tell the story because my Dad would not stop laughing.

No one thought it was possible. During my senior year in high school I excelled at wrestling. In fact, I was undefeated at the 175-pound weight class going into the final match to determine our league championship. Unfortunately, our heavyweight got sick, and we had no one to replace him except me. In order to wrestle heavyweight, you had to weigh 185, so I had to put on about ten pounds in two days! It was the last time in my life someone told me I had to put on weight.

It was like a movie plot. It came down to the heavyweight bout with the match tied. If I won my match, our team would be league champions. (I had dreamed about doing this.) My opponent outweighed me by around *forty* pounds or so. To make a long story short, with two seconds to go, I pinned my opponent to win the match and the conference championship. The sold-out gym went crazy and I leapt to my feet, hands up in the air and fists pumping and then I caught my mother's eyes, which were filled with tears. For me the whole arena went silent, and I couldn't take my eyes off my mother. I knew that if it were not for her, this victory would never have happened. I raced over to her and we hugged for a least two minutes, oblivious to the sounds of the cheering crowd and my teammates celebrating their victory. For my mother and me, it was *our victory*—our dream that I would walk again. We had done so much more.

Unfortunately, an opposing coach heard that I had wrestled heavyweight and knew that I had wrestled in the 175 class. Since I was the best wrestler in the region in that class, he appealed the decision that had been made to allow me to go up a weight class and then come back to my normal weight class for the state tournament. We lost in arbitration and I had to wrestle heavyweight in the state tournament, and I lost in the second round to someone who looked like a bull moose! I would have liked to have seen what I could have done in my weight class, but as my father reminded me, I went farther than anyone thought I could when I was stuck in an iron lung. I won the real battle. My mother gave me my passion for international affairs and cultures and taught me to walk twice in my life. I will be forever grateful that she gave me the confidence to make my dreams come true.

| II |

SOUTH OF THE BORDER: DREAMS OF A YOUNG MAN

Help me to fling my life like a flaming firebrand into
the gathering darkness of the world.
—Albert Schweitzer

Chapter Three

THE RICHNESS OF DIFFERENCE

*T*here's another world out there. I fell in love with Latin America in Cochabamba, Bolivia in the summer of 1967. I was sixteen and having a life-changing experience that has followed me to this very day. My grandparents had died a few years before, and after the estate was settled my family and I decided to take a trip to South America to visit missionaries who had gone to divinity school with my father. Even at that age, I had decidedly mixed feelings about missionaries. I perceived that they often acted in condescending ways to the native peoples they were trying to convert, implying that cultures not based on Christianity were somehow inferior. But in this case, having some connections with real people made the trip special—definitely outside the realm of a gawking tourist.

We visited Brazil, Bolivia, Peru, Ecuador, Colombia, and Venezuela. (We happened to arrive in Bolivia only weeks after Che Guevera was captured and killed.) Our family was taken to visit the family home of one of the members of the church our missionary friend started just outside of San Paulo, Brazil.

I was stunned by what I saw. The walls of his home were made of corn stalks and tin cans found by the side of the road laboriously sewn together with some type of wire. Their roof leaked because it was made out of cardboard, and the cardboard only lasted for one or two rainstorms, which occur frequently in the tropics. Their only piece of furniture was a soggy mattress on the dirt, or should I say mud, floor which the mother, father, and two or three kids shared. Their garden consisted of six onions, and their cook stove was a pile of rocks that burned whatever the family could scavenge and boiled water to cook whatever rice or other food they could get or scrounge. Usually, it was not much. Their source of drinking water was a fecal creek that ran about thirty feet from their home and often flooded during the rainstorms. The same creek also served as the sewer system for houses similar to this one as far as the eye could see. The father earned one to two dollars a day as a human mule, never earning more than five hundred dollars a year, putting fifty-five-gallon drums on his back and carrying them up a gangplank and then down into the holds of ships. His wife had cataracts in both eyes and no access to funds for an operation that could easily save her sight. Their only clothes were what they had on their backs, and the local laundromat was that feces-infested creek. It was hard for me to leave because I wanted to do something for them. Since then, I have never stopped asking myself, my students, and anybody in general—*why*?

Before or since, I have not seen many places elsewhere that have this level of poverty, and I have been to fifty-five different countries around the world—and forty-six of our fifty states plus the Navajo Nation. Later, I was to learn that although there are enough calories produced in the world to make everyone fat, it is a lack of political will that causes poverty and starvation. I still have not heard many presidents or world leaders express deep concern about human rights and hunger problems in their campaigns for office—except for Jimmy Carter, whom I hold in high esteem!

I stood in this man's yard, transfixed. I had never seen poverty like this before in Ohio. It haunts me to this day and motivates me to open the eyes of people from the first world who evidently do not care much about the poverty in the so-called Third World. Back then, at age sixteen I asked myself what could possibly create such poverty. As I grew up and matured, I gradually came to understand the causes and dreamed about changing this somehow, sometime in my life—and this overwhelming desire eventually led me to serve in the Peace Corps. But I digress ...

The Hoffers, the missionary family we visited in Cochabamba, Bolivia, lived in the only two-story building in town, next to the Central Market square. I spent hours up on their roof drinking in the scene of the Quechuan people (descendants of the Incas) selling their wares in the rough-hewn wooden stalls of the Central Market. The women were dressed in colorful native garments with white stove pipe hats on their heads. The brims of these hats were decorated with black embroidery that enabled a knowledgeable person to identify the women's hometown or province. There was a cacophony of sound from chickens tied together by their legs clucking madly as though they knew they were about to be dinner for someone. There were goats bleating and cows mooing and smells emanating from the cookfires and salsa music blaring from a bar across the market place. Off in the distance, the snowcapped Andes Mountains rose majestically and the setting sun reflected all sorts of lights off the snow.

While in Cochabamba, my mother had to use the public rest room. We didn't know it was a unisex bathroom with no walls between toilets. People of both sexes tipped their hat to her as she sat on the toilet and exchanged what we think were pleasantries. My mom could not move and didn't know where to direct her eyes, but my dad finally rescued her and she came out laughing sheepishly, highly embarrassed.

In Ecuador, we drove from the capital Quito over the Andes Mountains and then on to Shell Mera, which was located at the head-waters of the Amazon River. I noticed that there weren't many guard-rails along the highway (using the term highway very loosely)—and that in many places there was a huge drop off a cliff decorated by a bunch of crosses standing along the side of the road. When I asked why those crosses were there I was told that they marked the place where a car or even a big bus had gone over the edge, and all the passengers had been killed. It was easy to understand why, because the road had traffic going in both directions and was muddy and slippery and often had only a single lane. When there wasn't room for two big trucks to squeeze through, one or the other had to back up until they reached a place in the road where both could pass. Often, when I looked out the window of the car we were in, it seemed as though we were on the edge of a precipice. It turned out that we were, and I had every reason to be scared to death.

We made it to Shell Mera, where there was a missionary station and an airstrip where light planes could land. The missionaries were using that base as a way to contact indigenous people in the Amazon basin without getting killed by suspicious indigenous groups. We flew into an area of the Amazon basis where an indigenous group called the Aucas had been recently pacified or become Christians. Indeed, some Aucas had killed several missionaries who had tried to contact them about a decade earlier. So it was with some sense of trepidation that we were there in an environment that had previously been quite hostile. My family was not used to the fact that everyone there except for the missionaries were half naked, and yet we were not supposed to look them in the eyes. This meant that I did not know where to look and so I decided to look the indigenous women in their chin and kept saying to myself, *don't look down!*

After about an hour and a half, we flew back to Shell Mera and stayed there for the night, sleeping in hammocks with someone right outside to take us to the bathroom so as to avoid any snakes that had slithered into the room where we were sleeping or were along the trail to the bathroom or inside it.

For a small-town boy from Ohio, this entire trip was fascinating. It ignited a curiosity in me about other cultures that has never waned and was the beginning of my next dream—to celebrate the cultures and embrace the diversity of the peoples of the world instead of letting our differences divide us. I flew back to the US a changed person thanks to the dreams of my mother. However, at the time I didn't really know how much that trip changed me.

Author's Note

It was not until later in my life that I began to question the role of missionaries and their need to convert someone to Christianity or they would spend their afterlife in hell. To help authorities colonize, Christian missionaries, both Protestant and Catholic, often arrived at a new place with a feeling a superiority—not only from a theological point of view, but also from a cultural point of view. As a group of indigenous people became more christianized, more and more of the native peoples' knowledge was lost. This is true in what now is called the developing world, which includes Asia, Africa, and Latin America. The conquistadors were very destructive throughout Latin America in their desire to discover gold and promote Catholicism in the name of the Pope. Protestant missionaries were slaughtered in what was then called the Belgian Congo as it became independent— such was the hidden ire against missionaries. There are tons of medicinal plants in the Amazon rain forest that will be lost with the destruction of the rain forest by companies governed solely by the profit motive. I saw this later on during my years in the Peace Corps, watching the environment be raped in Costa Rica by mining and energy companies. I fear that, with the inauguration of Brazil's newest president, Jair Bolsonaro, given his anti-environmental predelictions, it will be open season on the Amazon rain forest.

| Chapter Four |

OSU vs. VIETNAM

I *had wanted to* join the Peace Corps ever since I first heard about it when President Kennedy broached the idea in one of his speeches. After my family's trip to South America, I began thinking more and more about it. However, there was such a thing as a military draft back then, and every American male had to register on their eighteenth birthday to prepare for the possibility of military service. When I first obtained my draft card, I felt it was quite an honor and was proud to possibly be able to serve my country. But the more I heard about the deaths of American soldiers in a weekly death count, the more hesitant I became. (Yet I still believed I could handle the physical challenges of a soldier because I thought of myself as an athlete who could handle any bodily challenge. However, I probably would not have passed the physical because of polio.) I remember learning that, after French colonials got their asses kicked in the Battle of Dien Bien Phu and were forced out of Vietnam, we (the USA) gradually took over the war even though we had no strategic interests there except for stopping communism. Eventually, this became part of my reason for joining the Peace Corps—to understand why people turned to communism if as, according to my father and many others, communism was inherently evil and Godless. Indeed, the Peace Corps was created in part to combat communism under the guise of promoting our concern for others much less fortunate than the citizens of the United States.

I was sitting on my lifeguard chair at Lake Pymatuning in Ohio in the summer of 1969 just after graduation from high school when I found out my draft lottery number. (The draft lottery had been established to provide a fair selection process. Rich parents could always find a way to get their sons an exemption from the draft, so the war in Vietnam was fought mainly by soldiers from families who were poor.) All 365 days of the year were placed on 365 ping pong balls and were drawn from a bin of some sort until all birthdays had been drawn. My birthday was February 13 and, as it happened, my draft lottery pick was thirteen. Because I had a 2-S (student) deferment, it meant I could not be drafted into the military until I graduated. I remember at subsequent draft lottery fiestas, a group of my male friends would get two bottles of Jack Daniels or some similarly appropriate beverage, and the one who drew the lowest number got one bottle because it was virtually certain he might be inducted into the military—and the guy who got the highest number (and therefore would not be drafted) got the other bottle—and the result was a lot of drunk people. Men who got a number roughly below 140 were likely to be forced to go into the military unless they had a 2-S deferment. If you had a draft number above 150 or so, you were unlikely to be drafted. However, if you took a quarter or a semester off, you would lose your 2-S deferment. Right after I was classified as 2-S, they stopped issuing this educational deferment. This meant I had to stay in school or I would be drafted.

The other kind of deferment which was often pursued was being a conscientious objector. But while I was thinking about whether or not to apply for this option, the United States Supreme Court ruled that one had to object to all war—and I only objected to the Vietnam War, so I didn't pursue it. The only other choice for someone in my shoes was to emigrate to Canada, essentially give up American citizenship, and risk being arrested if you ever returned. I never seriously considered this an option because it would mean estrangement from my family. But it might have been better than dying in a war that we never should have fought.

By fall of 1969 I was enrolled at The Ohio State University, where I graduated with a BS in Social Work in 1973 and with an MA in Student Personnel and Counseling in 1975. As luck would have it, in 1973 the decision was made to go to an all-volunteer army, so the draft was no longer a concern. However, I did participate in protests on and off campus and made at least one antiwar pilgrimage to Washington, DC.

I admired and loved my father. He could have gone to a bigger parish and made more money but instead chose to serve in a small town in rural Ohio and help people who often were and still are ignored. If it was within my father's abilities to help a person or a needy family, he would move heaven and earth to be of service to anyone. As a result, we never had much of a savings account, but we did not lack for anything. Dad was in the Navy during World War II as a rear gunner on an SB2C Helldiver bomber flying off the aircraft carrier *Hornet* in the Pacific Theater. He won the Distinguished Flying Cross for his bravery and the pictures he took flying over enemy ships. As a result of his military service, he was one of the "love America, or leave it" contingency. The worse and the more controversial the war in Vietnam became, the stronger my dad's feelings became to support it. And of course, I was going in the opposite direction!

As a first quarter freshman at OSU, I joined Navy ROTC mainly to please my father. That lasted about two months because they kept trying to march us around the campus decked out in full uniform to the to the tune of boos and anger from students protesting the war. One day, our ROTC leader started berating me in the middle of the Oval, which was the central gathering place for anyone affiliated with OSU. At the time, rallies protesting the war were also being held in the Oval, so the protesters could hear this fellow ordering me to brace at attention while he yelled in my ear. I decided I'd had enough and knocked the guy down into a mud puddle, sat on him, and then went to ROTC headquarters and turned in my uniform.

It became quite a game with the local police force as they tried to clear the Oval. We students would disperse and, knowing the sidewalks well, would fill in behind the advancing police line. Then the cops would turn around and march back across the Oval, and the same thing would happen all over again. They marched back and forth across the Oval several times before they got wise to our game. So then they started firing tear gas at us, but more often than not, the wind would blow it right back at them. Finally, when they overcame that problem, I went and got my scuba tank and diving mask and some thick work gloves and began throwing the tear gas canisters back at them, causing them to run. It ended when the police decided to shoot us with rock salt, so I turned tail and ran. I normally couldn't run very fast and found it accordingly more difficult to run wearing a scuba tank. As a result, I was hit on my butt and my back a couple of times with rock salt, which permeates your skin and burns quite painfully—so I retired from battle.

On the one hand, I respected my father and military men and women everywhere. On the other hand, I did not see the need for a war in Vietnam. And it was an unwinnable war. It did not matter that our soldiers were well-equipped, well-trained and courageous— some of the best we ever produced—nor did it matter how many North Vietnamese were killed or how many villages were destroyed. It seemed that the North Vietnamese would be able to fight literally forever, even though they might lose every battle. Eventually, US armed forces would leave and go back home. It did not matter if it took ten years or twenty or one hundred—at some point we would leave with our pride wounded, thousands of casualties, and a country divided. We would be the losers. *And we were.*

A good book on this subject is *The Ten Thousand Day War: Vietnam 1945–1975*, a book that was recommended to me by a person who had been a Lieutenant Colonel in the United States Air Force and served two deployments in Vietnam. He said he could never understand why the US lost the Vietnam War until he read this book. In my opinion, we have not learned these lessons from the Vietnam War and we are and have made the same mistakes in Afghanistan, and when we leave, and we will, the Taliban will have won a very similar war to Vietnam. Currently, in Syria our president is guilty of a mindless swing to the complete opposite. Having stood alongside Kurdish forces for years to stem the tide of ISIS, we now are prepared to walk away, leaving our allies twisting in the wind.

My head and heart were already stretched to the breaking point with the turmoil surrounding Vietnam. Then May 1, 1970 became one of the worst days of my life.

Chapter Five

MY WORLD FALLS APART

*T*hings were getting pretty hot around the campus due to protests against the war in Vietnam. So I hitchhiked home. I went straight to Pierpont, got my car, and went to see my girlfriend, Lynn Buckett, who was and is a wonderful human being. We were in her parents' basement, probably making out, when Lynn's mother came down the stairs and said, your dad's on the phone and it sounds urgent. I came quickly and got on the phone. Dad said, "Your mother has been in an accident and was killed."

Mom was hit by a drunk driver while coming back from showing our home movies of the trip to Latin America to a women's club at another church. The drunk crossed into her lane and hit her head-on. She probably died instantly. She was only forty-two.

I stood there stunned. I told Lynn and her mother what had happened. They gave me long hugs and were worried about me driving with such emotional distress. I don't remember the drive home, but I am sure I went too fast. I pulled into the driveway and parked my car in a haphazard manner and bolted to the door of our house. I opened the door, and there sat my sister Carol, my two brothers Don and Pete, and my dad—all crying their eyes out. We all cried together for a couple of hours and then tried to sleep, but sleep was impossible. Sometimes the door to the breezeway would be blown slightly open and we all would react to the sound, looking anxiously to see if it was Mom returning. It obviously was not, so we finally oiled the door to keep it from making that damned squeak.

The next few days were a blur. Dad was well-known in Ashtabula County, so people came to the calling hours from all over Ohio and the US. I alternated between absolute depression and uncontrollable tears—and then anger at God and the world. At one point, I asked if I could be alone with mother, and when I was alone with her, I told her—thank you for all you've done for me. I was glad that, two weeks before her death, I had told her the same thing in person.

I still haven't gotten over my anger at God for taking away such a good woman, one who had rescued my ability to walk. Twice. Years later, my good friend and Nobel Peace Prize Laureate, Betty Williams, reminded me that fifteen thousand children under the age of five have died and still die each day from preventable causes like polluted water, lack of sanitation facilities, malnutrition, and no medical care of any kind. *Where was God in all of this?*

The day after the funeral, my father said we should take a drive. We needed to pick out a tombstone for my mother's grave. We did just that, so if there's any chance you might be in Pierpont, Ohio and visit our countryside cemetery, my mom's grave has a rising sun on it—some consider it a setting sun. It has meaning to me both ways. We drove aimlessly for awhile, but then Dad said to stop and turn into a certain driveway. I'll never forget that name on the mailbox. It was the name of the man who killed my mother. Turns out he had been drinking and it was not the first time he had been caught driving drunk. It was the first time he had killed someone, though, and it had to be my mother. My dad identified himself to the man's wife and sister, and they immediately started crying and begging forgiveness for their husband and brother. My father went into the bedroom where my mother's killer was recovering from the minor injuries he had sustained. Dad knelt beside his bed and prayed and proceeded to forgive the man that four days prior had taken Mom away from us forever. I stood at the end of the bed ready to cry and/or kill the man who had murdered my mother. I still don't know how my father could forgive him, and I chastised Dad for doing this deed as I was fantasizing about running the man over with my car if I ever had the chance. Turned out my father was right and I was wrong. It took me years to admit this, which happened only due to some counseling, which helped me finally realize that forgiveness was as much about me as about the forgiven—and that I had to forgive so I could live a life without bitterness and hate. I have my bad days even now, when these memories overwhelm me and I need to pout and cry a bit. But at least I have learned to let my mother's life set an example that I should do my best to follow. Yet I have little use for the expression that *everything happens for a reason*, which assumes it is for a *good reason*. In my view, there are indeed reasons for something happening, and they can be bad or good or somewhere in between. My mother's death was awful, but I have survived and thrived by trying to make her good life my motivation. This is another dream that I am still trying to fulfill.

Later in life, I came to appreciate forgiveness even more as Martin Luther King, Jr., Archbishop Desmond Tutu, President Nelson Mandela, and yes—even Albert Schweitzer—spoke and wrote about the need to forgive someone who has wronged us in order to survive and become whole again. They were and still are right—and it is their example, as well, that I try to emulate.

On May 4, 1970, the day of my mother's funeral, four students protesting the US bombing of Cambodia were shot to death by the Ohio National Guard at Kent State University. I knew some students who attended Kent State, and they were tremendously upset. I felt like my world had fallen apart. There was no good reason for this to happen. And the memory of the assassination of Martin Luther King and Bobby Kennedy a few years before added to the perception that my life and my country were broken and in shambles. I wondered openly if America was acting in a way that was hypocritical to the principles expressed in the Preamble of our Declaration of Independence: *that all men are created equal, that they are endowed by their Creator with certain unalienable Rights, that among these are Life, Liberty and the pursuit of Happiness.* I wondered if these principles applied outside the United States and if not—why not? I wondered why we were in Vietnam in the first place and soon learned that we were in Vietnam in part to combat the communists from taking over the world, and this inordinate fear of communism was to govern most of our foreign policy initiatives from 1945 until the Soviet Union fell in 1991.

Author's Note

> *We justified the Vietnam War based on the Gulf of Tonkin Resolution, which claimed that without provocation North Vietnam had attacked our ships. Our aircraft carriers scrambled some fighter jets, and they flew to the scene to confront the North Vietnamese attackers. One of the fighter jets was piloted by Admiral James Stockdale, whose son Taylor attended Colorado College, where I worked for a few years in the eighties as an Associate Dean of Students. Admiral Stockdale, who later on was Ross Perot's running mate in the 1992 presidential election and the longest serving POW, looked for any ship that could possibly be construed as an attacker—and saw nothing. He circled the area for several minutes, as did other members of his squadron, and there wasn't even a fishing boat in the bay. But we based our involvement in the Vietnam War on this attack on our naval vessels—which did not happen! As Admiral Stockdale said, the war was born in a lie and therefore had no chance of succeeding. The powers that be in the US knew it and lied about this important event. There were and are more lies for me to discover. Disillusionment would begin to set in for me as these lies were slowly uncovered.*

After my mother's death, Kent State, and the Vietnam debacle, it took a long time to put my life back together philosophically. But I did eventually learn the importance of forgiveness for me and for others.

Chapter Six

OHIO STATE:
A GREAT UNIVERSITY

*M*y *life at The* Ohio State University was otherwise generally enjoyable, especially in 1973, when I had the honor of
being named one of ten Outstanding Seniors. One of the
things I was most proud of was that I had led the efforts, along with
one other fellow member of the Ohio Stater's service organization, to
establish the first undergraduate recognition dinner for our women
athletes. I happened to run across several of them while they were
discussing how they would raise money for a small celebration and
whether they could collect enough among themselves to underwrite
a few keepsakes for memories of their athletic prowess. I was stunned
because each male athletic team enjoyed their own banquet and booty.
The football team had a huge festive dinner and got sport coats, dress
pants, and ties—plus a special school ring and a Rose Bowl watch.
At the same time, our female athletes were making their own awards,
baking cookies and cakes, and not getting much support or attendance
at their meets, matches, or games. That did not seem fair, so I went to
a women's basketball game at the invitation of Julie Brewer, the team
captain. I recognized at once how good these athletes were, and it
seemed practically a crime that they were not receiving any recognition at all from anyone other than themselves. We had some difficulty

getting the athletic department to acklowledge this until we met with the president's wife. The day after we met with her, I got a phone call asking me to come to the president's office and was told that we now had the money for a nice banquet and bracelet charms for the members of each women's athletic team. It was about time. *I am reminded of this on the day of a tickertape parade for the women's soccer team in NYC that just won the world cup. You (and our society) "have come a long way"— but it has taken too long!*

Although the OSU professors I had were well-versed in their subjects, the real world kept intruding on my education. For two summers I worked with the South Side Settlement House in Columbus as part of a summer internship at their Triple S Camp. During the first summer, I was the head life guard, and in the second summer I was a counselor for a teen camp composed mostly of urban youth—mainly African American, some Hispanics, and some white sons and daughters of welloff Board members who were there to maintain a cultural mix. It was there that I first heard the N-word used extensively by the African American campers, themselves, in loud conversations or disagreements with each other. I also heard the term (which I regret writing but feel that I must) "yellow nigger." I did not know what that meant because my upbringing was essentially white. The urban kids got used to me being a very naïve country boy and tolerated my questions. I learned that *yellow nigger* was an insult flung at a light-skinned, teenaged, African American camper when she exploded—yelling, "my daddy and mama are just as black as anyone else's parents." Then she seemed to be defending her blackness all summer. I finally learned that there was a hierarchy in the African American community based on skin color— and the lighter and whiter, the better. I also learned that only African Americans could use the N-word among themselves, which puzzled me as to why anyone would want to use a pejorative word rooted in the evils of slavery—even among friends from the same culture. I never really understood this, even as it became a topic

of conversation in the teen camp, and I still haven't heard a good justification for its use.

The camp was located about an hour south of Columbus in the
Hocking Hills, near Lancaster, Ohio. When I was asked to accompany
one of our black woman counselors on a trip into town to get some
needed supplies, it turned out that this part of southern Ohio was like
the South in its perceptions of black people. This lovely woman was
very friendly in the camp, but once we got into town she acted like I
didn't exist. Naïve me did not realize that an interracial couple was
not an acceptable sight in this part of Ohio. I had been enjoying our
expedition together and was asking questions and telling jokes when
she suddenly hissed at me—telling me to shut up. Back at camp, I
asked her what gives, and she ran it down to me, telling me about how
interracial couples had gotten their asses kicked merely for going to
a movie together. She added that the Klan was active in this part of
Ohio despite the recent gains of the civil rights movement. This was
quite an awakening for me.

Author's Note: America—love it, or leave it?

> *Back then, just as I do today, I abhorred the rise of hate and white*
> *supremacy groups that made our friends of color fearful for their lives. As*
> *I write this, forty-nine people have been shot and killed and many others*
> *wounded in New Zealand by a white supremacist. (To me, it is getting*
> *worse instead of better.) These days I still think about what I should do if*
> *my country is doing something unethical? Is it really America—love it,*
> *or leave it? Why can't it be America—love it, or fix it?*
>
> *I remember stories and have watched documentaries and speeches*
> *given by Dr. Martin Luther King, Jr. He was arrested numerous times*
> *for calling for voting rights and civil rights and organizing marches*
> *and staged sit-ins at lunch counters for all to see that people of color*
> *are human! Today, some of my conservative friends seem to think that*
> *refugees should be repatriated so as to get in line to cross the border and*

immigrate legally, a process that could take eight to ten years. Hence, the people of Central America are caught between a rock and a hard place. They leave their homes headed for the US in order to escape the high rate of crime and drug gangs that have de facto power in their countries. Women go north knowing that the cost of the journey is to be raped several times by their so called "escorts" while also risking getting caught and being sent back to their home countries. Most of them will try again and will have the same expectation of being raped again. Additionally, climate change is affecting the ability to grow food in many parts of Latin America, and many do not have the education to enable them to do something other than eke out a living and hope their children don't die because they may have little to feed them each day.

I ask myself, by what authority do we have the right to deny these immigrants—who are only trying to cross our border to seek protection and/or a better future for themselves and their families—a chance to find "Life, Liberty and the pursuit of Happiness"? I think that when someone arrives on the border trying to escape poverty and danger, we should immediately vet them for a criminal record, and if that record is relatively benign, welcome them to our country. Then we should support them in finding a job, or an educational opportunity or training program, and help them get established in the States or somewhere else in the world that needs their skills.

I think of Nelson Mandela and the laws he broke to end the evil political system of apartheid which stripped black people of their dignity and made many of them live in poverty. I think of Mahatma Gandhi and the laws he broke to bring independence to India. And our Native American friends would. have many reasons to break laws and treaties that had been forced down their throats. Talk to them, as I have, about how many treaties were broken over the years by white settlers.

I think that anyone reading these words would do the same thing— break any law that would help them care for their family and give their kids a chance at life. These people should be viewed as refugees and be provided sanctuary until such time as they can feel safe going back to their country. We should not build a wall; rather, we should invest that money in education and health á la Costa Rica.

For those of you who will think that there is no such thing as an unjust law, you are sadly mistaken. Read Nelson Mandela's Long Walk to Freedom *and you will see the story of a man who tried to work according to the law but eventually had no choice but to break the laws of South African apartheid. These refugees/immigrants coming across our borders today have no choice if they want their families to live. The Declaration of Independence should be applied outside our borders. If you read the Declaration again, you will find that our forefathers broke laws early in our country's history. Jefferson wrote: "Governments are instituted among Men, deriving their just powers from the consent of the governed,—That whenever any Form of Government becomes destructive of these ends, it is the Right of the People to alter or to abolish it."*

Was Nelson Mandela correct to have fought and endorsed violence towards the goal of ending apartheid in South Africa even though apartheid was the law of their land? He worked for years non-violently to change the system so he and his South African families could live in dignity.

My main concern is that white superiority is raising its ugly head again today at a time when I think the battle should have been won. It's true that we have had a black president, but racial incidents actually increased after Obama was elected president.

Since I began writing this memoir, a new museum opened in Montgomery, Alabama called the National Memorial for Peace and Justice, which tells the story of forty-four hundred African men, women, and children who were "...hanged, burned alive, shot, drowned, and beaten to death by white mobs between 1877 and 1950. Millions more fled the South as refugees from racial terrorism...."[1] There were laws restricting African Americans from voting, and I fully support the

---

[1] https://museumandmemorial.eji.org/

disobedience toward many of these laws despite the fact that some choose to believe that you shouldn't disobey a law but wait until it is changed. Wrong!

| III |

THE PEACE CORPS/ COSTA RICA: DREAMING THE IMPOSSIBLE

I decided that I would make my life my argument.
—Albert Schweitzer

Chapter Seven

IN PURSUIT OF THE DREAM:
COSTA RICA-BOUND

*B*y 1977 *I was* all set to go to join the Peace Corps in Jamaica. Then two of their volunteers were killed there in the midst of a revolution, which prompted the Peace Corps to close that program. So I took a position with the Residence Hall Program at the University of Delaware and began to read up vociferously on Latin America. I enjoyed the company of Brian McAree, Larry Adamkevich, and Michael Eilbaum on ski jaunts, trips to the beach, playing and dancing to "oldies" music, and having some of the best discussions about things that mattered philosophically, politically, and theologically. These conversations, together with memories of the poverty I had seen during my Latin American trip that kept coming back to haunt me, were important forces toward driving me to reapply for the Peace Corps.

An unpleasant experience I had at the University of Delaware also sharpened my desire to pursue that dream. While working as an Area Coordinator in the Residence Hall System, one of my staff members came into my office with a big grin on his face and said to me, "Guess what we did last night." I said I had no idea, and he replied that he and a group of friends had gone "trolling for niggers." In the grip of a slow burn, I asked him what that entailed. He said, with grin fast fading, it meant that they would get large wooden paddles and drive around looking for a solitary black person—male or female. When they found a likely victim they would stop the car and sneak up on that lone person of color and smack him or her on the behind. Then the culprits would run back to the car, laughing and bragging that they had scared the shit out of that nigger. I fired him on the spot. His direct supervisor came to see me fifteen minutes later saying that he was a good guy, and they were just having a little fun. The young African American woman at Triple S Camp instantly came to mind, and I could imagine how she would feel—scared to death and that the world was against her. I was ashamed to be white.

I was finally accepted into the Peace Corps in the fall of 1980 and was assigned to Costa Rica as a community and school gardens promoter. I went with the intent of finding out why people were hungry in this world today when there is enough food produced worldwide to make everybody fat, and also to find out why communism was so evil.

On November 6, 1980, I flew to Miami for an orientation process and then landed in San José, the capital city of Costa Rica, on November 10 with around twenty other people hopefully destined to be community and school gardens promoters. Another dream was coming true—thanks, Mom—thanks, Dad.

Chapter Eight

LETTERS HOME

Author's Note

The following letters were written in 1980, 1981, and 1982 during my time in the Peace Corps. I have not changed anything I wrote during my Peace Corps service. When I have needed to clarify or expand on my thoughts, I have done so in Author's Notes.

For my first year, I was stationed two kilometers from the Costa Rican/Nicaraguan border in a town called Los Chiles to be a community and school gardens/nutrition promoter. Los Chiles translates as "the joke," therefore, it was an appropriate place for me to be. It also turned out to be a staging area for clandestine military operations, so I was only in Los Chiles for ten months because my safety became a growing concern. When I wrote these letters and wrote about communism and Christianity, I often had my father in mind. We argued and discussed the issues in our hand-written epistles—no internet back then! It was my dad who gave me my passion to help poor people, but he also thought communist ideology was godless, and he couldn't stand that. I would argue with him today if he were alive, that it is possible to be a Christian Marxist. I think you might notice that my political, theological, and philosophical inclinations and beliefs evolved during my time as a Peace Corps volunteer.

NOVEMBER 13, 1980—SAN JOSÉ, COSTA RICA
(my first letter home)

Dear Dad,

Have been here two days and I am being treated very well. Costa Rican people are some of the nicest people I have ever met. The first day here we went to the Center for Human Development with whom the Peace Corps has contracted to conduct our training. The first thing we did was hit the garden and construct two raised-bed gardens designed to channel the rainwater away from the plants so they would not drown in the tropical rainstorms. We then proceeded to plant mustard, lettuce, Chinese cabbage, radishes, and coriander. I also planted string and black beans and cowpeas, learned about fertilizers and insecticides, and got many blisters and a sunburn. (A chicken just ran through the house followed closely by a goose. I may be eating the chicken for supper.) I was then taken to meet my host family, and they were very nice. Three families living in a six-room house—and I have one room all to myself. Then I returned to the Center and had a three-hour session in Spanish. Today up at 6:00 a.m. Classes start at 7:30—four hours of Spanish and four hours in the garden. Am surviving and I basically feel good, but it is quite a change.

Well, the political situation in Central America was starting to heat up when I got here. There is some communist activity in this country (which I am in sympathy with because they are organizing some very poor people). There is a possibility of civil war within Nicaragua; the government in El Salvador is eliminating (as in killing) the opposition without fear of reprisal now that Reagan is elected. His stated position is that he prefers strong alliances rather than human rights in countries here. This gives hope that negative effects of our foreign policy down here are corrected because there is going to be a lot of bloodshed in the name of anti-communism or in the name of strong alliances. I may see some of it or the results. Please tell people to look beyond their country and see the needs of people in other lands. We must become a lot more cognizant of some of the blatant lies espoused by our government if we are to survive as a respected and inspirational nation. We cannot, as a supposed Christian nation, or as moral human beings, make alliances with countries in the interest of stability and not consider human rights. People in the US have no idea of the things that have happened in Costa Rica and the other countries that make people scoff when it is said that we are a Christian nation. I was beginning to realize that we have acted in ways that have increased our economic well-being—especially that of large companies like United Fruit!

Love,
David

Author's Note

> *Reality-check alert: I was recently watching a news program analyzing our current president's affinity for strong men who are otherwise known as dictators. Historically speaking, our presidents have often undermined democracy in Latin America by supporting authoritarian regimes! An example is that FDR supposedly remarked that the dictator of Nicaragua, a guy named Somoza, was a son-of-a-bitch, but he was our son-of-a-bitch. The commentator on the above-mentioned program said that there are dictators who the US likes and those who we don't like. Now we seem to like dictators like Putin and Xi Jinping, and that these leaders have great strength—which is what Trump admires. Additionally, Trump is meeting with the dictator of North Korea who is an absolute son-of-a-bitch to his own people. Yet the democracies of Europe and elsewhere are being relentlessly criticized by the current administration for their supposed failings, despite their dedication to democracy. If we continue undermining democratic values, it is at great risk to our country and ourselves.*

November 18, 1980—La Garita

Dear Dad,

Well, here it is, my first week of training is over. One down and twelve more to go—and *boy*, is it intense. This is by far the hardest thing I've ever done. On Sunday all twelve of my host family's immediate relatives came over bringing with them their two or three kids each to meet me. They all talked Spanish very rapidly and all at once. The kids were screaming and the dogs, cats, turkey, and a rooster joined in. They are also offended by the American definition of privacy ... . There is none!

On the bright side, my mother here washes and irons my clothes every day. On the dark side, she hangs them on barbed wire. So much for my unpatched wardrobe. On the bright side, they are very nice and talk to me all the time. On the other side, I can't understand them.

You have heard of the Palestinian, Cambodian, and African refugees. Well, there are El Salvadorian and Guatemalan refugees here—and in bad shape. Will be spending some time with them in another month. There is so much pain in the world, and so few people do anything but put bandages on it. Would that I could change the system. Well, am learning *mucho* and am glad to have made the decision.

Love,
David

December 20, 1980—San José

Dear Dad,

My site for the next two years is going to be Los Chiles, two miles from the border with Nicaragua. Yes, I requested it because it is the most needy. Yes, there are Sandinistas operating in the area and, yes, there are refugees from El Salvador who I am interested in meeting. I have to go in by plane or boat because there are no roads, or they are too bad. Boondock City.

Also, Costa Rica is in an economic crunch because of a depressed market for bananas, coffee, and cacao. As a result, I may not get things I need for teaching kids how to plant crops and teaching their families how to eat right. I specifically will need money for seeds because I think I can make or beg other things that I need. So, if anyone needs or wants a fund-raising project, tell them all money will go for seeds and vaccines for chickens or cows, and I will be administrating any donated funds. (Countries like Costa Rica used to be self-sufficient, and by that I mean that Costa Rica used to grow a wide variety of crops and vegetables. But with the advent of large companies wanting land to produce coffee, bananas, and cacao for export—Costa Rica (and other countries) lost their agricultural diversity and became agricultural monocultures instead. That made Costa Rica more and more dependent on one or two crops, which meant that if the price of coffee was high, all was well. But when the price of coffee dropped, Costa Rica and other coffee-producing countries suffered until the price went back up. This is what was happening when I arrived in Costa Rica in November 1980. I became more and more cognizant of the need for biodiversity, especially for small farmers. When the market for coffee or bananas or cacao dropped, the farmers I worked with could normally turn a huge profit growing marijuana, for which there was a steady demand.

Went shopping in Miami to buy presents for my host family down here but had a hard time deciding what to buy because I can afford to buy more now than my host family has ever owned. There is more money in my four pairs of shoes than three of my host family brothers have together in their entire wardrobe. I think I'm getting more and more radical here and will upset people upon my return. But I guess Christ is more interested in poor folks than rich folks. In many ways, Americans are pharisees who think that because they give some, they are better than other people. I wish our schools would teach better about people in other lands. So, Carol, I'm going to try to send you stuff to use in your class when I can. I also am going to rewrite the history books. I hope I live to be a hundred because there is so much to do.

I was taken by my host family brothers to see a soccer match of the highest professional level in Costa Rica between Alajuela (known as La Liga, and fans are called Ligistas) and Heredia. Two of my brothers were ligistas and two others were fans of Saprissa, which is a perennial league champion in Costa Rica along with La Liga. Playing for La Liga was a legendary player known as "El Surdo" Jimenez which means the lefty because he used his left foot often to pass and shoot. That day, he scored two goals and assisted on two others and Alajuela won the match five to two, and so my brothers who were fans of Alajuela were very happy—especially when they found out that Saprissa had only managed a tie. I found out that it was essential for one's education to understand that soccer was like a religion in Costa Rica and that this would be true throughout most of the rest of the world.

It was also essential for one's vocabulary, because I learned all the swear words that could possibly be used at almost any soccer game, at any level. Words like *jue puta arbitro*, which means the referee is a whore, or *ciego*, which means blind—or another phrase that loosely translated implies that the referee and/or the opposing coach/goalie/player has had sexual relations with his mother.

Love,
David

JANUARY 17, 1981—LA GARITA

Dear Dad,

I'm back in La Garita now and what a trip I just had to Los Chiles (my site). And I thought I had culture shock when I arrived here two months ago! Actually it wasn't that bad or that small but what really hit me was the isolation of the town. It was only a thirty-minute flight from San José, but it is necessary to travel by air or go by boat. For only two months of the year is the place accessible by anything other than a horse, or a four-wheel-drive Jeep with chains, or a big tractor. The cost of the flight is 150 colones one-way, which is between twelve and fifteen dollars. But it's beyond the reach of most people in my town on any basis. The town is Pierpont-sized and is the center for commerce in the region. There are a lot of frijoles grown there. There are four flights a week and two boats a week that arrive basically when they feel like it. (Airplanes have some type of schedule—you know the day they will arrive.)

Around this time, my host family decided to have a family gathering on a Sunday, which is a normal thing to do for any family in any part of Latin America. It turned out that my host family had two daughters and one son who were also hosting Peace Corps volunteers-in-training, so it was a big gathering with rice and chicken and refried beans and fried platanos and cabbage salad—the works. The other PCV in training also came and kept asking me questions about how I felt and was I being treated OK and if I liked the family, etc. It wasn't until after I was out of the Peace Corps and getting together with the same group of Peace Corps volunteers-in-training some six months after completing our two-year stint in the Peace Corps that I found out the real reason everyone gathered that Sunday for lunch—much to my embarrassment and to the universal glee of my friends when they heard the story.

About two weeks into PCV training, I woke up at about four in the morning and I knew I had about twenty seconds to make it to the bathroom, which was in the other section of the house. However, someone had locked the door to the other part of the house where the bathroom was located, and I was desperate. I pounded on the door but nobody in the house moved. Then, clad in only my underwear and a T-shirt, I ran towards the gate at fast as I could, recognizing that I had to keep my butt cheeks as tight as possible for as long as possible. I made it just outside the gate towards the corner of the house when there came the worst case of explosive diarrhea I have ever had. I got some on the wall around the house, the grass, the bushes, and I think—a lonely banana tree. When all was done, I had a mess to clear up and nothing to clean up the mess with, except banana tree leaves. I had to do this because Ticos were getting up early and I kept having to hide in the bushes so that my host family neighbors would not see me running around scraping up and/or covering up the gigantic mess I had made as they went to work. I did the best I could and thought I had gotten away with it but, alas, I had not even a chance—although it rained hard and some of the evidence floated away. It turned out that my host family had sent for their other members hosting PCVs-in-training to find out why their gringo had taken a dump outside their front gate, and that's why they asked me all the questions about my well-being. We all laughed uproariously when two-and-a-half years later we all found out the real reason for their visit. I also checked the door to the inside of the house every night and was never locked out of the bathroom area again anywhere I slept.

I have a house with electricity for about thirty dollars a month. There is plenty of ventilation (i.e. holes in the walls) and I get to have a separate building in which to go to the bathroom. I have a small area of land to plant and grow chickens on and my own barbed wire clothes line. My stove is a hollowed-out table with sand in it in which I can make a fire. There is no chimney, however, and so the smoke goes in the house. I guess I'll be able to smoke chickens. I did see a dead leopard that was being skinned, which they said was *pequeño* but looked *grande* to me.

I have to buy a horse and if anyone comes to visit, I'll have to rent another one. They'll have to deal with the fact that there is a considerable amount of influence from Nicaragua and I met several "nicas" one of whom talked very openly with me about problems in Nicaragua. Later on, a person who overheard us said that the guy from Nicaragua "might be in trouble when he goes back home because the walls have ears." I'm hope to go there as soon as I can since I'm only two-and-a-half miles from Nicaragua, but I have to get permission from Peace Corps. That may not happen.

Love,
David

JANUARY 22, 1981

Dear Dad,

I'm in the last two weeks of training and I'm as exhausted as I've ever been. The new info keeps flowing all the time and I don't have time to absorb it all. Everything is in Spanish now and although I understand almost everything, it takes intense concentration—like the concentration you need for counseling—and that goes on for twelve to fourteen hours a day. This has been going on for two months plus, and I am just trying to keep my sense of humor up.

I have to give a talk Wednesday to my classmates on how to vaccinate a chicken, in Spanish, and I need to prepare for it. It should be wonderful experience for all as I can't find the verb for "to prick." I hope "to poke" works.

Love,
David

JANUARY 30, 1981

Dear Dad,

I am delighted that the church voted to send me money for seeds. I could use any amount you ever have for vaccines for animals. I will be teaching the students in the schools and the cooks about nutrition and trying to introduce other cheap crops that would improve their diet. I also know how to raise fish in fish culture ponds and might use money for this.

Only one more week of training and I'll be done. I'm probably going to arrive at my site on my birthday, so be thinking of me. I'll be home next Christmas and I'll probably talk for two to three weeks straight if I remember English.

Love,
David

February 6, 1981

Dear Dad,

Well, good news! I have passed everything! I received exactly what I needed to pass the Spanish exam and am now at the level of someone who can get along in this country. I made a number of mistakes in grammar, but I passed. I now know enough to be dangerous in technical aspects. I've studied fish, chickens, rabbits—and can kill and dress a chicken, grow twenty to thirty crops, know if there are pests, diseases, controls—can graft fruit trees, can fertilize anything, make compost, know organic controls—and can make fish ponds and build a chicken coop—all of which I have done and more. I am going to be sworn into the Peace Corps on Feb. 9 and will be at my site for about two or three weeks. Then we will return to San José for three to four days of orientation with the Ministry of Education, under which our program is located. While I'm in my house my carpentry skills will be sorely tested because I have to repair the holes in the walls of the house I rented. (Peter, where are you when I need you?) I have to build an outhouse and a tool shed and buy a horse. Also, Carol will be interested to know that the only bad thing on my evaluation was that "he needs to weed his garden more," but I call it the no-till method of farming!

Love,
David

Chapter Nine

LOS CHILES AT LAST: CUCARACHAS AND THE JUE-PUTA DAIQUIRI

FEBRUARY 14, 1981

Dear Dad,

I arrived today in Los Chiles at about 1:00 p.m. and went to a hotel here until I could check on the house that I rented. I spent this afternoon digging a hole for my outhouse and putting in my electricity with my landlord. I am going to spend tomorrow covering holes in my walls and disinfecting the whole house. I will also buy a bed, and will spend my first night there tomorrow.

I was taking a cold shower after work and I became aware of lots of eyes looking through the holes in my walls while I was bathing. I dried off and opened the door to my house and watched a few neighborhood kids scatter when one said to another "he's white all over!" I died laughing.

Throughout my time in Costa Rica, one of the things I enjoyed the most were the various mistakes I made in Spanish as there are several words that with the adding or changing or forgetting a vowel or consonant changes the meaning of the word often to great comic

relief! After a few weeks in Los Chiles, it came time for me to introduce myself to the teachers at one of their conferences. There were
over twenty elementary schools in the Los Chiles district and a high
school, and each school sent at least three teachers to each conference, and it would be my opportunity to impress them. So, I practiced
my speech and looked up all the verb tenses in my handy dandy 501
Spanish verbs book and was ready, I thought. My job was to plant
vegetable gardens in each school and get the harvests into the diet
of the school children, as there was a basic lunch every day of rice
and beans and not much else. In the middle of my talk a teacher had
the nerve to ask me a question and completely screwed me up. She
said, "Señor, can you get us some spoons for our kitchen?" The word
for spoon is *cuchara* and I wasn't sure what it was and didn't hear it
well—and I wanted to respond fast so she would think I knew what
they are talking about—but I used the word for cockroach instead of
spoon and I wound up saying that I could get them all the cockroaches
they wanted. Cuchara and *cucaracha*—spoon, cockroach. The teachers
broke down and laughed for a long time and then told me—no thanks,
they had enough already. The teachers teased me for the rest my time
in Los Chiles.

Another time about six weeks after arriving in Los Chiles, I went
to eat lunch with some friends at a little *pulparia* and I wanted to have
some ice cream for dessert. I was sure my Spanish could handle it but
when the waitress came to take our order I mixed up the word for ice
which is *hielo* with the word for ice cream which is *helado* and wound
up asking the waitress for a glass of water with ice cream in it to make
it good and cold. The waitress looked at me as though I were crazy so
I repeated myself. "Quisiera tener un vaso de agua bien fria con helado
a dentro." She went back to the kitchen and I heard them laughing
and talking and opening the little serving window and pointing at me
saying that's the gringo who wants ice cream in his water. Finally, they
came to me with a dish of ice cream on a tray and a glass of water next

to it and if the gringo wanted to have ice cream in his glass of water, he could put it there himself. We all laughed heartily!

The funniest thing that happened to me and about which I was teased unmercifully by my friends in Los Chiles occurred after about six months of being in my site. I was invited on a Sunday to the home of the family of the bank president of the local branch of the National Bank of Costa Rica. This is quite an honor because this does not happen very often as Sunday is a family day, and I had to use deodorant, take a bath, and generally spruce myself up and be on good behavior. Somehow the bank president's grandmother who was about four-foot-six (okay, I exaggerate, but she *was* short) had gotten the idea that gringos could make a drink she mispronounced until I finally realized that she wanted me to make a daiquiri (or *deqiri*, as she was saying it). I finally understood, and they had some type of rum and I asked for some coconut to shred and some lemon juice and some kind of lemon soft drink and some sugar and some of the local hootch that had been broken out to welcome me. Unfortunately, I asked the grandmother if she had a scraper to shred the coconut—only the word I used meant prostitute. I had asked the bank president's grandmother for a prostitute to help me make the daiquiri. Her face went white and she dropped the glass she was holding on the floor and it shattered. I was horrified to realize that I had said something terrible, and the bank president had just entered the kitchen where I was, and so I said, "I only need a little one," thinking she needed a little glass. The bank president laughed uproariously and could not stop laughing for an hour or so, and his grandmother's face gradually regained its color and she began laughing as well, but I did not find out exactly what I had said until the next day—because every time the bank President started to tell people what I said he began to laugh again. To be honest, the word I used was worse than prostitute, but I will only tell the real word if I know you or you send me something to assure me you won't sue me for the word I used. (Have to have a sense of humor to learn another language)!

Love,
David

FEBRUARY 23, 1981

Dear Dad,

Here I am, celebrating my one-week anniversary in Los Chiles. I'm still in my adjustment phase but am doing very well considering that I haven't spoken English for a week. My Spanish is improving all the time but I still make my share of errors. If you have gotten the tape by now, I think I talked about my running battle with cockroaches which start coming out of the wall at about 6:30 every night. Usually, by the time I go to bed I have killed eight to ten and ignored eight to ten others because those little buggers are fast.

I am beginning to get a little used to Los Chiles now. It is bigger than Pierpont and has about five bars and restaurants , seven stores, an "airport," and a telephone system like the phones we used to have when we called the operator and had her ring a number.

Yesterday I went on a riverboat ride and saw the border with Nicaragua. In parts I felt like I was on a jungle river with big trees, vines, coconut palms, and the squawking of big birds with big noses. It can seem very idyllic here and very peaceful. Los Chiles is not that bad-off developmentally and there are no people starving. There are some serious problems with nutrition and the further you get away from Los Chiles the more problems you see. Also met my first Sandinista, which was very interesting because he regarded me with a great deal of suspicion—wanted to know if I was with the CIA, and I don't think he believed me when I told him I wasn't.

Love,
David

MARCH 14, 1981

Dear Dad,

I'm here in Los Chiles and I am finally unpacked. It is a little difficult to unpack because each time I arrive here, it is an event. Usually about five to ten kids pile in after me and since I usually arrive with boxes and bags full of stuff, they are very curious about what I have. They always ask how much everything is, and when I tell them their eyes widen and then they look like they don't believe me when I say it is not very expensive. I went over to the house of the lady who does my laundry who had heard of all the things that I had brought with me. (This was only a half-hour after I arrived, and she lives on the other side of town.) She asked me, "Where did you get the money for this?" I replied that I got it from the Peace Corps. She said, "How many dollars do you have?" I replied, "Not many." At this point she looked at me rather frostily and stated, "I am bothered by gringos who think they are poor. Are you able to go home right now if you had to? Are you able to buy medicine if you need it? Can you buy food when you want it? Can you buy clothes when you need them?" And since I was sitting there wearing a new pair of shoes, holding a new pair of boots, and sporting a nice haircut, I said sheepishly that I could do all of these things. She replied, "I can't." Enough said.

I'll try to answer your questions now. The cockroaches range in size from a half to two-and-a-half inches long. My house has a floor and is about six inches off the ground. Whoever designed the house designed it so that there are plenty of cracks in the floors so that the cockroaches can get through. Nice of them.

My sink is constructed of wood and is a box about three-foot square that someone stuck on the side of the house with a water spigot that runs into it. Yes, there is running water and electricity. The electricity is generated from the nearby river. The town has about eight hundred people in it. There is no paved anything up here. The streets look like someone plowed them with about a three-foot blade. The only thing that gets around up here is a four-wheel-drive jeep with chains—and *they* get stuck.

The birds around here are like jungle birds. We have plenty of parrots, toucans, and related birds. I may get a parrot for a pet. [*I didn't.*] The trees I don't know very well, but we have lots of palm trees and banana trees and fruit trees. I have a banana tree and an orange tree in my yard, and anytime I want, I go pick one. I am going to plant flowers in my yard, but I have to figure a way to prevent the wild horses that wander around town every night from eating them.

They play baseball here, and I think I may get involved with a team from here if they get a league going. Soccer is also very popular—in fact, I've become quite a fan. However, when I play I've found that they can do things with their feet that I can't even do with my hands. I also learned all the slang and curse words I need at the soccer camps such as *hueputa arbitro.* It has something to do with the referee and his ancestors I think, but you can figure it out.

I go to both the Protestant and Catholic Church in town, and I tell them that I am a Christian and that I like and dislike both of their interpretations of the Bible. I can't discuss theology yet as my Spanish is not up to speed to discuss theology—but poco a poco.... (The more time I was there, the more disillusioned I became with organized religion and wondered where God was!)

Love,
David

MARCH 22, 1981

Dear Dad,

Well, another week has gone by, and it is hard to adjust here. (I haven't yet gotten used to my war with the cockroaches…) I know through the books I read that this is normal behavior for anybody adjusting to a climate (not just weather) that is radically different. It still doesn't make it any easier.

I especially don't like the way men treat their women here. I know from my counseling that a lot of men don't know the first thing about how to treat women in the US, but the men of the US would be like kings to the women down here. There is a saying here that the men say all the time, which is "I'm not married, but my wife is." Women here actually expect their men to be going out, messing around with other women. The director of the high school here, for example, has a house near Alajuela. His wife and family live there. He lives here with a woman on the main street of town and has two kids by her. He has a total of four kids by two other women (one of whom I know). They also think nothing of hitting their women, and I've seen some women with some pretty nasty scars and wounds. I am not sure what to do about it. And if the abuser is confronted about his actions, there is no real action taken and the abuser may take it out on the abused woman, thus making it worse for her.

Another problem is that I'm expected to behave and treat woman in the same manner, and I won't. The women seem so appreciative when I treat them like I normally do, and the men think I'm homosexual. I tell them that I'm not—and that no one can pressure me to do something I really don't want to do—and that I'll decide with whom I'll have any sort of relationship. Down here it helps to have pictures of girls with my arms around them, but they are freaked out when I say most of them are just good friends. They can't see women as friends, which is sad!

Love,
David

MARCH 29, 1981

Dear Dad,

What an eventful week this was! Monday night I helped organize a rescue effort for two babies that were sick in the night. Since Los Chiles is inaccessible except by plane and boat, and the nearest hospital is two-and-a-half to three hours away when you can get through in a four- wheel-drive jeep, we had to organize an emergency lighting system for the airfield. This consisted of all the cars in town and building bonfires along the edge of the runway. The landing and takeoff came off without a hitch and reminded me that I didn't want to get sick here and have to leave in a hurry. The babies survived. During my tenure in Los Chiles, we only had to do this one more time, when a young man was bitten by a poisonous snake. I had to walk for an hour and paddle a dugout canoe for an hour through a swamp and river and walk another half hour to get to the patient. The evacuation was successful!

When the MD and nurse assigned to Los Chiles are not there, sometimes people come to me for help. I am not much help, although I am certified in advanced Red Cross first aid and I have a book called *Donde No Hay un Doctor* (*where there is no doctor*), and I try to help as best I can. So, I can put bandages on cuts and I have a bottle of Tylenol to help with pain, but I can't do much more. What would help is better nutrition, which is the main reason why I am in a program to cultivate vegetables for the diets of the children.

I've become a popular person to give someone a shot in their behind when that has to be done and the doctor and nurses are not available. It seems that when you give a shot in someone's behind you kind of make an imaginary circle and you give the shot in the upper right quadrant so you don't hit an important nerve and paralyze the person getting the shot—or something like that. However, it has got out that

I make the sign of the cross over the patient's behind just before a shot in the butt, and that has made the people feel like God is helping me and keeping them safe. I do not deny it!

I eat my meals, breakfast and dinner, at the home of Elba and Anselmo Miranda Calix— and lunch is on my own—often eaten at one of the schools where I was working or a local restaurant, using the term restaurant loosely, very loosely. During my first meal with the family, after working in the gardens all day in the hot sun, I was famished and ate too much, as it turned out. The men in the family eat first, then the boys, and then the girls, and then the women—in that order. I took too much rice and beans, and by the time it was the women's turn to eat, there were no beans left for them. Since rice and beans are a complementary protein, that means that the women folk did not have protein in their meal, even if they were pregnant. I felt bad when I noticed this, because I realized that my gluttony had caused malnutrition in the women in the household. From then on, I made sure I took smaller portions. In fact, when I encountered a pregnant woman, I pointed out to the medical folks that there could be a male baby inside that woman—and that started to change the diets of pregnant women in Los Chiles. I, of course, didn't care if a female baby came out, which I think helped some of the pregnancies that occurred in Los Chiles. Sneaky.

On Tuesday, I went to visit one of the schools. When I arrived, I found a one-room schoolhouse with a blackboard that was cracked and chipped. There were two long benches, handmade with tables that wobbled a lot. The kids were dressed in ragged clothes, and there were about ten of them ranging in age from six to twelve. The kitchen consisted of three stones with a flat pan on them, and on this was prepared their meal of rice and beans and fried plantano which is a type of fried banana. Not bad for protein and starch but not much else. We worked to prepare a garden so they could have some vegetables in their diet, but I quickly realized that I would have to do two things: One is to plant peanuts to fixate nitrogen into the soil so that vegetables can grow. In the tropics there is no dormant season when the soil can be replenished with fallen leaves as happens in the United States. Tropical top soil is only four to six inches in depth and will wash away when there is a lot of rain. So I paid kids the equivalent of about a dime for each bucket of manure they could bring to my own garden, and I made kind of a horse and/or mule manure soup in a fifty-five-gallon drum and spread it onto the garden area. I also tried composting with any biodegradable plant I could work into the soil.

The second thing I realized was that I needed to build some sort of fence around the garden to keep the pigs out. Each pig had two long sticks of wood attached to the pig's neck forming a sort of X that blocked the pig from entering the garden. And if you had two or three strands of barbed wire every five inches or so off the ground to an overall height of twenty inches, the pigs could not pork out on (get it?) your vegetables. Anyway, we started preparing the land for the garden.

I arrived back in town to find four ophthalmologists from the States in Los Chiles—and only one translator. So, I translated for them for the next two days, and we examined the eyes of over 650 people. More than half had serious problems with vision, and of that half, half had problems that we couldn't help that were caused by the lack of knowledge and/or lack of access to medical help, and/or a bad diet. One of the saddest things I've had to do in my life was when I explained to an eight-year-old boy that he would never be able to see again. I'll never forget the look on his face when he finally understood my Spanish. We haven't known comparable sadness. And it could have been prevented if he would have had access to medical care. But we were able to help more people than we couldn't, and so the good and the happy outweighed the sad and the bad. This morning I helped kill a pig and butcher it. They use every part of the pig, including the fat and the head. I'm constantly amazed at what I eat. I am going to eat pig's feet tonight and maybe the ear, too. I just hope I won't throw up in front of everyone because they're always watching to see how I'm going to react to new things. I would almost kill for a decent pizza right now!

Love, David

APRIL 5, 1981

Dear Dad,

Hi there! I just finished mowing the lawn— and *boy*, am I tired. The job here is a little different because the lawnmower is a machete and a stick. You keep the stick in your left hand and the machete in your right hand and after you've swung the machete, you swing the stick to knock the grass back up so that it can be cut. Understand? Anyway, the natives are really good at it, and I'm terrible. My lawn looks like about ten cows laid down all around in it and left depressions in the grass. It is awful looking, and I'm going to hire someone to do it right tomorrow.

This week was slow because the teachers were in meetings for the first three days—and were they *boring*. But I got to know them much better, so that was good. Spent some of the money the church sent for seeds and to repair a motor for a boat so I could go visit the schools that are along the river. Am coming out of Los Chiles this Thursday because I have to buy more seeds and also fight for some tools—because I have to get the seeds in before the rainy season starts or I'll never get them in. I also have to get a gamma globulin shot to prevent hepatitis, so I'm going to take a break. I'm looking forward to it because I can relax a little when I don't feel quite so much on display. Interestingly, many people down here don't understand why I would leave my family for two years. They want to know if you're mad at me or vice versa, or whether I don't like the US, or what. I try to explain that I want to learn about their country, and that I want to change things in the US, and that I love my family and friends a lot. So you guys are on my mind frequently and I'm looking forward to seeing you all at Christmas and having a hot shower and a pizza!

Around this time, I encountered a shirtless young man with a backpack sprayer outside my house, patiently waiting for me to return home. I opened the door for him, and before I could say much, he started spraying a white substance around my house (using the term "house" loosely). I stopped him and asked what he was doing, and he said this was a part of the Costa Rican mosquito control program to prevent malaria, and it was mandatory for all structures in an area where malaria had been or was continuing to be a problem. I went over to the burlap bag that carried the insecticide and saw the words: USA Department of Agriculture—DDT. I was shocked to learn that I would have to live in a house that was regularly sprayed with a chemical that had been banned in the US because it was so poisonous for the environment. I tried to explain to the young man that he should cover his skin with a shirt of some kind and always wear a white filter mask over his mouth and nose to keep from inhaling it. All my words were to no avail, and I realized I would have to move to another area where malaria was not as much of a problem. Later, I found out that DDT and many other poisons are being sent (the correct word is *dumped*) by chemical companies to many other impoverished countries for use in agriculture without much warning to these unsuspecting third-world countries as to the poison that was in use in their fields. It turned out that the mother of the home where I ate my meals in Los Chiles had had six or seven miscarriages, and I have often wondered if DDT was the cause of her losing so many pregnancies. Malaria is a serious problem in many countries, but I think the cure has often been worse than the disease. However, I am quite sure that chemical companies did not have many pangs of conscience, as selling this product in the developing world is quite lucrative, I understand.

I also have had the chance to visit banana and palm oil plantations.

There was no sound—no birds chirping, no animal life, no nothing at all because of the great amount of chemicals used to keep the bananas in production. The chemicals are destroying any chance for a normal, healthy ecosystem, but we are sure to get our bananas while the plantation workers are often sick. In Nicaragua, there has been the same problem in sugar cane fields, and there were many people who harvested sugar cane who died from the use of agrochemicals. They were even buzzed and sprayed by crop-dusters while working in the field—sometimes several times. This ignorant behavior often caused a horrific disease from which the sprayed Nicaraguans began to die in an especially awful manner. The internal organs begin to implode and the worker often drowns in his or her own blood. No one really cares though. At least not those in power. For those with further interest in this subject, the disease caused elevated creatinine levels due to chronic kidney disease.

Love, David

April 13, 1981

Dear Dad,

Have been in San José for the last three days, and this week I'm going to beaches nearby for some very welcome R&R. I just need a break from the mental strain of being in Los Chiles right now, and hopefully, I will get back there next Monday rejuvenated and ready to go again. I wish I could get through this adjustment phase faster because I sometimes have no energy—or feel drained from a combination of the heat, the constant rain on some days, and being on edge because you are always being watched and people are making generalizations about America through you. It's a responsibility I take seriously and hope that I do a good job of representing you all. (I am told that many people of color feel the same way in our country.) I'm going to hit the sack.

My love to all, and remember me in your prayers,
David

Chapter Ten

THE CIA NIGHTMARE

APRIL 24, 1981

Dear Dad,

Here, it is Friday in Los Chiles, and there is the annual fiesta going on now which kind of reminds me of the county fair. Only there are only three food booths, a bull ring, a dancing and music area, and a drinking area. The bull ring is very interesting. They bring in these mean bulls and put them in the ring, and the men take turns trying to catch one and ride it. There were bodies flying all over the place last night and more than a few injuries and gorings. But it is a real macho thing, and they go and get drunk and try to do it. They were trying to get me to do it, but I couldn't get drunk enough. Nor did I try. I was the only one with a first aid kit and who knew what to do with a cut or a scrape.

Something funny happened at the fiesta. The equivalent of a School District Superintendent was dancing very close to the woman he was living with when his wife showed up—and *boy*, was she upset. She took a swing at him and nailed him on his chin. However, his heel caught on the roughhewn dance floor, and it looked like she knocked him on his butt. He took more grief about getting knocked on his butt by a woman than he did for getting caught by his wife living with another woman! In fact, men seemed to be expected to do this. One saying here is that "I am only married in my own house."

A really thought-provoking thing happened to me on a recent trip to another isolated school called Medio Queso. I arrived there a few weeks ago at about four p.m. and still had a little light left before the sun went down, so I checked out their school garden to see if there would be any use made of the seeds I had given the teacher. After a few hours of work, I was invited to dinner by the schoolteacher, which consisted of rice and beans, and one egg. It happened to be the only egg in town and was given to me as the honored guest, so I couldn't turn it down. As I prepared to go to sleep on one of the wooden benches, I was asked to join them to watch TV and drink beer (warm beer, which I dislike—but there was no refrigeration or electricity.) They had managed to get an ancient portable TV to work by hooking it up to a battery, and I watched the *Dukes of Hazzard* and *Dallas* along with the twenty to twenty-five people who live in the village of Medio Queso. *Dallas* was showing a particularly obnoxious episode where everyone seemed to be sleeping around, and there was a lot of backstabbing going on, and there seemed to be a lot of very expensive new cars. The *Dukes of Hazard* showed lots of women walking around in bikinis and many car-chase scenes with lots of accidents. No matter, because in the next scene, they had a new car which they promptly wrecked again in yet another scene. Finally, as the beer flowed freely it seemed to act as a truth serum, and the questions for me became more pointed—especially two of them: Why, if women ran around in bikinis and anyone could get a new car anytime they wanted, would someone like me be in Medio Queso—and was I an agent for the CIA? The last one really hurt me because I was in the Peace Corps for totally altruistic reasons and hadn't heard much at all about the CIA. So I read some books and talked to people about the role of the CIA in Latin America and was horrified to learn that almost every country had a story about the CIA or about an inappropriate intervention by the US military. I discovered that John Foster Dulles and his brother Allen—the former being Secretary of State and the latter being the Director of the CIA under Eisenhower—had orchestrated the overthrow of a freely elected government in Guatemala because the president of the country, a guy named Arbenz, would not do everything that United Fruit wanted him to do. Did I mention that both Dulles brothers were also on the Board of Directors of the United Fruit Company? And the more I read, the more I learned that they were constantly looking for leaders of countries to overthrow to stop communism, even if they were not communist. It seemed to me that if someone threatened US interests, they would often be labeled a communist, which made that leader fair game for the CIA to neutralize in many different ways. This is a nightmare to me, for we often say we are a beacon on a hill—that we promote democracy—that is, until the interests of the US are threatened, and then that threat is neutralized.

One of the most egregious examples of their stupidly was that they orchestrated the overthrow of the freely elected Prime Minister Mossadegh in 1953 at the behest of Great Britain, which wanted to regain control of the Iranian oil fields. (What was all that English oil doing in Iran?) Indeed, the coup was planned and implemented by President Teddy Roosevelt's grandson Kermit with the support of the Dulles brothers. I maintain that this event is a direct link to the instability of Iran nowadays, and is at the root of the problems we have had ever since in that part of the world. Had we left things alone and stayed out of their internal politics, we would have had and would still have a democracy in Iran, had democratic traditions not been undercut by the supposedly main promotor of democracy, the US. (Democracy continues to be undermined, even today, through the efforts of the leaders of Russia, China, and the US.)

There is also a relative calm here now in the wake of what happened here last week. Sandinistas crossed the border and killed a man about fourteen miles from here in a place where I have a school. The

Sandinistas have been restless ever since Reagan cut off part of the aid for Nicaragua, and since relations between Costa Rica and Nicaragua started deteriorating. So there have been some border incidents since then, and the police have taken to carrying rifles. But Costa Rica protested, and Nicaragua said they were sorry and that it wouldn't happen again. Yet it isn't all that reassuring. I'm kind of staying close to Los Chiles until it blows over and the Peace Corp checks it out a little. But it makes me think a lot of heavy thoughts, and I am tense when I'm traveling now, even though there is no apparent danger. The man killed was a member of Somoza's National Guard, and gringos aren't too popular there either. But I don't feel in real danger because I have met several Sandinistas here—I think some of the ones who were in on the killing—and they seem real cordial to me. I hope I'm right.

Am still having problems with transportation because the horses I have looked at to buy look dead, and the good ones are too expensive. So I've asked Peace Corps to give me a motorcycle (and now I can hear Peter giving me a hard time about that!). But it will be better for me if I use one because it is faster, and I can visit more schools.

Love,
David

APRIL 28, 1981

Dear Dad,

Well, some of the danger of the past week seems to have passed. The Sandinistas have calmed down and apologized for the killing of the man, and I even met some more of them. I am told that I met one of the big guerilla leaders of the revolution, but I don't remember what he looks like. (It seems to have been Commandante Zero—or according to his real name, Eden Pastora.) Oh well. But the situation seems manageable now. The situation was also helped along by four days of fiestas, which I think I told you about.

Have a list of projects that I might need money for. Have a friend in town here from Nicaragua who is very concerned about the youth of Nicaragua not having much to read. He is a Christian and wants to start a Christian library to take to his town in Nica so the kids can learn about God and things other than communism. This takes a lot of courage, and I told him maybe our church could help him out. One hundred dollars would be a start, and anything more would enable us to hire a boat to get them in. Also, I would like to buy a refrigerator so I can start buying and storing vaccines for chickens and other animals. Most of them need to be refrigerated. And there is always a need for more seeds, tools, fertilizers, boat gas. Am liking things better now…

Love,
David

APRIL 30, 1981

Dear Dad,

Things are actually *going* better. Yesterday I was able to get to a school in a boat. Such fun, but since gas costs three bucks a gallon, and I needed six gallons, it was expensive! But I had fun going on the river and saw some good jungle, a big snake (I didn't stop to ask what kind) and beautiful birds. It was great, and when I almost dropped the motor in the river and capsized the boat all at the same time when I was putting it on, I didn't even get mad. I also did all this in front of about twenty people and have had to take all kinds of kidding ever since. Oh well, at least I learned how to say "dumb gringo" in Spanish!

Also, the monsoon season is here, so it rains about three times a day and there is more mud than I've ever seen before in my life. My pants are muddy after walking twenty feet, and I am constantly sending clothes to the laundry lady. It is difficult to walk to the store, let alone to schools, and I still don't have a horse or a motorcycle. But when that gets solved, I'll be a lot better.

That's all for now as I have to go chase a chicken out of my garden!

Love,
David

MAY 7, 1981

Dear Dad,

Just got back from what was supposed to be a long weekend. I found out from a boss at the central office that if I went to San José and got permission from someone else, I could get a motorcycle. So, I did, and I rode it back today. It took six hours—and most people only take two or three! I don't know how to drive a moto in mud very well. By the time I got here, I had fallen in two mud puddles and gotten stuck once—and my backpack refused to stay tied onto the back of the bike and fell off at least ten times. As I did all this, I was afraid that the cycle would stop and I would be left in the middle of nowhere. But I made it and caused a good laugh among the people here when I arrived because I was covered with mud!

Now that I have a motorcycle I should be more effective in my work and have more of an impact. Things have settled down here a little since the Sandinistas crossed and killed that man. But it weighs on your mind and reminds me of how lucky I am to have a family like you guys and the support of the people in Pierpont. It seems that I can't emphasize this enough but hope that everyone really knows. I understand on a gut level what it is like to not have the security that we have in the States and I get even more motivated when I think that some of the reasons people live in fear here has to do with the actions of the States' foreign policy. I hope that you all are listening to what is going on in the world around us and remember that everyone is equal in the eyes of God.

I also was able to procure a horse from the auspices of a local farmer. I rode it once to visit a school before I got the motorcycle. When I swung my leg up to get on the horse, because my saddle girth wasn't tight enough, I kept right on going and fell off the other side, landing flat on my back in some mud, which cushioned the landing. When I finally did get properly situated on the horse, the horse turned his head and looked at me like—are you for real—is this some kind of nightmare? I finally got the horse going, but it seemed that, with each step, he was on the brink of death. I visited the school and went back to Los Chiles without any further protests or baleful looks from the horse.

About a week later, I wanted to use the horse again, but the caretaker/farmer said it had died a few days ago. I asked how, and the caretaker/farmer said it had died from a snake bite. I asked where was it, and the farmer didn't know. When I told this story to my fellow Peace Corps volunteers, they were less than sympathetic. One volunteer named Jerry thought that the horse had committed suicide rather than face another day with me on its back. Very funny!! But I didn't buy another horse, either.

Love,
David

MAY 14, 1981

Dear Dad,

It's been raining here in Los Chiles for two straight days, and I'm not able to travel because the roads are so bad that it is impossible, and I can't plant my garden because the ground is too wet— and I'm bored stiff. I leave Saturday for La Garita for a week-long workshop in Spanish. At least I won't be bored anymore. We have a workshop every three to four months so we can learn to use more verb tenses and learn more grammar. Maybe I'll actually be able to use this language well someday.

Before all the rains started, I was able to visit several schools and I went to the town where that man was killed. That was quite an experience. The road to there is like a motocross course complete with gullies to cross, bridges made out of two logs, steep hills, and a washboard surface. It is really a lot of fun to go to this place. I got chased by a bull down a hill, and since the bull was gaining on me, I didn't slow down at the bottom. Well, there was a jump there that I didn't know about, so I jumped across a three-foot gully on the motorcycle. Scared me to death, but I made it and got out of there! When I arrived at the above-mentioned town, it was like arriving at an old deserted town in a western movie—where you don't see anybody, but you know people are watching you. The town consisted of about four buildings and the school, and luckily there was one guy there who worked for the Health Ministry who recognized me. He came out, and then his family, and then the rest of the people in town. And since they knew that I was in just as much danger as they were, they talked quite openly about how they always check to see who is coming and if they are armed. They seemed to think the guy that was killed was a Somoza supporter, so they weren't in real danger—but they weren't sure. Anyway, these people shared with me their food and hospitality and their fears about death—and it was quite moving! (There is no safety net for many people living in poverty.) I hope nothing happens to them, because they are good people!

Monday I was at another school and got caught in a rainstorm on the way back—and an hour trip turned into three-and-a-half hours since I was learning to drive in the mud. But I didn't have any big problems, except that the mud gathered in the back wheel, and I kept on having to clean it out.

Love,
David

MAY 28, 1981

Dear Dad,

You asked me to describe my job more when we talked on the phone.
So here goes! My biggest problem is transportation, so when I get up
in the morning I check to see how bad the roads are because if it has
rained very much, I can't use the motorcycle. So the next thing I do
is check the boat. If a teacher isn't using the boat without permission
(like this week) I can go to the six schools along the river. Except that is
expensive and costs 250 colones for one tank, and because four tanks
of gas eats up a third of my salary, I'm careful with that. When I finally
get to a school the first thing I do is check the garden to see what needs
to be done. Sometimes the land needs to be cleared, or the soil loosened,
or raised beds built, or weeding done—yuk. (That's right, I still hate
to weed!) So I either tell the teacher what needs to be done, or I work
with the students and do it. We spend from one to two hours working,
and then I go to another school if there is one close enough. If not,
I find a school with a few wooden benches and I go to sleep on the
bench. There is no bench wider than 12 inches—and it is most uncom-
fortable—and I keep falling off because the legs and the ground are
uneven, and the slightest movement can topple me onto the ground,
which may also be wet from extensive rain. So then I stay overnight
as best I can and go to another school nearby the next day. I also have
given talks in Spanish to the kids on seed germination, compost piles,
garden design, companion planting, erosion, and lots of other things. I
hope that gives you a better idea of what I am supposed to do.

Love,
David

Author's Note

> *I had just gotten a letter from Dad in Lake George. I pictured the old cabin there and us sitting at the table making English muffins (with soup cans on top of them to toast better). I thought I would give nearly anything to have a meal like that right now—an omelet with lots of cheese, English muffins, jelly, and bacon. My mouth was watering, but I knew that in a half-hour I would trudge off to get my daily injection of rice and beans.*

JUNE 6, 1981

Dear Dad,

It's been raining for a week now, and this marks the beginning of winter down here. The mud is so deep on the road that a horse got stuck this morning. A horse! I couldn't believe it. A horse had fallen in a hole up to the top of his back. This hole was in the middle of the road—the main road out of town! *Boy*, did I feel isolated after that. If you even get two days of sun, the road dries enough to travel, although you have to find the right ruts. But the minister of health is going to lend me a horse, and I guess that will help. It is just that the horse is twenty kilometers away, and I can't get to it unless I struggle through that mud. And it's going to be a long winter, so I've started working with house gardens. I'm going to do this because I won't have to travel and I can have a good effect. It also looks like I will be using my boat a whole lot more to visit other schools. The bad thing about it is the cost of gasoline. Oh, well. At least I'm learning about the problems of a developing country firsthand. And when this is all over, remind me that at times it was a pain.

Love,
David

Dateline June 17, 1981

Dear Dad,

Today, when I returned from San José I took a bus to Cuidad Quesada and then a small plane from Cuidad Quesada to Los Chiles. Because the clouds were so bad (ground to 5,000 feet) we took off and returned to Cuidad Quesada two times before finding a break in the clouds to go through. The pilot kept going near the ground to look around and see where we were. When he finally found out where, we were almost out of Costa Rica and in Nicaragua—and had to go into a steep turn to avoid crossing the border. I felt like I was back in the beginning days of aviation and the barnstorming that I have only read about. But it was quite exciting, and I don't think I'll ever lose my love of flying. I finally recognized the river that I also used for travel, and we flew up that river, which had sharp turns. And when we arrived in Los Chiles we flew down the main street about fifty feet above the buildings, buzzed the runway to get the cows off it, and then landed the plane. We sat there on the plane, unable to move, and the pilot grinned at me and said—what fun! Nothing that happens on a big passenger plane (like a 747) even phases me now.

Love,
David

June 17, 1981

Dear Dad,

Got back to Los Chiles yesterday from a two-week working vacation, where I went to a beach and had several boring meetings. The beach was called Manuel Antonio and ranks up there with the most beautiful beaches in the world. It is very isolated, with very little development, and it is possible to camp there for about twenty cents a night about twenty feet from the ocean at high tide. The beach was shaped like a crescent, with white sand and various rock formations of different colors out in the sea. The jungle is behind you with beautiful palm trees and vines growing, with monkeys and beautiful birds (parrots, macaws, etc.) in the trees. It was gorgeous!

There wasn't much new in Los Chiles when I got back. Life is still hard for the majority of the people here still, and hostility for gringos is rising. Have experienced quite a bit in the last month from various people in various forms. One night, two drunken Sandinistas berated me about the evils of the United States (alcohol is sometimes a truth serum) and the fact that everybody in Central America is going against America. They made me so mad that I defended Reagan, (although there is nothing about his foreign policy that I like). I argued with them half successfully about the good things we have done, but was limited by the fact that my Spanish goes to pot when I have to talk that fast—because if I stopped they would start talking again. The problem is that I agreed with many of the causes of their hostility and I can't defend many of the actions of the US. But I did want them to see the other side of US motivations.

I would like to explain some of my feelings. I am proud to be an American and a citizen of the US. But I think what happens to many Americans is that we confuse American patriotism with Christianity. As I understand the Bible, God is concerned and will be angry, if he isn't already, about injustice in the world and the mistreatment of poor people. Read Amos and Isaiah again and the part of the Bible that talks about the years of the Jubilee. Then read a history of whatever country (except Costa Rica) you want in Central and South America, Africa, or Asia—and you will find a history of exploitation, and/or rape in the figurative and literal sense, and/or power in the hands of a few who use the poor people to keep them that way. I have read histories of almost every country in Central and South America, and some of the countries in Asia, India, and Africa—and find that the good is outweighed by the bad things the US, France, England, Belgium, Germany, Holland, Portugal, and Spain, have done. (See, I spread out the blame.) For example, take Latin America. Since independence from Spain for most countries in Latin America occurred by 1820 or so, there has been 160 years of war, exploitation, ruthless dictators, and hungry people there. That is a long time to build up antipathy towards the colonial powers of first England after Spain (which continued to about 1900) and then the US taking over the role of hegemonist until the present day. I think I can make a case that the US government or American businesses were behind most, if not all, of the problems in Nicaragua for the last 160 years. William Walker, a gringo, tried to take over the country to make it a state of the United States; he was President of Nicaragua for a short time before he was assassinated. Indeed, the airport in Costa Rica is named after a young man who fought against William Walker and was killed: Juan Santamaria.

Costa Rica is one of my favorite countries in the world! This is not only because of its great natural beauty and the kindness of its citizens. It is because of its dedication to democracy and the fact that it does not have an army. Also, Costa Rica, when it was settled by the Spanish, did not have a settled indigenous population that could be enslaved or exploited. So the population of Costa Rica was much more egalitarian because the land owners worked side by side with the other workers in the fields. I should clarify and say that there were some indigenous peoples in the Costa Rica area, but they were not settled into cities á la the Incas, the Mayans, and the Aztecs. They were nomadic, and fought the Spanish, and were eliminated.

I would like to mention a hero of mine, although I never met him. His name is Pepe Figueres, and he was a general in the Costa Rican army when there was an attempt to overthrow the freely elected new president in the 1948 elections named Ulate. To make a long story short, Figueres raised an army, overthrew the government that had stolen the elections, and put himself in power. He was in power for eighteen months, and during that time he created a *Junta de Gobierno*, which wrote the new constitution of the country. Then he did something unheard of in the annals of Latin America governments; he gave the presidency of Costa Rica to the man who had won the elections even though he (Figueres) was not of the same political party as the winner. Unheard of! Astounding! Normally, in many countries it is: one man–one vote–one time. (The late president of Venezuela, Hugo Chavez, is an example of this—as is Nicaraguan president, Daniel Ortega.) And while Figueres was in power, he eliminated the army and thereby freed up the money for military expenditures to be used to build schools, train teachers, and organize a nation-wide health system.

It is no accident that Costa Rica has one of the highest literacy rates in the world, above 90% in most surveys. Most countries in the developing world do not need a military of any kind, but they do need a police force. So I love Costa Rica, not just for its beauty, but for its love for democracy. And this country should be an example for many countries to emulate.

The best thing that has happened to me in the last four years is a gradual change from being a citizen of only America to also being a citizen of the world and trying to look at America through the eyes of other countries instead of the red, white, and blue glasses we normally look through. (It is that I am proud to be an Ohioan, and a citizen of the USA, and a citizen of the world. These identities are not mutually exclusive.) The fact is our policies have killed and exploited more people than our aid has helped, and one has to remember that some of our aid is military aid to further our own interests as a country. (I will admit that there are some wars I would fight, though, like World War II against Hitler.) We can have some good discussions when I come home in December.

Well, am going to get this in the mail today, so I'll catch you all later.

Love,
David

While living in Los Chiles, I became friends with the local head of the Communist Party, whose name I forget, but who I will call Don Pedro. I had long conversations about the pros and cons of capitalism versus communism, and he could not be moved from his extremely negative fiew of capitalism. When I was forced to leave Los Chiles, Don Pedro was waving at me at the local airport as my plane took off. He looked rather smug, as I recall—as if he felt that communism had won the engagement with the gringo representing capitalism. He might be very poor, but he was not going to abandon his constituency, such as it was.

About five or six years after I left the Peace Corps, I visited Los Chiles again to see my old friends. Pedro was one of them and I was pleased to see that he was well-dressed and looked healthy. He furtively glanced around to make sure no one was looking and then said, "I am not a communist any more. SHHHHHH!" Pedro was selling rocking chairs made out of different colors of very strong wire and some other odds and ends. He was now a venture capitalist and did not want to hear anything about his days as chair of the Communist Party. He had found some degree of hope for his family earning money selling furniture. I bought two rocking chairs and kept continuously teasing him about being a decadent capitalist. But the moral of the story is that if a person does not have hope for a better life, he or she will look for the best theology or political party that promises and delivers food and shelter for his family and the hope for a better future. Humankind must be allowed to dream and to accomplish those dreams for themselves and their families, or the result will be violence.

Chapter Eleven

LIBERTY LOST?

Author's Note

> *The following letter describes an incident that crystalized and reinforced my belief that the principles stated in our Declaration of Independence should prevail everywhere in the world. Although I was completely inno-cent, the actions of a so-called friend caused me to be accused of drug traf-ficking, jailed, and nearly sentenced to eight years in a hell-hole prison. But I was lucky—I had the full weight of the Peace Corps and the US embassy behind me, so I was able to walk away from it after two awful days and nights of miserable physical conditions and gut-wrenching fear. Had I been a poor Tico, would I have been "created equal" and endowed with a God-given right of a fair trial and, ultimately, "Liberty"?*

AUGUST 11, 1981

Dear Dad,

Well, I've had some adventures in the past couple of weeks and I don't mind if you write this up in a letter to my friends.

About ten days ago, on a Wednesday, I went to the aduana, which is the customs office—the place to pick up packages in Costa Rica. (I was in San José for an all-volunteers conference and for the embassy to check on my security situation in Los Chiles because there have been some more border problems with Sandinistas.) I picked up the package, which was a cassette from Dad, and then a friend arrived and asked me to pick up his package because he needed to go somewhere in a hurry, and it takes hours to pick up your package. I agreed, which turned out to be the biggest mistake of my life because inside the guy's package was half an ounce of marijuana, and when I left the aduana, the Costa Rican equivalent of the FBI were waiting for me. They showed me their badges and asked me to accompany them to their headquarters so they could ask me a few questions. I said okay and went with them, not having the foggiest idea what they wanted because I hadn't opened my friend's package although someone else had opened it. On the way to the headquarters, they asked to see my ID and were surprised that my name did not match the name they had received. (The aduana opens all packages that come in and someone had called the police.) When we arrived at the headquarters, they opened my friend's package and showed t to me. They said, "This is marijuana," (jamming the package under my nose for me to smell) "and you are in big trouble and under arrest for trafficking marijuana." I was completely shocked but figured that when I told them my story and found my friend, everything would be all right and I'd be back on time for supper. Little did I know!

I was detained at around 2:30 in the afternoon, and when I asked to call Peace Corps, they told me I couldn't call for about forty-eight hours, if then. This made me mad and scared—since I had visions of Papillon and getting stuck in jail. I was incensed and humiliated to be fingerprinted and photographed for mug shots, all the while protesting my innocence. I was placed in a holding cell and told to take off my shoestrings, my belt, my chain necklace, and my watch—and put my money and the things I took off in a bag, which I never thought I would see again. The holding tank was pure cement with a toilet in the corner covered with excrement, and the cell looked filthy. I was told I would spend the night here and I might get to call Peace Corps in the morning. I said I'd better call now, and they laughed and said lots-a-luck, which made me madder. There is nothing like being in a disgusting jail (having done nothing wrong), having no one know where you are, and being powerless to do anything about it. I can't imagine being any more upset than I was at that moment. Until later...

At about 6:00 that night, the arresting officer came and asked me how to contact my friend, and I said that Peace Corps could contact him if I could call Peace Corps. With that, they took me into a room where five men sat in a semicircle around me, firing questions at me in Spanish as fast as they could, trying to get me to admit that the package I had picked up for my friend was mine. We wound up yelling back and forth until they finally agreed to let me call Peace Corps, which I did. I called the directors, Pepe and Jean Lujan, and they proceeded to bring the wrath of God down on the police. (I must say, Pepe and Jean treated me with love and support throughout the ordeal and were directly responsible for getting me out as fast as I eventually did.) But right then, things looked bleak for the home team. Peace Corps found my friend, the police arrested him, and he proceeded to confirm my story. So I said, then let me go. The police responded that I had to stay the night, make a statement in the morning, and then could go. Since that was the best I could do, I shut up and tried to resign myself to a night in the pig sty with the drunks that were starting to come in for the night. I wasn't allowed to read anything, couldn't talk to the guards, and the rest were too drunk to understand. And my friend was in another cell because they were afraid I would deck him! I wouldn't have, but I sure felt like it. So I passed the night measuring the cell and trying to keep the drunks from vomiting on me. I didn't get much sleep, had a lousy supper and bread and water for breakfast on Thursday. Finally, they came for me at about 9:30 a.m., and by 10:00 I had made my statement and thought I would be out. At 10:30 the police came for me and my friend, and we were told that

I had to appear in court. Because I had been arrested, a judge had to let me go. By the time we got to court, it was closed, but we talked to Jean and Pepe, who said that our hearing was at 2:00 p.m. and at least I would be free by afternoon. So they took us downstairs to a holding tank to wait for our hearing. But at about 12:45, the police came for us, handcuffed us (for the first time), and instead of leading us to the court, put us in a small, cramped paddy wagon. When my friend and I asked where we were going, no one would tell us, and I started to get upset again. Finally, in the paddy wagon we were told that we were being placed in San Sabastian, which is the maximum-security prison for Costa Rica and which made the other place where we had been held look like the Waldorf Astoria. As soon as we got there, I started talking because I was mad, had been psyched to be free, and was afraid that I was getting a real runaround. But it was to no avail— and I was stripped, made to take a shower, and outfitted in prison blues with my own pair of bracelets. I was analyzed by a psychologist, a social worker, and a lawyer—and my friend and I were put in the minimum-security part of the maximum-security prison. Thank God. The next part was a scene from the movies.

We had to go get our mattresses in the maximum-security part of the jail and had to walk a gauntlet of men in cages to the room that held the mattresses. It seemed that every inmate had heard that two gringos were coming, so we were greeted by every epithet and filthy word in Spanish and English that you can think of: "Let's kill them— fresh meat—let's fuck them…" and so forth. That was the longest two minutes of my life. Never in my life have I felt so much hostility. We got our mattresses and made it back to our cell, which we shared with thirty other guys. The jailhouse lawyers were giving us advice when Jean and Pepe showed up with a very good lawyer who swore he could get us out the next day, which was Friday. I didn't believe it because I thought I should not have even been there in the first place and prayed like heck that night. We went back to our cell and ate dinner,

which was disgusting—served on plates that had crud cakes on them
and which we had to eat with our fingers. I didn't want to touch it let
alone eat it, but I did since I hadn't eaten since the stale piece of bread
in the morning.

The night passed uneventfully, except that our blankets and mattresses were stolen while we were talking to the lawyer, and here there
was a real advantage to being big. I walked up to two inmates and
asked them where my blanket was. They both handed me theirs and
said they didn't want to fight. I laughed for the first time in days and
said I didn't want to fight either and took the blankets!

The next morning my friend and I went to court and we both made
statements again in the presence of our lawyer. But as the police statements were being read to me, the scariest thing happened. The police
had tampered with the evidence and had lied in their statements. They
said that, while at the aduana I had opened my friend's package, and
that the police had reopened the package in my presence at the aduana.
This is critical because it implied acceptance of the package and a fore-
knowledge of its contents. I had hardly even touched the package. I
then was asked to identify the package, and it was *a different package*
than the one I had picked up. But the dummies had forgotten to put
stamps on it, so I asked how it could have been mailed without stamps.
Later, I was told that that got me out because the police were caught
saying that I had picked up a package that was impossible to have been
mailed. Anyway, we went back to jail while the judge read our statements, and we were finally let out with the charges pending at 3:30
p.m. on Friday. The effect on me when I drew my first breath of fresh
air was great, and I savored it. It was a great feeling to be free again.
I had hated being in handcuffs, and in a prison uniform, and being
paraded around in public where everyone will think you are a criminal.
And since I had done absolutely nothing wrong, the loss of freedom
was doubly distasteful. But Jean and Pepe were great and were as upset

as I was—and Jean kept crying when she saw me in cuffs because she knew I shouldn't be there.

On Sunday of that week, my friend told me that he was going to receive more marijuana in the mail and that he had received marijuana (in envelopes instead of packages) before. Up until this point, I wasn't all that mad at him, but this was absolutely stupid because it put his friends and the whole Peace Corps program in jeopardy. He was really stupid. And since he was going to receive more, that put both of us in danger of going back to jail. The decision was made to get us both out of the country—and my friend out of the Peace Corps.

So I am now in Honduras visiting people I know here. Why did I leave? I was not going to go back to jail for anybody or anything because of the way the police manipulated the evidence. But I have the support of the Peace Corps and they want me to come back. I do, too. But if I can't, I will transfer to Honduras and work here. I had the permission from the Department of Immigration here, my lawyer, and Peace Corps to return to Los Chiles—and everyone thinks I'll be back, and I even bought a round trip ticket. So by the time you get this, I may be in Los Chiles again. Although there is an ongoing concern about my security in Los Chiles, we don't think the situation is serious enough to prevent me from going to back to Los Chiles. That, however, was a cover story.

Honduras is a country that is poorer than Costa Rica where there is almost no middle class, just very rich people and very poor people. In Costa Rica there is a middle class, which I have learned is an important indicator of the economic health and stability of a country. Honduras consistently ranks as one of the poorest countries in the western hemisphere and has often been under the rule of a dictator.

Here in Honduras almost everyone is poor. It is common to have families that have had fourteen or fifteen children with six to eight of them dying before the age of five. The roads here are terrible. The buses worse. I helped to rebuild a road so the bus I was on could go through.

With an hour to go in my trip to a friend's house, darkness fell and the headlights on the bus didn't work. We were in the mountains, with cliffs like those in Ecuador all along one side of the road!

A baby died of malnutrition in a village where I was visiting a friend. In another house, my friend and I helped get worms (not earthworms—the kind babies get from bad water) out of the mouth of a child of a family we were visiting. The child of another family had a swollen belly because of worms and infected cuts on the belly where the mother had tried to let out the gas.

Physically, Honduras is beautiful, but the people are struggling for each mouthful of food. So it's been quite an experience over the past two weeks.

Today I'm at Copan near the Guatemalan border visiting some ancient Mayan ruins. I had to take a break and get away from it all. I've felt and seen too much pain. I think it will last me a lifetime. Although I'll be all right, now I need a break. The effect of all these adventures on me has served to radicalize me again. I am incensed that people around the world are incarcerated without a trial and without having done anything criminal. The Jews in Russia, the dissidents there, the people who have disappeared without a trace in Brazil, Argentina, Uruguay, Chile, South Korea, the Philippines, South America and many other countries. It pains me that our government supports many of these repressive regimes, and this has made me value the rights of political prisoners all over the world. And although, comparatively speaking, my experience wasn't bad at all, I never want to lose my freedom again and I want to help people who have lost theirs for no good reason at all.

If my friends get this, I want you to know that I probably thought of all of you while I was in jail—and the good times we had and I appreciate, and all. I really missed you! That goes double for my family, whose love and support I cling to in my mind. It brought me a lot closer to God because, for a while, it was just me and Him, and He seemed very real to me.

Some of you guys didn't get letters I was planning on writing because of all this. You may not for a while, either, because I need to sort things out in my head about what has happened to me in the past two weeks. But I will pick it back up when I can, and I know I can count on your support in the future, as always!

Love to all,
David

Chapter Twelve

RETURN TO LOS CHILES

Dear Dad,

Hi there! Well, yesterday, no—the day before, I arrived back in Los Chiles. At long last! I never thought I would actually miss the place so much. But it was good to be back and the people were glad to see me. I had called the family I eat with and let them know I would be back, and several people came out to the airport to greet me. On the way into town I felt like I was on parade. It took me two hours or so to go one kilometer, as I had to talk to everyone. When we (my boss from the Peace Corps was with me) arrived at my house, we found that the Health Department was there spraying my house with DDT to kill mosquitoes to stop malaria. They thought they were doing me a favor. But DDT is one of the worst poisons there is and they use it all over the place and indiscriminately. American and European companies are dumping these poisons down here since they are banned in the States and Europe. The guy spraying my house very proudly showed me the bag of DDT which said "Made in the USA." I was hoping it came from somewhere else because problems with chemical pollution are becoming a real problem down here. We often dump chemicals in the Third World that have been banned in the US because the residents of the developing world don't know that they are being poisoned. Indeed, one farmer thought that the chemical he was using to kill mosquitos in his house (again DDT) would cure a wound to his horse. So he put DDT directly on the wound his horse had for a couple of days, and his horse died as a result of this "medicine." He was poor and didn't have the money to get even an old nag. He had used his horse to work his fields and produce food for his family, and now that was gone.

I proceeded to show my boss around town, and he was impressed with all the gardens around here. It felt good to see kids eating the fruits of the things that I had planted with them. There were some problems with the radishes, however, since they need to be thinned every once in a while in the early stages so that the roots develop well. That hadn't been done, but at least they were eating something. Towards the end of the tour, I dumped my motorcycle into the mud and my boss and I fell into the biggest and deepest mud hole I have ever seen. No one was hurt, but I was laying on top of him laughing so hard I couldn't get up. He kept sinking in mud, which made me laugh harder, and by the time we both got up, we were another color! We were still laughing about two hours later.

In answer to some of your questions on the phone—here goes, about the political situation and my dislike of Reagan. He, in his foreign policy, is doing the same things over again that got us into trouble down here in the first place. He is basically supporting the elite, rich minority in almost every developing country in the world against the poor people who usually are in the majority. This plays right into the hands of communism. I've just finished reading two books about Marx and Engels (Engels was Marx's sidekick) and three books about the history of the times and economic theories. Marx, in my opinion, wrote (when the *Communist Manifesto* was published in 1848) as a reaction to excesses or evils of capitalism, which in the 1840s and 1850s was famous for having children chained to their factory machines working eighteen-hour days and receiving a pittance for their work. The horror stories about this time period are awful, and there was quite a disparity between the rich and the poor. This is critical, I think. When there is such disparity between rich and poor, no way to redress grievances, and no prospect in the near future to change this—you eventually get the poor people mad at the upper class.

I think I can make this argument, this scenario, about whatever country in the world that is "fighting communism." If you read Mao Tse-Tung's "Little Red Book," you will find that he says that the source of communists' power is in the frustrations of the majority of the poor people. Why not, then, undercut the legs of communism as it is practiced and make sure people simply have enough to eat, a place to sleep, clothes, and medical attention—and most importantly, the security to expect those things in the future? Your vision of a communist is a godless zealot with no morals or scruples who sacrifices all for the state, while a communist down here can be a poor farmer who goes to church and wants to have his babies live and enough to eat. Why then is there any logic whatsoever to arming the rich elite with helicopters and going into a village of poor people with all guns firing on the helicopter and having men, women, and children die on the pretext that there were some "communists" there. (This has actually happened in El Salvador and Guatemala a number of times. While in Honduras I talked to refugees who had lost several family members in this way.) What happens to the people in this situation? Does it scare them into never seeing a communist again? The answer obviously is: *no*. The reaction is—I am going to pay those xxx guys back—and as more incidents occur, the resolve gets stronger and stronger. When poor people feel that there is nothing to lose—*which they do down here and all over the world*—it is very hard to beat them.

Please tell the congregation thanks for the money. So far, I have used the money for seeds and fertilizer and gas. I have bought radishes, mustard, beans, frijoles, corn, carrots, beets, peppers, tomatoes, onions, eggplant, and okra—and have had around fifty-five gardens in the area ranging in size from one meter wide by ten meters long, to an acre. I also used the money to buy 10-3-10 fertilizer and to buy gas to be able to visit these schools and communities. Hopefully, I will get more gardens going soon, since a month layoff affected things a little bit.

Thanks for all your love and support through this past month. It's been rough, but I learned a lot from it.

Love,
David

Author's Note

Now, as I am in the process of editing my book, I feel that I am one of the few North Americans that has spent time in a Central American war zone living with hopelessly poor people for several months. When I see our current president speaking so ignorantly about the threat those caravans of refugees are to the citizens of the USA, I am dumbfounded to think that so many people believe him—rather than someone like me, who has lived the experience of total poverty in Honduras, Costa Rica, Nicaragua, and Guatemala—and returned there many times since my years in the Peace Corps. I know what poverty looks like on the faces and in the eyes of someone who is starving, having seen this for the first time on that fateful family trip to Brazil when I was sixteen.

On one of my first trips to Guatemala, I befriended our bus driver Luis. He had lived and worked in New Mexico for about two years to earn some money so he could take better care of his family. The first time he attempted to cross into the US, he was caught and sent back to Guatemala after a short stay in one of our detention centers. He tried again about a month later and this time he made it and was able to help his family by wiring them half his paycheck every month.

When I asked him what the journey was like, his eyes would get a sad, faraway look, and he would mumble something about being very upset about some things that pained him greatly. Finally, he described the need for what they call "coyotes," the guides who are hired to help the refugees (as I prefer to call them) cross the border—and in many cases, the desert—and charge thousands of dollars for their services. In his successful trip across the border, the composition of that group was about ten men, four women, and three or four "coyotes who were well-armed with guns." They slept as a group out in the open with a distance of about twelve inches or so between each person. My friend Luis was therefore about twelve inches away from a woman on one side of him and another woman on the other side of him. Each night, the four women were raped by one or more of the coyotes, and Luis could do nothing to stop it, or he would have been killed. He said he was and will always be haunted by what he saw—the stoic faces of the women as they endured this humiliation. Upon questioning, these women told Luis that BEFORE they left on the trip they knew they would be raped and felt it would be a necessary evil to endure for the good of their family. One can only wonder how bad it must be in the small towns and villages throughout Central America where their women think that they don't have any better options than to endure rape by their so-called escorts along their journey. Why on earth can we not spend some of the money for that damned wall on building schools and educating teachers, businessmen and women—and constructing clinics and training doctors, nurses, and physical and occupational therapists—to create a healthy social and economic climate throughout Central America. I guarantee you that if this would happen, no one would have to flee his or her country.

| *Chapter Thirteen* |

MUCHO GUSTO!

Dear Dad,

It was good to get mail from you. It was a very supportive letter and made me feel really good. I'm very pleased that so many people are concerned about me and praying for me. But you were right when you said that I wouldn't come home. I'm needed here and I will stay.

I am going to talk a little about my danger situations here because, in comparison to other places, I'm having no problems. I will admit, however, that things could heat up real fast if anything occurs in Nicaragua. But when you are here, there are times when the village will be actually boring. We are under no attack and do not have the constant pressure that people from Guatemala and El Salvador have, and which I was able to view firsthand while in Honduras. If there is a civil war in Nicaragua, I will be in serious danger and will get out. I have cut out a few villages along the border that I was visiting and am trying not to put myself in situations where something could happen.

On the other hand, when I talked with the refugees from Guatemala and El Salvador, all the people I talked to had lost at least two members of their families to government troops who murdered them. There are stories of helicopters flying into villages firing indiscriminately at anything that moves and killing a lot of innocent people. One guy I talked to had his whole family wiped out this way. Another woman was forced to watch her husband tortured before they finally killed him. I could go on ... I thought my heart would literally break and I'll never forget the eyes. They were dead—and also full of hate and unspeakable pain. Made me recommit myself to what I am doing.

I also wanted to react to your part about missionaries down here. I know that missionaries are doing good work down here and in many parts of the world. But I sometimes react against missionaries because I think that they put their emphasis only on salvation and I think it should be justice. So, what I think has happened is that some repressive governments have welcomed missionaries because they (the missionaries) can help placate the masses of people while the government does what it wants. On the other hand, I suppose you could argue that the people in a country like this need that comfort even more, so I suppose that it isn't all bad and probably balances out. What I saw of World Vision I liked because they are involved in correcting physical needs as well as spiritual.

Actually, today I'm rather bored because it has been raining a lot (four days straight) and the ground is too wet to plant anything or work it. But, *boy*, do I have ideas for you to do in my house when you get here, and you're going to do some physical work in the garden. You both should have a good pair of work boots that lace up about your ankles because there are some very poisonous snakes down here that you see every now and then. One just killed a horse a couple of months ago.

Author's Note

I am not sure where to fit this in, but I had gradually been changing my theological beliefs from what I was raised to believe. My father was a fundamentalist Presbyterian Minister and believed that everything in the King James Version of the Bible was inspired by the word of God and was literally true right down to the commas. I was often called on to give testimony in youth groups as to the healing power of God because I had recovered from polio and become an athlete through the power of God and the power of prayer.

As I reread the Sermon on the Mount when I grew older and had exposure to different cultures and religions in my life, I began to wonder if the Christians in the US really did care about poor people. My friend Betty Williams, the 1976 Nobel Peace Prize Laureate, first shared the statistic with me that thirty thousand-plus children under the age of five die every day of preventable causes, and although there has been some improvement, a lot of kids die every day from preventable disease (fifteen to eighteen thousand, depending on your source of information). Yet my dad, who believed in helping poor people wherever they were, voted for Nixon and Reagan, who were not as supportive of human rights as, say, President Carter.

I began to seriously question the power of God when my mother, who had dedicated her life to making sure I could walk again, was killed by a drunk driver. She was practically a saint in my eyes, and I was angry that she had been taken from me and my family. There is a scripture verse that says, "All things work together for good to those who love God, to those who are called according to His purpose." (Romans 8:28). I did not see how the untimely death of my mother worked together for good in any way, shape, or purpose. In Philippians: 4:13, it says, "I can do all things through Christ who strenthens me." Well, I couldn't keep my mother safe, but what I do with my life comes from my mother and still does inspire me.

Another verse (or maybe it's a saying) is that "everything happens for a reason," implying that eventually something good will come out of everything. I have come to dislike this saying intensely because in my mind sometimes there is no good reason for an event to happen, or someone's child or mother to die, or to get a terminal disease. When they die or maybe are injured—what good comes out of that? I did not see any. And I still don't!

When I had Guillain-Barré in my forties, by that time I had a whole lot of relationships with people from a myriad of cultures and countries who prayed for me, lit candles for me, had a mass especially said for me, had prayers go up to God from Mormons, Buddhists, Presbyterians, Native Americans, Muslims, Baptists, had good wishes from Atheists, Hindus, Jews, polytheists and I wasn't sure what actually helped if anything. It felt good to have so many friends supporting me but I wasn't sure there was a God and what happened to someone was not just the luck of the draw.

When my father forgave the man that killed my mother, there was an otherworldly presence in that man's bedroom that I still cannot describe but I am sure was there. My father was right on this one—as regards his ability to forgive this man who killed his wife within twenty-four hours of the funeral while his son was at the foot of the bed with the urge to kill. It took me two years to go to counseling and work out my anger issues. It was something I needed to do even though I didn't know it. My dad was angry, but his anger was directed at God. Yet he would never admit that—and he often asked "Why, God?" I don't think he ever got an answer.

As I grew older, I learned of the efforts of Dr. Martin Luther King, Jr., Archbishop Desmond Tutu, President Nelson Mandela, the Dalai Lama and—yes—even Albert Schweitzer himself, who in their writings and teachings talked and wrote about the power of forgiveness and theneed for the recipient of the harm to forgive the perpetrator. I had the opportunity to visit Nelson Mandela's tiny cell on Robben Island. I didn't understand how any person could come out of twenty-four years in a cell not much bigger than a closet without becoming mentally and emotionally unhinged. It boggles the mind. Yet later, as president of South Africa, Mandela invited his former prison guards to his house for lunch, and it was Mandela's ability to forgive the people who imprisoned him that made a huge difference in being able to set South Africa on a course towards democracy. Although it has been almost fifty years since my mother was killed, I still get angry, but most times I am at peace about her death. But I am not at peace over the violent deaths that occur around the world for no good reason.

So now I consider myself a religious agnostic or a shaman polytheist or a Schweitzerian.

SEPTEMBER 20, 1981

Dear Dad,

Hi there! Well, it stopped raining for two days, and I got out of here to visit some schools and communities. I had never been to one community before, so I made an all-out effort to get there. It's called Sabagal and is only accessible by a tributary to our main river, and you can only get through this river when there has been a lot of rain. So since the conditions for this had been fulfilled, we went. It was beautiful—one of those days when it feels great to be alive! The jungle looked vibrant and green with those long hanging vines all over the place. It did not look at all foreboding, but vibrant. We saw packs of monkeys all over the place and I finally learned that these monkeys made this noise that I had heard a lot that sounds like a growl of a tiger. (The first time I heard this, I was on my motorcycle in the middle of nowhere changing sparkplugs. It scared me to death, and I think I changed the sparkplugs in two-seconds-flat and got out of there. When I got back, I asked everyone if there were tigers here, and they said—not many! The sound is a howler monkey. I didn't believe it then, but I do now.) One monkey threw a coconut at us. He missed me, but I think he could pitch in the big leagues. Then—for the first time, I saw eight or nine of these half-size alligators that everyone says are in the river but I had never seen before. Let me tell you they are in the river, and I'm not going swimming in there again. They are ugly and have a big mouth. Like Alexander Haig!

Anyway, there were four or five parts of the river that we had to cut our way through, and I felt like I could be the star of a movie with Humphrey Bogart in the African Queen. It was great. They kept telling me to watch for snakes, but we didn't see any. Along the way we stopped when we came to houses where one or sometimes two families lived, eking their existence from the ground—to see if they were interested in having a garden. Some were and some weren't. So we will probably go back with some seeds when you guys are here, since it is such a great trip!

One of the places we stopped at had a ramshackle shack on it full of holes in the floorboards. It housed a lonely old man with whom I sat and talked for a half-hour or so. He is from Nicaragua, and he told me that he had worked this farm for twenty-two years and now he was sick with rheumatism, gout, and something else I didn't understand. He was barefoot and had pants on made out of burlap bags that were very old and raggedy. His shirt was worse and his skin was blotchy from not getting enough to eat. He had no teeth, couldn't see, and was worried that the snakes that sometimes came up through the floorboards would bite him, and this would be how he would die. So, I helped him cover some holes with loose boards and rusted cans as best I could and sat down and drank coconut with him. (I don't like coconut juice right from the coconut, but I drank it.) I left feeling sad and hoping that he would be alive when I returned.

When we got to the school we were going to, the teacher hadn't even started a garden and the kids were pathetic-looking. Oh well, I guess there is a disappointment or two in this line of work. It was still a good day—a good day because I learned and I understood more. But I also have a long way to go.

Love,
David

OCTOBER 9, 1981

Dear Dad,

I thought that I would tell you a little bit about the people you and Don are going to meet. The first person is Francisco Mora, or Chico, my best friend here in Los Chiles. He works for the Ministry of Agriculture, and I share his office with him. He has the responsibilities of visiting the farmers in the area and helping them with their cows and crops. He also visits some of the schools and helps out with my gardens. He uses some of the seeds your money has purchased with his farmers, and I have also worked with his farmers. He has an interesting background and has lived in Los Chiles all his life. He lived here when there was no road whatsoever, and you could travel for a day without finding a house. He got up at two or three in the morning to milk the cows by hand, worked all day long with a machete (which is very tiring work), and went to bed at 7:00 p.m. every night. He did not know cars existed, or televisions, or many other things. He is not afraid of the poisonous snakes that abound here and is a natural in the saddle, as he virtually lived in one on the round-ups. It took a month to get to the railroad here, and he would be riding from dawn to dusk. He personally knows what it's like to be hungry, sleep dirty, have raggedy clothes, and wonder how he was going to eat next. But he was basically happy, he says—until the day he realized there was another world out there. He became bitter because he couldn't share in the riches of the world, even though he and his family worked like dogs to be able to have the bare necessities. It was a big treat when they were able to get twenty-five centimos (which is less than a cent) to buy a small piece of candy. That happened once every two months or so. He was able to work himself up in the world because of a fierce determination and an innate and quick intelligence. He studied hard when he finally went to school, and it was with great pride that he graduated from high school here. But his life is directly out of a western movie, only poorer. As of today, he still retains a good amount of disrespect for US policies and understands why a person becomes communist—although he hates communism passionately because he says, "there is no freedom." But they offer a light at the end of the tunnel to a man living in dirt, hungry, and sick—which we fail to do. He is glad to see me and the seeds because now there is a small glimmer of light where there once was none. He'll be a good friend for a long time. (He's twenty-five.)

The village is getting prepared for your impending arrival. They want to know how many words of Spanish you speak, Dad, and so—start practicing! Don't forget your canteen and a hat, because the sun is hot down here. Don't forget your boots because there is mud down here! Don't forget Kaopectate because there is d— down here. Don't forget the plane tickets. Don't forget money. Don't forget film and the movie camera. Bring me a box of Velveeta cheese and Ritz crackers, and I'll be in heaven. I'm serious! But don't put the cheese on the plane!

OCTOBER 30, 1981

Hola amigos,

Haven't written for a while because I've been busy with work and a friend of mine that came to visit. Even though Dad and Don will be here next week, I'm writing to remember my thoughts later because a lot has happened, and as time goes on, the events tend to run together. I can't seem to write in a diary because my letters serve as my diary.

Mario got here on the 17th of October, and I met him at the International Airport. We had a really good week together, but we were constantly reminded of the different way of life down here and the closeness of death. At least I was. Mario and I spent the first couple of days in San José sightseeing and doing work for my job, and we arrived in Los Chiles on Tuesday, the 20th. I started out by showing

him around Los Chiles and the gardens I have there. Then later that
night we found out that there had been several deaths of small children in a town nearby called San José de Amparo. It seems that their
drinking water was bad and the children were too malnourished to
resist the disease. I had worked with some of the families there, and
we were in the process of making some gardens. So Mario and I tried
to go there but were turned back by muddy roads and a big rainstorm.
(The mud is so thick and sticky here that, when it collects under the
bumpers of the motorcycle, it slows the wheel rotation down and you
have to stop and clean it out. We were stopping every hundred yards or
so, and the strain on the moto became too great.) I have since made it
there, and indeed there have been some deaths of kids under four years
of age. Kids that I played with when I visited their families. Kids that
should be living now. Kids that needed just a little bit of milk, good
water, and more vitamins. It doesn't seem like it is too much to ask.

Mario and I visited a couple of places by boat and saw some alligators and monkeys and beautiful jungle birds. We shared a lot of
our memories and times—and created new memories. Then on the
Sunday after the dance, I received a radio message from the Guardia
Rural that Peace Corps was trying to contact me. At that hour and by
that method, it had to be an emergency. It was. Mario's father had died
unexpectedly of a heart attack after having had a physical check-up
three days before he had the attack. It was a painful thing for both
of us because it was the first time Mario had lost anybody that close
to him—and for me it brought back memories of receiving a similar
phone call eleven years ago from my father saying my mother was
dead. I also felt close to Mario's father, although I had not spent nearly
the amount of time that I would have liked to have shared with him.
Mario's father had escaped from Cuba about two years after Castro
took over—and his story is quite interesting and thought-provoking.
It hit me that this man had also had a dream, and that dream was simply to be free and live in peace to raise his family. He would have loved

to stay in Cuba because he always loved his country, but he loved his freedom and family more. Since Mario's father had influenced me to develop an interest in Latin America, I hope that the greatest tribute to his memory I can do is to continue helping people realize their dreams. He was a fine man and will be missed by all who knew and loved him.

Yesterday, rightist extremists hijacked a plane of the Costa Rican National Airlines called Sansa. It is the airline I use to reach Los Chiles, and I was going to be on it, but I came back a day early by another route. Their demand was that political prisoners in Nicaragua and Costa Rica be freed and that they be allowed to fly to Honduras with their comrades. They are a radical right group that is anti-communist whom I consider to be more dangerous than the communist groups around here. They threatened to kill one of the twenty-two passengers on board every forty-five minutes until their demands were met. At 6:00 this morning Costa Rica let some of the prisoners go, and this mollified the group enough so that they let their hostages go and left for Honduras. But it was a reminder once again of the deep divisions in this part of the world and the lengths that a splinter group will go to try to accomplish their purposes. It is a little scary and will probably get worse before it gets better.

Well, I am going to sign off now and put this in the mail. I am really looking forward to seeing Dad and Don next week and sharing my life with them. I hope nothing goes wrong and they don't do something stupid like miss the flight. I'll have a cow!

Love,

David

Voluntario de Cuerpo de Paz

Author's Note

> *I sent instructions to teach my father two phrases: "mucho gusto,"*
> *which means much pleasure, and "igualmente," which means "equally,*

I am sure." When Dad first got to Costa Rica, we were hanging out with my English-speaking friends and so he didn't have the opportunity to practice his Spanish enough, although I tried to make him do it. When we arrived at the airport in San José we met a friend of mine, so my dad had a chance to shine and speak one or two words of Spanish. Using the honorific title with impeccable formality, I said to my friend, "I'd like you to meet my father, don Leland," and my friend said, "Mucho gusto"—at which point, my father was to say, "Igualmente." Instead he said, "Leche," which means milk. My friend stifled a laugh, and when he got off the plane in Los Chiles he headed out rapidly telling my friends and neighbors what my father had said. By the time I passed by with all of our luggage, neighbors would come up to me and say "mucho gusto" followed by "leche"! All that practice, and my dad blew it. It eventually became the joke of the town and we all enjoyed it and my dad was a good sport about it.

Before my adventures in Honduras, I accidently got a girlfriend named Grace, who was the Spanish teacher in town. There were several teachers in the local high school who were in their twenties, and we often hung around together or went out dancing. I knew Grace liked me by the way she looked at me even when she was dancing with someone else. I tried to avoid dancing with her too much as I did not want a girlfriend because I needed to spend time with a lot of the teachers. We were all at a special concert by a salsa band that made it into Los Chiles, and we were all dancing and having a good time. Then a slower music song came on, called a bolero, and Grace glommed onto me with both arms wrapped around me so that we were dancing with one shadow, as they say, and only when a couple were boyfriend and girlfriend did anyone dance together that closely. So when I got up to dance I was single and when I sat down, someone asked me if Grace was my girlfriend, and I said I didn't think so—but my friend said that I had a girlfriend now and you better *like it because the other female teachers would not like it if Grace was not treated well by me. So I accepted the fact that I had a girlfriend.*

I spent some time with Grace, and she was most interested to know that my father and brother Don were coming to visit, so invited us to dinner. I accepted with pleasure and we set a date for the dinner. When we arrived, we noticed that there were only only three place settings at the table, and we took our seats wondering where Grace was going to sit. It became obvious that Grace was not going to eat with us, but was going to serve us and meet our every culinary need. We all protested, but it was also obvious that she would be serving us no matter what we said. Anytime one of our plates was empty, it was refilled automatically without asking. (And the food was tremendous. Grace had gone all out.) Toward the end of the meal, I reached for my glass of water. Grace stopped me and took the glass from my hand and held it up to my lips for me to drink as a gesture of her desire to serve me. My brother made a sound like somebody choking and said something about needing to use the bathroom and headed for the out-house, his shoulders shaking silently with laughter. My father, being the most mature of the males in the house, did not react and managed to control himself. It took Don fifteen minutes to stop laughing and return to the table, making under-the-breath smart-ass comments that were funny, but I couldn't laugh.

After dinner, we all went to my friend Chico's house for dessert—but instead it was a full-fledged meal. During dinner, Chico said that he would like to learn more about each one of us and that he would like each person to talk about himself or herself. Don went first, and he tried to mess with my mind by picking the most obscure topics for me to translate because I was the only bi-lingual person there. My Spanish was decent at the time but I did not have the vocabulary to translate Plato or Socrates or transcendentalism or the ideas of the Buddha—so, of course, that's what my brother started talking about with undisguised glee at my stumbling efforts. My father went to the bathroom, so I told my brother to f-off very sweetly and I made up something he said and told him to shut up. Next was my father, who once again was the mature one in the group, and he spoke as a minister about his work helping others and his belief in God and the importance of his Christian ideals—all very translatable for me. Next came Grace. She talked about her life in a small town in Costa Rica and how she became a Spanish teacher. Then she said that her life was very grey, with a lot of clouds in the sky until recently, when the rays of the sun broke through the clouds and gave her life hope (ready for this?) when she met me. And I had to translate this! I looked at Chico, who had a shit-eating grin on his face but was no help, so I translated it as vaguely as I could—but when my brother understood what Grace was saying he made another choking noise and had to go to the bathroom again! For the rest of the trip, he made a constant stream of smart-ass comments like "Morning, Sunshine,"—or "Here comes a ray of sunshine," or if it was raining, he asked me to part the clouds. Very funny.

When Dad left for home, Don stayed on a bit longer and came with me to a workshop on tree-grafting in La Garita.

NOVEMBER 22, 1981

Dear Dad,

Getting back from La Garita was not without its events. On Thursday, Don and I were at the airport to return to Los Chiles. While I was at the ticket window I received a call from Jean and Pepe Lujan (PC Director) saying that I had to return to the Peace Corps office because I was not going to be permitted to go back to Los Chiles. It seems that Peace Corps/Washington had sent an order that I was to be taken out of Los Chiles because the situation was becoming too dangerous for me. I was disappointed, but Don and I packed up, got our baggage off the plane, and went to Peace Corps. When we got there, I found that the directors had received an order from their supervisor that I was to have my site changed. I was upset because I had spent the last nine months gaining the confidence of the people and had a number of projects going besides the gardens. I think that I am in very little danger here comparatively speaking and that I am needed to help with the nutrition problems and to counteract negative influences on the image of America. So I am going to fight to get the order reversed so that I can stay.

I ran into some friends of mine from Los Chiles at the airport and explained what had happened. They were upset, and several of them called Peace Corps to explain that I am still safe and, hopefully, the decision will be changed. I may work for a month outside of Los Chiles in another part of Costa Rica, but I don't even want to do that. Vamos a ver!

Still, I have to admit that the situation is worsening. Nicaragua is upset about recent statements by Haig and Reagan saying that intervention by the States in Nicaragua is a possibility, and two days ago a large group of Costa Rican National Guard left to kick out some Sandinistas who were using areas near here for training. Don thinks I should get out, but I don't think the danger is all that great. We have Peace Corps volunteers in worse situations in other countries, like Guatemala—and the people here can't just pick up and leave at the first sign of trouble. I don't want to, either.

Since this is most likely to be my last letter before I get home for Christmas, this will have to serve as my Christmas card to all of you. There are many times that I think of all of you and the good times we have had. I thank you for the memories and support while I have been down here. I hope that you have enjoyed receiving the letters and that you have learned something from them. I hope that next year will be one of continuous growth and awareness of others and their needs.

May God bless you and love you and give you peace in this holiday season and throughout the year. Stay in touch.

Love and kisses,
David

Author's Note

> *There were some people in the Costa Rican government that were and are still sure that I was removed from Los Chiles because the CIA did not want me to see what they were doing, as it was illegal for them to use Costa Rican territory for a staging area or for any other nefarious purposes. A friend of mine whom I met well after my Peace Corps experience and who worked with the Arias Foundation had first-hand knowledge of how the then-director of the CIA William Casey would fly down to Costa Rica, arriving at around 3:00 a.m., and would demand that the Costa Rican government officials meet him at the airport. Then he would bully and intimidate the Costa Rican officials to get them to allow the US to use Costa Rican territory (near where I was a volunteer) as a base for their clandestine operations against the Sandinista government in Nicaragua. Despite intense pressure, President Arias never caved in to the demands of the Reagan administration and allowed the US to operate in Costa Rican territory. It is one of the main reasons that I consider Arias a hero, because he could have been neutralized if the US thought they could get away with it.*

Chapter Fourteen

STARTING OVER

JANUARY 19, 1982: SAN JOSÉ

Dear Dad,

Well, I'm out of Los Chiles officially. I have just returned from getting the rest of my things from Los Chiles, and it was quite sad. When I arrived, the news had changed from rumor to official: there was and still is a small group of counterrevolutionaries who had camped right along a road I used to travel. There have been several small battles around, and about twenty people have died. That includes, I understand, a couple of kids who got caught in the crossfire. There were many people to say good-bye to, and some tears were shed. Questions and comments included: "Where are we going to get more seeds— who is going to help us—I know you are CIA now—you said you were staying for another year —don't they understand we need you here—*WHY*?" If I would have had any choice or enough money, I would have stayed.

The thing that bothers me the most is that the communist organizers are still there. They were there when I got there and they're there now. I can't do anything to combat their influence now. (And maybe I shouldn't.) If anybody ever reads any Mao Tsetung, they'll find that the way he thinks a revolution should be organized includes people living in the target area for *as long as it takes* to convince them that communism is better. There is no way for me to tell the people that Uncle Sam cares about them—for where am I? There will be no way to say that I will be there when I am needed. There is no way to say that I understand your suffering—for when the suffering starts, who is there to help? I cannot say here's something to help you eat when the communist agitator points out that the US has launched another submarine, built another bomber or cruise missile, which can't be eaten. Things don't seem all that dangerous to the average poor person there. Why did the gringo leave? Who's there for the other side now? There is only one side now...

It looks like I will be down in Puerto Jimenez on the Osa Peninsula. It isn't all that bad and may actually be more isolated than Los Chiles— as I understand that it takes two days to get there, and there is no electricity and lots of snakes. I hate snakes, and since the Osa Peninsula is the only virgin jungle area left in Costa Rica in a large area, snakes are all over the place. It also has small tigers (ocelots, I think) and some abundant bird life. It is a fascinating place from a naturalist standpoint, and it also has a lot of poor people. Also, there are several large fruit companies there which I will be able to check out since this is another strong interest area of mine. I want to know first-hand the effects of businesses like this on the people down there. I also would be working with 4-H clubs and kids a lot—and also with Native Americans, all of which sounds really interesting. I hope that it is and that I am ready to leave some effect down there.

Well, all for now. I'm fine—sad to be out of Los Chiles but looking forward to new adventures and life in general. I had a great time at home and one of the best Christmases ever.

Love,
David

FEBRUARY 1, 1982—TURRIALBA

Dear Dad,

Now I'm in a city called Turrialba because I'm going to take a course on how to organize 4-H clubs. More on this later! But for the past week and a half, I have been traveling around the country a bit making arrangements for my new site, which still is on the Osa Peninsula. I am changing ministries from the Education Ministry to the Agriculture Ministry and will be working with 4-H clubs in this zone in addition to what I was doing with school and community gardens. So since I am going to work with 4-H, I have attended a course on how to organize them. But the only problem is that I think they have crammed into two weeks what could be done in one day. Each guy gets up and says the same thing about how to organize things in different words, and I am bored stiff. Another big part of the course is traveling around visiting some of the clubs in outlying areas. We can't do that since the two vehicles that are available to us are broken and there is no money to fix them. So I'm bored today!

Last week I traveled to see my new boss at the Ministry of Agriculture in a city called San Isidro del General. To get there, we had to go over a group of mountains called El Cerro de la Muerte, which is "the mountain of death." I was to find out why when we saw a very serious accident. I have always been somewhat suspicious of vehicles here as I often notice bald tires on heavily laden trucks and buses. On that day I was traveling with my Peace Corps boss over this road which is characterized by hairpin turns, steep grades, high cliffs, no guard rails, and crosses marking where people have died. In places where a lot of people have had problems, the crosses constitute a mini-guardrail. As we passed a truck while coming down the mountain, we saw what we thought was exhaust fumes, but which turned out to be burning brakes. About a minute after we went by, the truck lost its brakes and came barreling down the mountain after us. It made the first curve, but not the second—and just after passing us, it flipped over, spilling its cargo over the edge of the cliff. The truck itself was barely hanging on—thanks to a small rock that happened to be in the way, which prevented it from following its contents. I was the first on the scene and expected to find some dead bodies—but, amazingly, there were four people crammed into the cab, and I think that this prevented anyone from being thrown very far. All were very banged up, and there were some broken bones, but nobody was dead. But the next day, someone went over the cliff where the accident had occurred. The mountain had claimed another.

We are in the final week of the presidential campaign here, and I have never seen anything like it. Everybody is excited and carrying banderas of their particular parties. I think that I have found where the excitement about democracy has gone—because down here it escalates every day. Here, a political event is an event for the whole family. If a candidate comes, the family packs a lunch and goes to listen and has a great time—even if they don't belong to the party he represents and have no intention of voting for him. It is a social event and a time for listening and then having lively spirited discussions about what he said, how he could help the country, what his wife wore, and whose colors were prettier. It reminded me of a big-time football game at Ohio State when everyone arrives at the stadium dressed in the colors of the Buckeyes, which are red and gray. In the stadium, the atmosphere is electric and the important characteristics of each team is analyzed, cheerleaders ogled, drinks are drunk, and fellowship is shared by everyone. The whole football game can take five to six hours, including before and after parties. That's the way it is here about their candidates, their freedom, and their issues. It strikes me as quite a difference in the level of importance. If anyone ever tells me again that people in these types of countries can't handle democracy, I may have to sit on them.

Love,
David

Chapter Fifteen

DEMOCRACY WITH ENTHUSIASM

Dear Dad,

Today is my one-year anniversary of being in the Peace Corps. A little less than a year from now and I should be home for a while—anyway, before I go off on another adventure and/or job. As always, when I look back on the year, it went extremely fast, but I remember some times that went extremely slowly. Like the first couple of months in Los Chiles, when I didn't know the language very well and I could hardly wait to go somewhere where English was spoken so that I could be understood. Many times, I went to bed early because when I was sleeping, time passed more quickly. And when there was a lot of rain for three and four days straight and it was necessary to swim to supper instead of walk, the days seemed pretty long. But today, as I reflect on my first year here, it seems like it zipped right by.

I'm still stuck in Turrialba learning how to organize 4-H clubs. And this particular time period is very boring and slow because there is no particular course and I have to follow this guy around who is a promoter of 4-H clubs. And although the program seems useful, everything is in a lull here because of the elections. So here I sit, waiting for lunch.

Elections here were a gas! For months preceding the elections, people were aglow with enthusiasm for politics. In the last letter, I talked about how the elections seemed like a football game. Well, the last two days before the elections were crazy, too. I was in San José and there were cars everywhere covered with the flags of their particular party festooning every inch of the car until it seems that the drivers can't see. The horns are constantly blowing, with each candidate having their particular cadence. Monge, who won, had one long blast and a short one. Calderon had three shorts. Echandi had one short, one long, and one short. And every group was having a constant battle whenever they saw an opposing representative of another candidate. It was jubilant celebration of democracy. The day of the election was clear and the excitement mounted. I went to a polling place to see how they run the election. First of all, you show your ID to the electoral judge who verifies your existence. Then you pick up three ballots: one for president, one for congress, and one for municipalities. Then you go and dip your thumb in indelible ink and put your thumbprint next to the party of your choice. The ink on your thumb does not wash off and thereby prevents someone from voting twice. It is also a remarkable badge of honor; anyone who does not have a darkened thumb is hounded unmercifully until they vote. I believe 95% of the people in Costa Rica voted. I was embarrassed to tell them that only about 50% of the people in the States voted in the last election. The Costa Rican I told that to could not believe it and said something to the effect that those people were pretty dumb or unappreciative of democracy. I couldn't have agreed more!

The area outside the election was a fiesta. All the street vendors were there hawking their various wares and the paraphernalia of the campaign. People unashamedly wore the colors of their party—T-shirts, hats, and carried flags denoting their allegiance. It was a cacophony of sound and a kaleidoscope of color mixed up with a country-wide celebration of the good things of democracy. It was a day when the

Platonic theory of government seemed remote and insensible and made me ashamed to think of how hard it is to get people to the polls sometimes in the States. Amazing!

Well, I'm also coming up on birthday number thirty-one and I find it disconcerting. Ten years ago I was a junior in college and I thought I was old. I am starting to think very seriously of what I will do when I get out in a year. A PhD in something really attracts me right now as there are a number of universities that offer full scholarships to former Peace Corps volunteers. One is Ohio University in Athens, another is Columbia in N.Y.C., and there are several more. I would also be interested in working with Bread for the World, and I would be interested to know if Dick Watts from Swords to Plowshares would know of any similar positions with churches in the States.[6] So any ideas would be appreciated!

I have to go back to class now. I hope I make it through the next three hours without falling asleep!

Love,
David

Author's Note

> *I had the good fortune since Peace Corps to work/volunteer for the Carter Center in their election monitoring program. I went to Nicaragua twice and Venezuela once to monitor elections there. All the election monitors arrived for a couple of days of training, and then it was off to the town where we would be based for two to four days. As election monitors, we had no power to intervene for any reason. We could only observe and then report our findings to the central command post if we saw any irregularities. We were allowed to ask questions such as how's it going or any problems. I am happy to report that I never saw any election irregularities in the areas for which I was responsible. I am sorry to report that I helped give Chavez to Venezuela, which has been an unmitigated disaster.*

My favorite story about my experience as an election monitor centered around the town of Ocotal near the border with Honduras. (It seems I live a border line existence!) It was a requirement for each election monitoring team to pick a polling place and observe it as it opened, and then go back to the same polling place and watch it close. The poll workers helped everyone with understanding their ballot. After they filled out their ballot, it was deposited in a large cardboard box, one box for each political position that was being contested. There was one box for president of the country, one for government representative,s and several more for each contested position. There were at least 5 representatives of each major political party as observers, plus poll workers, plus international election observers. From the time the polls closed and all the boxes were sealed and totals agreed upon for each position—all observers had to be within sight of those boxes until a big official truck came to pick up the boxes. An observer couldn't even go to the bathroom. I was immensely impressed with the observers and the poll workers because all were women (not well educated, but very smart and hardworking, and very proud to be bringing real democracy to Nicaragua). However, the truck was at least an hour late, and these women needed to go to the bathroom, which was outside of our polling place and down the street. Finally, the women could stand it no longer and they decided to march to election headquarters about two miles away in Ocotal. They assigned two monitors to each box, and I trailed behind and watched over everything. It was a march for democracy—and the women began singing songs—and this event became a parade—and the women were very proud to be helping their country take tiny but important steps towards democracy. As soon as they arrived at election headquarters, they all made a beeline for the bathroom. I was impressed with how every poll worker at every voting station I visited felt a sense of pride because now Nicaragua could become a true democracy.

I am sorry to say, but as I write this, Daniel Ortega has turned Nicaragua back into a dictatorship and has undermined people like those nine-plus women who worked so hard and were so dedicated to bringing democracy to their own country. Life has become very hard in Nicaragua as the tourist industry has been decimated and it does not seem like things will get better quickly. It pains me because I have some friends I love down there, and they are in a tough spot.

Chapter Sixteen

PUERTO JIMENEZ

FEBRUARY 22, 1982

Dear Dad,

Well, get out your maps again as I am in a different place. This letter is coming to you from Buenas Aires, Costa Rica (not Argentina) were I am embroiled in another boring course on how to organize 4-H clubs. Last weekend, I gave my boss a hard time about coming here, but I had to anyway. It seems to me that I have wasted the last month and a half, and that is a very poor way to spend your taxes. But it will end this week and I will be productive as soon as I get to my site.

I'm going to use the two hundred dollars (from the money given to me when I was home) for my projects in my new site. There are a million more small projects that need money. It is actually easier to get loans for large amounts and big projects than for the small amounts and small projects. So any money that is sent will be used well and for directly helping poor people.

I arranged to fly Miguel Angel, the deaf boy, in and out of San José for appointments. That went fairly well. I took him to two doctors (one for the hearing test and one for the school referral), and it was determined that he is deaf in one ear and half deaf in the other but with sufficient ability to hear so that he can learn to speak if he gets the training and a hearing aid. It was the opinion of both doctors, who were very competent, that no operation that can be done anywhere will help, because his mother had German measles during pregnancy. He can hear loud sounds if you're on his good side, and hopefully that will enable him to learn to speak. I got him admitted to any one of three schools in Costa Rica for the deaf, and now it just depends on where we can find money and a place for him and his mother to live. For all of the above, I figure it will cost about five hundred dollars or more, depending on inflation.

In the teacher's opinion who tested him, Miguel has the capability to learn enough after just one year in the school for the deaf to begin attending the regular school in Los Chiles. She held up pictures of various animals and made him watch her mouth, and he could imitate her mouth movements and make sounds that were similar to the words. In my mind, there was no doubt that he could learn, and it was a very uplifting and exciting experience to be helping in so obvious a way. He also seemed to know, and he kept grinning at me in a way that made me melt. Now I want kids. Anybody want to get married?!

Miguel did throw a few temper tantrums when I wouldn't let him do things since in the past couple of years he is pretty used to getting his way. I wouldn't let him go to a room where some friends of mine were trying to sleep, so he threw this cheap little helicopter toy that I bought him against the wall, smashing it to smithereens. I had been patient through other such temper tantrums, which is difficult because you can't communicate with him at all except about the various methods of excreting substances and ingesting substances. So I sat there listening to this kid howl and I thought about all the development theories I had been taught from Piaget to Montessori to Maslow. I thought about the Rodgers methods of counseling in being warm, client-centered, and accepting of others—and I finally came back to Skinner and operant conditioning, smacked the kid on the behind and had no further problems. I'll be burning my psych books when I return.

Dad, while I'm thinking of it, could you find out how much hearing aids are that would fit a six-year-old? It may be cheaper to buy a hearing aid up there and send it down with someone who is coming to visit me. Right now, the hearing aids are stuck in the customs house because they need dollars to get them out. It costs two hundred dollars apiece to get one out and I can do it with the money. Costa Rica doesn't have the money to get the hearing aids out and so there are about eight hundred sitting there and a waiting list of five thousand people to get one. I guess the people will have to wait—another of the small tragedies that doesn't get much play up there while the International Monetary Fund figures out how to squeeze their money out of the country. More on them in another letter.

I attempted to go to Puerto Jimenez, my new site, last weekend since Buenas Aires is halfway there. I took a three-hour bus ride and got there five minutes after the boat to Puerto Jimenez left. No more boats. No more buses back to Buenas Aires. And it was hot! How hot was it? It was so hot I saw two fire hydrants fighting over a dog! (Thanks, Mario.) It was so hot that Dante would have gone back to hell! (That's a literary reference.) It was so hot... Send in your best lines, folks. The winner will win an all-expense-paid trip to Costa Rica, where the Tidy Bowl man will give you a thrill. Anyway, I went to the beach and watched dolphins playing in the bay, and they were having so much fun that it put me in a silly mood which I have yet to get out of, even though I got back yesterday.

While down here I've had an opportunity to finish two books that were two of the best books I have ever read. One was *Inside the Company, A CIA Diary* by Philip Agee, and the other was *Open Veins of Latin America* by Eduardo Galeano. Both are damning indictments of the United States' foreign policy in Latin America. The first book details a former CIA officer's career in Ecuador, Uruguay, Mexico, and Washington, D.C. In it he details the dirty tricks played by our government basically in support of big business and in the name of anticommunism in order to get our way in their countries. It includes the planting of false documents on opposition leaders, inciting riots, hiring goon squads to attack people and disrupt meetings, throwing stink bombs into meetings, turning off the power in the middle of an opposition speech, burning buildings that are the headquarters of opposition parties (not necessarily communist), the use of torture, and many other things. The other book compares the development of the US to the development of Latin America and says that Latin America was literally raped by its conquerors ever since it was discovered. The conquistadors started by taking every bit of gold and silver they could find out of Latin America on the backs of Indians—and that has continued until now and still characterizes the relations of Latin America with the developed world, mainly the US and Europe. There are very few national companies of any size in these countries—just extensions of US and European multinationals. With the help of the US government these multinationals take the raw materials out of Latin American countries and return them already processed and between two and ten times more expensive. The profits from the raw materials goes only to a relative few in the country of origin. Processed material marketed elsewhere is taxed by the US and Europe so as to render it uncompetitive with their own products. There is no such thing as a free market in the US. The theories of Adam Smith seem to be applied only when it is convenient for us.

Another point I want to make is that when we as a country fight hard to place in power a government sympathetic to our economic needs as defined by big business, we eliminate the middle of the political spectrum. What I mean is this: usually, in whatever country you might pick, there are a few people on the radical left who might be represented by people like the Khmer Rouge in Cambodia. On the far right, we would find people like those in the Ku Klux Klan, with the vast majority of the people spread out in between. When we pick a side in the countries in Latin America, it is usually a side tending towards the far right, a side made up of the oligarchy that is made up of maybe 10% of the population and has been in control of the country for a long time. These people have been, and are, amenable to our economic interests as long as they get a slice of the pie in the form of a bribe or a percentage of the action. There is a wide discrepancy in economic level between this 10% and the rest of the population. Soon, the population begins to point out the discrepancy in various forms and ways. We support the 10% in power by the dirty tricks already alluded to and begin to alienate the rest of the population. Anybody who doesn't support the government is labeled a communist, which is far from the truth. Gradually, the reasonable middle (the ones who will make a reasonable compromise) are driven to become radicals and to fight for their fair share. The situation becomes polarized, like what happened in Cuba and Nicaragua, and is happening now in El Salvador and Guatemala. And we get stuck looking like the bad guys while anyone against us is labeled communist. It is just not that simple.

I thought I'd be in my new site a week from now. I'll write and describe the trip when I get there. Hope all is well at home. Thinking of all often,

Love,

David

Author's Note

> Understanding the history of colonization and the consequential economic development in Latin America is key to understanding what, in the mid-twentieth century, the US government construed as "communism." For hundreds of years, Latin America (like almost all former colonies in Africa and Asia) fell victim to some sort of mercantilist economic system in which the goal of the state was to accumulate precious metals and money.
>
> At the dawn of the sixteenth century, conquistadors arrived in Latin America with no other goal than to find silver and gold and send it back to Spain. Typically, they would return home and live regally off their ill-gotten gains. Most often, the illicit wealth arrived in Spain and then was

sent to England and the Netherlands from whence came the loans upon which Spain depended to finance a series of European and North African wars, as well as additional fleets of boats for seeking gold and silver.

Historically speaking, that system was utilized in one form or another for centuries. Governments in Latin America granted concessions which gave rich upper-class families the right to control certain franchises, such as cement, sugar, or tobacco production. The poor people who lived there existed mainly to serve the wealthy, and it took a lot of effort for a merchant/peasant/former slave/Native American, or ethic combination thereof, to reach the upper class. There was never any attempt to form legislatures, or a middle class, or any form of democracy in most Latin American countries. If a large group of people becomes frustrated because they cannot get ahead economically or feed their families, they will be inclined to become susceptible to nearly any political and economic ideology. When I was growing up it was communism, and a number of communist guerilla movements developed throughout Latin America. One example is Peru, where a Maoist guerilla group called the Shining Path formed and went to war with the Peruvian government. One of my favorite books of all time is The Other Path, *which documents the underground capitalistic economy that kept most people in Peru at that time living a little above subsistence level.*

On the contrary, most people who came to what would become the United States were essentially capitalistic. They came from countries that already had a democratic tradition (like England) to build a new life in a new country that was much more egalitarian. This is the huge difference between how North America and South America developed.

MARCH 2 1982

Dear Dad,

Well, eleven months to go and I am out of the Peace Corps. As I sit here in my new site of Puerto Jimenez I can't believe that sixteen months have gone by since I boarded the plane to Miami, leaving behind job, home, family, and friends. I still remember the scared feeling I had and how long twenty-seven months seemed. Now I feel that I will be home before I know it.

I flew in early this morning to Puerto Jimenez, and once again, I will be on the borders of civilization. I had to get up at 4:15 a.m. in order to catch the 5:30 plane at the airport in San José. I hadn't gotten up at the time in years and hadn't seen that time unless it was coming from the other end.

There are three ways to get into Puerto Jimenez: by land, sea, or air. Once again, by land it is only possible to enter three months out of the year because of the bad conditions of the road in and because of rivers that swell during the rainy season and lack bridges. It is a road that comes down from Puerto Cortez through Rincon to Puerto Jimenez. It is also possible to take a bus to Golfito and then take a boat across the bay to Jimenez. The fun thing about this, I understand, is that dolphins usually follow the boat and play in its wake. Today I saw the school of dolphins as we flew over them while they were frolicking below. The third way in involves flying the same type of plane as I flew from Los Chiles to Golfito and then changing planes to a small Piper Cub for the short hop to Puerto Jimenez. The runways are fairly decent, although the runway in Jimenez is like landing on washboard because it is made out of gravel. As I got here, the town reminded me of the stories of other gold rush towns in frontier days in California, Alaska, etc., which in fact is happening here. There are guys around here coming in from the outback with mules and pans, and they are actually panning for gold. Maybe I'll do that as a secondary project!

The town seems to be a little bigger than Los Chiles but with the same type of streets. It is a little easier to get here though, so the traffic in and out is greater, and there will be more gringos coming through here—unfortunately, because gold is attracting some scruffy types from the US and Europe.

Love,
David

MARCH 16, 1982

Dear Dad,

Well, here I sit in the Hotel Musoc at 9:00 p.m., trying to psych myself up to get up at 4:00 a.m. to be at the airport at 5:00 a.m. to make sure that I am on the 6:00 a.m. flight to Golfito and then Puerto Jimenez. I have a whole Piper Cub full of stuff, so I don't know where they're going to put the passengers! Maybe they'll swim!

I have been in Puerto Jimenez for about a week and two days now. I'm not sure I like it as there is a gold rush on and there are unsavory characters in abundance there, mostly foreigners. Once again, it seems to me that the money is going to benefit people outside the country more than in it.

But the place is beautiful, with beaches that stretch for miles without even a house. I have sat on a beach for hours sometimes and haven't seen a soul. However, a few beaches have these small black flies in abundance, and they like to bite your ankles. It makes for a short visit! The ocean is also teeming with fish and the bay has a resident pack of dolphins. I saw them once before when I was in Golfito and once again when I flew into Jimenez for the first time. But when I went to get my motorcycle, I took the launch across the bay because the cycle I was going to use was in Cuidad Neilly, near Panama. I thought I was on Flipper! The dolphins would race in circles around the boat and then alongside, eyeballing the people! They sometimes jumped together as though they were a synchronized swim team, and they also had a jumping competition across the wake of the boat. One would jump and then he would come half out of the water and stay there to watch the next one. As soon as the next one jumped, the other would take off and go get in line again. (There were six or seven dolphins.) I wanted so badly to jump in with them and play, but they could swim better than me! They were always smiling and seemed to be saying, "Look at me—look at me!" Now I want to be reincarnated as a dolphin! They know how to like.

I drove my motorcycle from the Pan American highway near Panama up around the foot of the bay and down to Puerto Jimenez. The road is basically good, except for about fifty kilometers near the foot of the bay. There the road goes from nice gravel to mud. And rather than being flat like Los Chiles, that part of the road is as bad as the movies—only it goes up and down big hills. It was quite a challenge to drive on, and it went through some of the thickest jungle I have ever seen. That was no good for my imagination because, as darkness was falling, I was still in the middle of the jungle. I thought of all the tigers and snakes around and prayed that I wouldn't break down! Then, when I got off the mountains and onto the peninsula part, the roads dramatically improved. The only problem here turned out to be rivers—five of them! And no bridges. So I had to ford them and one was about a foot-and-a half-deep in one narrow spot. That means that it almost got the spark plug (and this is the dry season). I also turned into a human mud flap as I absorbed most of the spray. I think I'm going to be wet a lot, and I'll probably have dishpan legs!

In deference to Peter, I'll close here and avoid any political commentary so he won't be bored! See you in ten-and-a-half months!

Love,
David

Chapter Seventeen

UGLY AMERICANS

MARCH 29, 1982

Dear Dad,

I am approaching the end of my first month here in Puerto Jimenez. I am fairly well settled in now, but I am not sure how well I like it. The house is rented out by these two rich gringos, who rented it to the chief of the immigration office down here, who in turn rented me a room in the house. I liked and still like the chief of the immigration office, and I like the idea that the house is next to the police station, which prevents robbers when I am gone. However, the two gringos, a man and his wife, bother me. She is actually pretty nice, but he is a coarse, sometimes vulgar, man who is a pain to be around sometimes. Also, they are down here looking for gold, and therefore are a minor example of that which I think is wrong with the area: too many foreigners getting the money for the gold and not even close to enough Ticos getting it. I also speak too much English when they are here, which has been one-and-a-half weeks out of the last month. The problem is that there are no other houses available in Jimenez now, and there would be none as secure. So I feel stuck.

A couple of days ago, I rode my cycle up to where there is a big concentration of miners and machinery. I was appalled by what I saw.

What had once been a beautiful jungle river had and is in the process of being raped. The roar of machinery shattered the stillness as the machinery shattered the rock and the banks of the river. For a hundred yards on both sides of the river, the jungle had been torn up, and great trees lay felled and smashed; the river had turned an ugly red brown instead of running crystal clear and the ground looked like an undulating moonscape. If they left it alone right now, it might recover in 5-8 years. But they won't.

As you approach the area, you have to go down a rough road through some beautiful countryside. Then you come upon the river, where you would think a giant plow had crisscrossed it a number of times. This mess lies abandoned as the large companies in here are under no responsibility to return the area to its natural state. Another kilometer further brings you in sight of the new work area. There are three or four workers taking a break. A couple of steam shovels are taking the dirt and dumping it into a sluice box where the gold settles to the bottom. It is obvious that there is no care about where the dirt pushed by the bulldozers to the steam shovels is deposited. Sometimes it blocks the rive,r which slows the river to a trickle and affects fish farther down the stream. Eventually the river fights back by finding a new course, but the damage to fish has already been done.

Only big companies are allowed to use machinery here because of licensing arrangements. But there are also seventy-five to a hundred men living in shacks along the river—as bad as the worst house you saw in the movies in Los Chiles. They work with shovels, picks and a small sluice box, and sometimes pans. Or they dig tunnels into the banks of the river and look for gold in these tunnels. The tunnels are not supported inside and have no ventilation. Many men pass out from the heat, and a few have died from tunnel collapses. The majority barely make enough to keep going and very few get rich. But occasionally someone gets lucky and finds 100,000 colones worth of gold which is around $2,000. That keeps them in alcohol and lets them live regally for a while. Soon they are back looking for a really big strike that will set them up for life. Few will ever get it.

From all accounts, the gold is not in a rich vein that runs through a mountain. Rather it is in the form of dust that has settled to the bottom of the river or is in microscopic layers in the riverbank. It is hard to imagine the desire that gold brings. People neglect their families, their small farms, and anything else—hoping to find their El Dorado. In a couple of years, the gold will be gone and the river ruined and the people will be back where they started from—poor, more cynical, and needing to develop the land sensibly so they can feed themselves. The rich will get richer again—and the poor, poorer.

Well, there is no gasoline in town today, so I can't travel. The gas should come in around 1:00 or 2:00 p.m. on the boat. I cut my thumb, so I can't grip my machete well and can barely hold this pen. So I'm going to sign off now.

Love,
David

APRIL 6, 1982

Dear Dad,

I am writing to you this week just happy to be alive! Two days ago, I was approaching a blind corner on the way to visit a project on my motorcycle when a truck careened around the corner and caused my life to flash in front of my eyes as I thought "I'm dead." There seemed no possible way to avoid a head-on collision from which I would be the sure loser. I headed for the ditch, hoping that I would be sideswiped and only have something broken as I didn't see how that could be avoided because the road is extremely narrow. At the last possible instant, the truck swerved and the tall section hit the front of the bike between the handlebars and the wheel, causing me to fly off the bike, land on my left shoulder, and skid along on the loose gravel. I am all right, however, and suffered no broken bones. I am black and blue all over and scraped in places I never thought I had. And so, as Easter approaches, I'm hobbling around and trying to take it easy. I am so stiff that I can't believe it. But I'm alive and will live to harass more people down here. I also had a doctor check me, and he said I will just be sore and stiff for about a week, which is better than being *a* stiff.

In other news, I was outraged last week by the gall of the foreign-owned mining companies in the gold region. In my last letter, I complained about the attraction that gold has and the fact that several small-time operators (four-to-five hundred) were up there eking out an existence chasing what (ninety-nine times out of a hundred) is a futile dream. This week though, the mining companies kicked out all the small-time operators for a number of reasons—saying that they had exclusive rights to the region, saying that the miners were a nuisance to them and that they were taking too much gold. To each of these claims, I say that it is not right, and I seem to have the preponderance of the community agreeing with me, including the lawyers that just arrived to investigate this thing. But the point is missed if one just looks at the legalities of the system, for even if the companies are right legally, there is a wave of antiforeigner resentment from most of the people here. The companies, for me, have once again set relations back in an undetermined way for a short-term monetary gain. The resentment is real, and I sympathize with the outrage that is generally felt—even though I feel that these small-time operators would be better off to go back and work the land agriculturally. They have a right to pursue their dreams, even if they are misguided in my opinion. To those who would reply that the companies also have a dream and a right to pursue that which is theirs, I would reply that I would theoretically agree but would not support policies that would jeopardize their own investments and the other investments of foreign capital in the region. As mentioned in the last letter, they are ecologically raping the land and now they have forcibly removed from the land some very poor people with nothing to show but dreams. They could have handled it in a myriad of ways, including helping the people to another part of the river or establishing procedures and/or times for them to work in the area. The point is that nothing was tried except brute force, and now the area is up in arms. The legal right to do this was questionable, but even if you ceded the legal right in a philosophical debate, the companies come out in a bad moral and ethical light and have planted the seeds for the resentment that will come back to haunt Americans later when they just might even want to do something good. The favorable climate for gringos here starts to go downhill, and the next batch that comes here will not be able to understand the undercurrent of resentment. No company has a right to do this, in my opinion, and they need to learn to consider the long-term benefits of cordial relations with a country rather than just a short-term quick killing. I feel that I am watching a microcosm of what has happened historically in Latin America—and continues to happen. I have seen companies that are starting to think this way, but they are few and far between.

Personally, I have had to endure some vituperative remarks and threats because I am foreign and a gringo. They do not know that I have no interest in the gold and don't believe me when I say so. I don't feel that I am in danger, but I always carry my machete whenever I go anywhere near the gold mines.

The rest of my work is going slowly but steadily, and I hope that things will be fine there—and as I come to be perceived as someone who is concerned about the poor, I assume that the remarks will cease.

I am happy to report that I will enjoy Semana Santa on a deserted beach near here, recovering from my physical and emotional wounds. I hope to reflect on the hope Easter brings us to raise my flagging spirits. It is to be a long fight!

Love,
David

APRIL 22, 1982

Dear Dad,

Have just arrived back from San José, where I had been for the past week getting seeds, getting my motorcycle repaired, trying to get tools for schools, trying to get paid for expenses, and many other things. It took me twenty-eight hours to get back. It was a twelve-hour bus trip, which includes one two-hour breakdown and a flat tire. I was distressed that the tire that went flat was the tire immediately under where I was sitting. I felt that everyone was looking at me accusingly, and I tried to act like it wasn't my fault! I don't know if I succeeded. Anyway, I missed the boat to Jimenez and had to stay overnight in Golfito. Golfito and sweating are synonymous. I can't find a room there that gives me a breeze and is mosquito-proof. I spent half the night sweating under a sheet and half the night getting bit. I think they had to wring out the mattress on the bed. Did I say bed? I mean hammock! It looked like a bed, you know—with a frame and a mattress—but when I lay down on it, it turned into a hammock! And squeaks. When I turned over, I thought mice had invaded the room.

You asked in the last phone conversation what it is that I do. I do essentially what I did in Los Chiles with the additional work of 4-H clubs. I get up every morning between 6:30 and 7:00, as that is when the symphony of animals becomes most intense. Dogs, chickens, roosters, ducks, and geese all go off together making it impossible to stay in bed until a reasonable hour. Besides, everybody thinks you're lazy if you stay in bed much past 7:30. I first decide two things when I get up. I look to see if it has rained and whether or not the tide is in. If it has rained too much, that means the rivers are up and I can't cross them. If the tide is up that means I can't go along the beach to visit some schools. The next thing I do is see if the local bank branch is using their horses, and if not, I use a horse to go to some schools, arriving each time very sore. Then I go visit schools and people's homes trying to promote gardens and 4-H clubs. I'm at the point now of being ready to have meetings and starting to plant. So, when I arrive at a school, I might give a talk on seed germination tests and then go work in the garden for a while on whatever needs to be done. Right now, we are chopping grass with machetes in most schools to clear areas for the gardens, and I am just talking about the benefits of clubs 4-S, as they are called in Spanish. Sometimes I work half a day and then go to my garden and chop there. Sometimes I work and travel until about 5:00. Sometimes I go to the beach at about 3:00 and reward myself for a good day or console myself for a bad day. Sometimes I go and kick the football around the field with the boys and make a spectacle of myself at around 4:00. I eat around 5:30 or 6:00 in a restaurant that caters to people on low budgets. It has a tin roof, one or two walls (depending on how you define wall), and a dirt floor. The place is decorated in early rustic, or I should say, early rust. It is an adventure to eat there because the chairs and tables tilt due to the unevenness of the floor and because of the varying length of the legs of said "furniture." The menu is extensive. You can have extensive amounts of rice and beans—sometimes soup, sometimes meat, sometimes cabbage and tomatoes—but always rice and beans. Morning, noon, and night. There is a nice restaurant in town that caters to gold miners who find gold, but this one caters to those who don't.

I hope that gives you a better idea of what I do, and that you will write more questions next week.

Love,
David

Chapter Eighteen

RICARDO

April 25, 1982

Dear Dad,

There are many times that I feel at peace with myself here, which may be hard to believe with all the agitated letters I write about this and that injustice as I see it. Tonight was also a good example of that sense of peace. I live with a man named Ricardo, who is the chief of immigration here and tonight he taught me how to cook beans because I made the mistake of saying that every time I cook beans (the entire two times I have cooked them) they turned out like bullets. So he showed me the secret of cooking them, which is to boil the heck out of them for a couple of hours, add salt towards the end, and start with fresh frijoles (beans)—all of which I thought I had done. Anyway, we joked and laughed about dumb things that gringos and Ticos do while cooking them and then had a nice meal together of tuna fish with onions, rice, and beans.

I also feel good after a good day of work, watching the sunset over the ocean—and waiting for the steam as the sun hits the water and the kids leaving after watching me shower and one of them saying, "See, I told you gringos bathe."—and riding my motorcycle along the beach with the fresh sea breezes blowing in my face—and always, seeing the excitement of the kids when they see the first buds of the seeds they planted pushing up through the ground. It ain't so bad down here as long as you don't dwell on the negative and you let yourself go with the many joys there are in life and the hope that each new day brings.

Last night Ricardo asked me what level of education I have. When I told him I had some hours toward a doctorate, he kind of blinked and took it all in. Then he said that he had had to quit school in the third grade and go to work in order to be able to eat. His work was this: he had a knife about the size of a butter knife, but much sharper; with this knife his work was to harvest rice one row at a time, each row extending for about three-quarters of a mile. He was bent over for eight to ten hours a day and could do no more than this one row at a time because otherwise you lost too much rice. He earned 9 colones a week (at the time less than a dollar a week, and this was when meals cost 2 colones a day). So in order to eat every day, he would have had to earn 14 colones a week. Sometimes the people he worked for fed him and sometimes they didn't.

He taught himself how to read and write better over the years after school, and after years of struggle he is now working for the immigration office in a good job. He says that back then there was more hope. *It soon will get better* was the feeling, and he recalls those times nostalgically. I looked at myself after we finished talking and compared our lives and thought about the many so-called "advantages" I had over him. More food, more education, more opportunity—more of everything. Yet this man knows more than I'll ever know about many things—from wielding a machete, to making beans, to being satisfied with life on a less developed scale. He doesn't have to reach for the stars as I sometimes feel I must. This morning we went out to mow the lawn, which consists of chopping the grass with a machete. I started flailing away at the grass and turned the small section I was working on into an area that looked like about a hundred beginner golfers had come through and taken divots out of the ground. When I stopped, pleased with myself, tired and sweating, he was watching me. He had finished the whole rest of the yard (seven-eighths of it) in the time it had taken me to hack up an eighth. His part looks machine-cut and mine needs to be resodded. He said to me, grinning, "You don't learn everything in the States." He's sixty-two years old.

Well enough is enough. Let me know if you like what I write, and ask questions.

Love and kisses,
David

Chapter Nineteen

FOUR "THATS"

Dear Dad,

I thought I'd tell you some little vignettes about my life here that sometimes slip through the cracks when I try to write. There were several times when I'd thought, "I should tell them about that." Well, here are four of those small "thats" that I haven't yet written about.

Eating Iguana

The first one is about the day the lizard/iguana died. I was driving down the road in an open jeep with the guy I live with. I don't remember where we were going, but whenever you drive anywhere here you see these flashes of green and gray which usually are these ugly-looking lizards about two- or three-feet-long from the tail to the head. They are quick, and you have only about a second to see that they are really ugly. Well, on this one day, one of the lizards decided to commit suicide by running under the wheels of the jeep we were in. There was a crunching noise followed by the squeal of brakes. Ricardo jumped out of the jeep, ran over, and picked it up by the tail and said, "What luck! We can eat this tonight." I said, "We can, huh? You mean *you* can eat it?" He laughed at me and said, "It's very good. Tastes just like chicken!" I grinned and thought to myself—we'll see. But he threw it in the back of the jeep and eventually we went home to where I learned how to skin, gut, and otherwise prepare a lizard for the kitchen table. The steps are as follows:

(1) Cut off tail. (2) Cut off head. (3) Drain blood. (4) Slice stomach and take out guts. (5) Peel skin. (6) Cut into bite sized pieces, fry, and put in stew.

The time came to try it when my friend, accompanied by three of his friends, brought me a little piece of fried lizard to see if the gringo would throw up or not. He didn't—because it *did* taste like chicken!

The Community Dance

Another thing that happens here quite often is the community dance. It is like something out of the 1950s because there are rigid social mores to observe: (1) Girls can never ask guys to dance, even if they are friends. (2) The girls are usually in small herds ranging in size from four to twelve. They stay grouped together and try to look cool all the time. (3) I always think they're having a terrible time, because they don't smile at you unless you are boyfriend and girlfriend. They also do not look at the boy while dancing because that means they want to go to bed with him. I always look at the girl while dancing and grin, and so I thought I was really doing something terrible that I didn't realize when she didn't smile back. (4) After the dance, they walk back to their table without looking at you again or saying thank you. They start jabbering again as soon as they hit the herd. (5) It is necessary to be a sprinter to get a girl to dance with you. As the first note of song sounds, you must dash to the table of the girl whom you would like to dance with and touch her lightly on the shoulder. She then gets up, usually without looking at you, and turns into an undulating ice maiden. You also have to learn strategy and learn to not appear too eager to make the dash to her table. You must note the competition and try to maneuver into a position to block out another's approach.

You can't try to engage in a conversation with her because she'll leave to dance with the next guy to ask her to dance.

I don't usually compete very well. I'm too soft-hearted. If I see that a woman has been dancing every dance, I think, "Well, I'll let her sit one out and then ask her." But just then another jerk asks her to dance, dances two dances with her, and the band takes a break. Last night I went toward a girl to ask her to dance, and before I got there, two guys got there ahead of me and took her out of the dance hall. I thought, "Typical. Beaten again." Turned out they were police and they'd arrested her for prostitution. A new problem for me—the lengths to which women will go to avoid dancing with me. Amazing!

There are many times when there also is nothing to do. I spent the morning today trying to repair my back tire on my cycle because it went flat over the night. Anybody that has ever worked on a cycle knows what a pain taking the back wheel off can be because of the adjustments that have to be done to chain, etc., especially when you don't have the proper tools. Then you have to get the inner tube out, find the holes, patch them, and put everything back together. Took me four hours to do everything. Then, no sooner was the tire on and I had gotten on the cycle to start, when the tire went flat again! I have two talks to give today and can't contact them to tell them I won't be there. Frustrating. I have always had very little patience with inanimate objects. I can't reason with them. I mean, after all that work, it just shouldn't up and go flat.

Am in the process of trying to get this little room to work out of in the nutrition outpost. They haven't used the room for a year because they've lost the keys, and nobody in a year's time has bothered to fix the door or change the lock. In order for me to change the lock, I have to get permission to do so from about four different people in four different cities, and who don't all have phones. It is going to be an interesting trick to do, so I think that I'll do it and let them yell at me about three months from now when they finally find out.

Last night I talked to a friend of mine in another part of the country who had invited a girl to go to a dance with him. He went to her house, picked her up, paid her way into the dance, danced a few times with her, and then they went to sit down. About five minutes later, she said, "I'll be right back." Two hours later, he was still waiting for her. He looked for her in the dance and finally left as she wasn't anywhere to be found. Poor guy was crushed. At least that hasn't happened to me yet!

An Alligator Scare

Every night when we are trying to sleep, we are serenaded. It seems that various members of the feathered species do their best to create hostility and resentment in fine upstanding young men like myself. Well last night, at the height of the concert about three or four of the local policemen could stand it no longer. They went and did something I have wanted to do ever since I arrived in Cost Rica. They got up, caught the biggest culprit (a rooster), placed him under arrest, cut off his head, cooked him, and ate him. They brought me over a small piece of the bird and I ate him with relish, that is to say, great desire as opposed to the condiment. I don't know whose rooster it was, but the police did it. I would have of course stopped the murder if I had known about it in advance, but cruel things just happen sometimes. I have to admit that I thought it was a very satisfying and gratifying midnight snack. Not very tasty, mind you, but very gratifying. The birds were very quiet for the rest of the night.

The commandos have also adopted a pet alligator which they keep tied to a tree beyond the police station. It has developed a nasty habit of biting the rope in half and making a mad dash for freedom. Most of the time they catch him because he is small (four feet long) and doesn't run very fast, but about a third of him is mouth (just like some people I know). He usually gets cornered and starts snapping at everybody until someone sneaks up behind him and kind of lassos him, cowboy style. I always feel sorry for him because I think he should be set free. This one night though, I was walking around the house when about two feet behind me I suddenly heard a sound similar to that of an alligator's jaws snapping shut. There are now claw marks about ten feet high on the house where I made a bid to become the first self-propelled human rocket! I was so scared I was glad my underwear was on its second day of use. (Contestants in the contest to finish this sentence, "I was so scared that I ...." Please send your entry to me in care of me. The winner wins an iguana, or a trip for seven days to Costa Rica. No nights—but seven wonderful days.) Anyway, I was scared to death, and it turned out that two guys were out walking the alligator (it takes two people to walk an alligator, otherwise it will eat the leash) and indeed it had snapped its jaws shut about ten feet behind me instead of two. But those turkeys saw me jump and haven't stopped laughing about it for days. I think I may put it in their beds. Now they also have a sack hanging from a tree out back with something in it that wriggles. I am afraid to ask about that.

I just had a frog jump on my foot while I was taking a shower. Startled me again. You see, sometimes the water doesn't make it all the way into the shower in the house and so you go outside to the shower there, which is a hose. It's kind of a group affair in the daylight because kids arrive to watch. After dark, toads become the menace to life and limb as they begin hopping around all over the place. I stunk and so I had to take a shower after dark during the deadly toad menace, and one hopped smack onto my foot and hung on. I turned into a toad myself, hopping around trying to dislodge the thing and did so after a few seconds. I was really "toad off"!

Reagan's Luggage

Somewhere around this time, President Reagan made a state visit to three or four Latin American countries, including Costa Rica, which meant all hands on deck (all US diplomats, their spouses, and all Peace Corps volunteers) to prepare for his visit . Because I was one of the biggest Peace Corps volunteers, I was drafted to be the person to carry President Reagan's luggage off Air Force One and see that it arrived in his suite. The Secret Service asked me to find an appropriate vehicle in which to transport the luggage and to give them the license number and make of that vehicle and warned us that—if any other vehicle approached Air Force One—quick and perhaps deadly action would be taken. Once the Secret Service had that vehicle's license number, the vehicle for the president's luggage could not be changed. We got a big Chevy station wagon, and I remember thinking that this vehicle was overkill since it was so big. President Reagan arrived on a Saturday, I think, and on Friday night bomb sniffing dogs arrived. The only vehicle available to pick up these dogs was the one designated to carry President Reagan's luggage. We did not think much about it, so I drove out to the airport with another Peace Corps volunteer to pick up the dog (singular) and take him to the hotel with his trainer. Much to our surprise, there were four or five dogs who had been in their respective cages for much longer than planned because the plane was about five hours late, and the poor dogs had deposited very smelly gifts in their cages (one had diarrhea)—and we had to put these smelly dogs in the car/truck that would transport the President's luggage the next day. We tried to fumigate that car and we washed the cages as best we could, but the smell lingered. To my shock, when I was handed Reagan's garment bag it was one of those cheap plastic models, and it had a rip in it, which meant that Reagan's suits were exposed to the smell of dog poop. However, we did believe that the Costa Rican president would be too polite to notice that the President of the United States smelled like dogshit. But anyhow, my friend and I decided to prepare ourselves for the onslaught, so we went and got drunk. Nobody said a word to us, and I have giggled about this for a long time. I did meet President Reagan and did not notice any smells, and he turned out to be friendly and solicitous about how we were doing and what our work was. Nice guy—but his policies helped screw up Central America because he made his decisions while looking through the prism of anti-communist rhetoric, which remains a problem in this region.

Love,
David

Chapter Twenty

MACHIAVELLI AND THE
EIGHT PIGS ON A LEASH

APRIL 30, 1982

Dear Dad,

In your comment about my comment about the responsibility of
the Costa Rican government in the rape of the land in the gold mining area, you are right in part. The government of Costa Rica has to
share some of the blame for not making the companies repair the land
after they are done. Indeed, that is part of the problem, worldwide.
Governments of developing countries have been, historically speaking,
in collusion with many of the companies that have come to their lands.
These collusions take many forms but usually it all comes down to a
few government members getting money for aiding the company in
their practices, or else for looking the other way. Here, I understand
that two former presidents of Costa Rica are involved with a few of
the mining companies. Dad, you have to understand that the benefit
to the economy that you speak of goes to a relatively few people in the
country. It may look good in their balance of payments deficit, but the
money *does not* get into the hands of the poor people of the developing
world. Costa Rica has historically been better at getting the money
more evenly distributed, but in this instance of the gold, most of the

money is not staying in Costa Rica; rather, it is going outside, as well as to a few rich people inside the country. The government then should also be blamed for being a government of few people. But I don't think that the gold helps the economy that much—only a few people in it. And I don't think the mining companies bear even at least half of the responsibility for the rape of the land. And if you had any idea of the Machiavellian manipulations that these companies do to get into developing countries like Costa Rica, you might think that they should take more of the blame.

Don't have any good friends yet except for Ricardo, but I'm getting to know some teachers who are pretty nice. It takes longer to get to know people here, as the people are distrustful of foreigners because of the gold. The heat and humidity here are about what it was like in Los Chiles but here there is a cooling ocean breeze that occasionally makes things better. I will have a little office in the nutrition center soon where I can put my seeds and do a little work. Last night I had a talk with the Puerto Jimenez equivalent of the PTA about 4-H, and I received good support. Will see if it translates into action. But in general, the work is going slower than I would like.

Love,
David

Author's Note

> Often, the source of the problem comes from our own political leadership. John Foster Dulles and his brother Allen were Secretary of State and Director of the CIA, respectively, and were also involved with the United Fruit Company as Board members. They were directly responsible for overthrowing governments in Iran and Guatemala when their interests were threatened. They made no pretense of promoting real democracy and instead acted forcefully to protect their economic interests, and the world is still suffering from their misguided actions and

hypocrisy. A book called The Brothers *supports my contentions. I began to realize that our government was using the fear of communism as a scare tactic and that I had been duped by this inordinate fear. If we had just implanted the Declaration of Independence outside of our borders, purveyors of communism would have melted away. Communism differs from Marxism, and the best thing one could do is read anything by my friend Dr. Anat Biletzki, who is an expert on this. I am at the point right now of dismissing any argument based on the bogeyman of communism as irrelevant, misguided, ignorant, and uninformed.*

MAY 18, 1982

Dear Dad,

I have just returned from a little trip to a place called San Isidro de General where my P.C. central office is with the Ministry of Agriculture. I had a few minor and comical adventures that I'm going to relate now, although at the time, I was angry. Last Thursday I got up at 4:00 a.m. to catch the launch out of Puerto Jimenez, taking my motorcycle with me. I was the first one on the beach to wait for the small boat that ferries people out to where the big launch is. Usually it takes about three trips to get the big ferry filled up, and they told me that they would come back to get me when the launch was filled with people. Well, needless to say, they never made it back but sailed off without me leaving me and another teacher stranded on the beach and no way to leave. I was so angry I could have had a cow! But speaking of which, I noticed another launch there that looked like a WW II landing craft that was loading a bunch of cows and pigs. So, I asked the guy if he could take me across the bay and he said he could if I helped him load the animals. So, seeing as how there was no other choice, with alacrity I agreed. We got the cows on with a minimal amount of fuss, although the cows are Brahmins or some facsimile thereof and kept chasing me.

They didn't seem to realize that they were supposed to be the ones to be chased aboard. They had no realization that we were under time constraints because the tide going out could leave the boat high and dry. The cows were nothing, though, compared to the pigs. The pigs, to start with, were panic-stricken and didn't want to go aboard for love or money—and we are not talking about baby pigs. We are talking about big mamas. They looked like I could ride them. I mean, they could have fed all of Costa Rica. The owner had them on leashes made out of nylon rope, and he took four leashes in one hand and four in the other and told me to do the same. I suppose I looked somewhat dubious, so he said, "Esta bien—estan acustumbrado." which is, "It's O.K. They're used to it." I got four leashes in one hand and had just gotten the other four in the other hand when all eight pigs took off at once—of course, in different directions! I felt like a wishbone on Thanksgiving. If you've ever had four hundred pounds of panic-stricken pork on the end of your arm, you know that something has to give. Eventually, I looked like a maypole on Mayday, so I let go of one group and dragged the other aboard. Then came the problem of catching the other four. Three of them we caught rather easily, but the fourth one was a pain since he had gotten in some mud and was like catching the proverbial greased pig. We finally caught it after some wear and tear on my clothes and pride. When we finally got the last pig on, we loaded my motorcycle, and I stayed in the hold to protect it from the pigs. By the time we got across the bay to Golfito two hours later, I smelled like rotten eggs. So I just walked into the ocean and dried myself off in the breeze on my moto.

Another time about a week ago, I was riding in a jeep down a very narrow road that had high grass along both sides when a snake that we may or may not have hit and that I saw at the last minute, struck the jeep. To make the kind of noise that it did when it hit the jeep, it had to be pretty big. I was very glad that I wasn't on my motorcycle, and I didn't stop to look at it because I hate snakes. (I may have mentioned this before.)

A friend of mine down here had the type of experience that I think is illuminating to a fundamental problem. That problem is the knee-jerk, negative reaction to the word "communism." My friend, you see, was accused of being a communist and threatened with being expelled from the country. Why did this happen? My friend, whose name is Jerry, came to Costa Rica in the same group with me and now works in the same program in another part of the country. He started working with very poor people called "precaristos" (or "precarious people"). As you may recall in another letter, when I started working with similar people in Los Chiles, I was warned that people might think I was a communist. Well, with Jerry this came true. In addition to this, Jerry made a statement saying that the Pueblo Unido (Communist Party) work more with the poor people than any other party here—which is true. They have no other constituency. But with this was the fact that he rented a house from a man who is suspected of being communist and in fact does do a lot of work with poor people. The combination of these three circumstances appeared threatening to the mayor of the town in which Jerry lived. The mayor called Peace Corps demanding Jerry's removal and also called the embassy. Jerry was forced to "lower his profile" in dealing with the poor and to go talk to this mayor and listen to abuse about his landlord, who is a good friend of Jerry's, and assure the mayor that he isn't a communist. The mayor also happens to be the owner of the only store in town and the landlord of many houses—and is characterized by charging exorbitant prices. Of course, he is going to try to crush anything that could change the status quo. Soon, however, the poor people who are being gouged are going to change their requests for more reasonable rents and prices for his products to demands that he give them the house and/or militant demands/actions. All the guy would have to do would be to charge more reasonable prices, and he would undercut their demands—thereby lessening the appeal of the seductive powers of communist whispers that go like this: "Go with us and you'll have more and cheaper food." "Support us and you'll have your own house." Take that appeal away and you kill their manipulations. It's like trying to deal with cockroaches. You can kill them once, but they keep coming back after time. But take away the food or cover it up, and the cockroaches have lost that which attracts them!

Chapter Twenty-One

SANDINISTAS IN LOS CHILES

MAY 22, 1982

Dear Dad,

I think that we should be concerned about my friends in Los Chiles, or I should say, *our* friends. I heard on the news this morning that the Sandinistas attacked Los Chiles and burned some buildings. I had spoken to Dona Elba last night—called up just to talk—and they told me that they might have to be evacuated and they are very worried. She didn't say anything about the buildings being burned or the Sandinistas, so I thought the danger was not imminent. But when I heard the news this morning, I tried to call Los Chiles but have not been able to get through. I am very worried about them, and I hope that you'll ask the congregation to pray for their safety and that of Chico and all my friends there.

Once again, I have all these mixed emotions about being in a relatively safe place when the people I care about are in some sort of danger—I know not exactly what. I am impotent to do anything to help them, except pray, and I feel that if I was there I would be able to protect them. On the other hand, if I was there, the Sandinistas might be looking for me, thereby putting my friends in danger who might be around me. During the last time period when I was there,

I understand that there was quite a fuss across the border about the CIA agent in Los Chiles, *which was me*. My worst nightmare is that the Sandinistas are looking for people that knew me and doing who knows what to them for associating with me. I hope and pray not, and will let you know if this is true.

In other bad news, yesterday England invaded the Falklands, and I am appalled that those islands are going to have such broad political repercussions, and that a war is being fought over something so silly as two islands. The fact of the matter is that the big loser in Latin America will be Uncle Sam. More than one person has talked to me about this situation, and none of the people are sympathetic to England, and most feel that the US is showing its true colors by supporting a colonial power in the oppression of a fellow Latin American country. I happen to be sympathetic to the position, although most people assume that I support the States' position. The islands were robbed in the first place by Great Britain 149 years ago, and Argentina has been trying to get them back ever since. Wouldn't you get a little frustrated after 149 years? On the other hand, I don't like the method Argentina chose for getting the islands back, and I despise the Argentinean government because they, I think, are trying to divert attention from an abominable economic situation and an abysmal human rights record. Having just finished a book called *Prisoner Without a Name, Cell Without a Number* by Jacobo Timerman, I have read one man's account of the torture and the damnable political system there. There are powerful factions within the government, and especially the army, over which no one has control, and they do what they please. I condemn the Reagan administration for ever cozying up to them and giving the Argentineans the idea that if they are against communism, anything they do is okay. Once again, the danger of seeing a "Red" behind every tree and having a foreign policy based on this assumption backfires. By our encouragement and preoccupation with anticommunism we failed to recognize or deal with root issues in Argentina and gave them the idea that they could get away with an invasion of the Falklands. Now the communists will gain influence because they can support Argentina and help them and say that they will help fight Yankee imperialism. And I think more people in Latin America will listen and wonder. I noted with interest that two of our staunchest allies in Latin America, Venezuela and Costa Rica, spoke out strongly against the US tilt toward England. Venezuela offered to send troops to help fight and Costa Rica said that we should move the capital of the Organization of American States elsewhere to a country that will support Latin America. It's a sad day for us, and I personally have felt more of that coldness towards me as a result. I think that both England and Argentina deserve to be condemned for their actions and that we should have stayed neutral in this conflict, but if you limit the discussion to simply who should have the Falklands, I think Argentina should.

Give my love to everyone and pray for Los Chiles,
David

Chapter Twenty-Two

RAINING CATS AND DOGS
AND SNAKES

JUNE 3, 1982

Dear Dad,

Well, I haven't got any mail for a while, but this time it is nobody's fault as the mail plane to Puerto Jimenez has stopped coming, so no one in town has received any mail for about two weeks. I don't know when they'll resume, but I hope it's soon because I really look forward to mail call every week. And I also don't know when this letter is going to go out because it depends on the launch that goes to Golfito every day, and it hasn't been going sometimes since the other major problem is that now there is a gas and diesel shortage. This is because Costa Rica doesn't have the dollars that are needed to pay for gas from OPEC. Puerto Jimenez is especially vulnerable because it is relies on food stuffs from the outside. If Costa Rica doesn't get gas soon and resume transports to Puerto Jimenez, the food supply will become cut-throat as the food supply dwindles. The prospects can be frightening!

On the bright side, the rain has let up finally and I've not run into a snake for two days. You may have heard that a big storm hit Honduras and Nicaragua. We got the tail end of that storm and we had rain pretty steadily for about two-and-a-half weeks. After the first half-a-week, the water was high enough so that snakes started to climb trees, nest in roofs, and in short do anything to get off the ground. I ran into snakes in the trees while walking along a path and while working in my garden. A typical encounter went like this. The Dutch lady in whose yard I have my garden went to the bathroom. After she finished, she looked up in the eaves and saw a snake curled around the room support looking at her. Very calmly, she comes out and yells to me, "David, you want to kill a snake." I think, "no-o-o," but I go over anyway. Now you have to understand that I hate poisonous snakes like I hate sharks, and sure enough, the snake is a small fer-de-lance, which is one of the most poisonous in the world. The snake can grow to two or three meters long, and is as thick as a boa constrictor and as fast. This one was only two feet long or so, but it was my job to knock it off the roof beam and then kill it. So, I poked it with my machete and nothing happened. It didn't let go. So I poked it again as hard as I could, and this time it plopped to the ground and headed for me. I went into a frenzy of chopping, and when I was done, the snake was in eighty-two pieces and I was sweating like a stuck pig!

But to talk about the other pleasures of my work is nice, too. Yesterday I went to a place called Rio Nuevo, which is about one hour by motorcycle and then about an hour by horse or an hour-and-a-half by foot, slogging through some of the worst bogs I have ever seen in my life. When I walk there, I am so worried about falling in the mud that I don't pay much attention to the beauty of the place because it goes right through the jungle to the school at Rio Nuevo. But yesterday, the people knew I was coming and sent a horse to meet me where the road becomes impassable for motorcycles. So I didn't have to slog through the mud. The horse did—with me balanced precariously on top of him. On some of the hills we climbed we kind of skied down, which is a new experience—skiing on a horse. But I did have time in the dry parts to look around and enjoy the unusual jungle vegetation and bird life. The jungle is very thick in places and has luxuriant, exotic plants and flowers everywhere, interlaced with vines that are as thick as a man's arm. White-faced monkeys peek out at you, chatter a bit as if discussing the preposterous invaders of their terrain, and disappear. Sometimes you can see rainbow-colored parrots with long, streaming, red tail feathers as they swoop and dive among the trees. The scene seems to be right out of the movies, and I felt very peaceful there. In addition to feeling a part of nature, when I got to the community, everybody there was in the school to meet me and listen to my talks about 4-H clubs and about gardens and about funds that are available from the Dutch and US embassies to improve schools and do other projects. The people are dirt poor there, but they are interested in improving their community and have already built a building to serve as a school. I use the term building loosely because the building consists of six poles that hold up the roof, which is made out of zinc sheeting. The sheeting is old, however, and there are many leaks when it rains. There are rough-hewn planks nailed to the walls that were made with the town's chainsaw, and these had two in gaps in them. The blackboard was rescued from somewhere and looked like swiss cheese with cracks around the holes. The teacher had become very adept at raising the chalk to prevent it from breaking when it came to a crack or hole. Unfortunately, I broke some chalk as I was writing on the board. While I was there, men were bringing in loads of rock in grain bags and old clothes, and spreading them inside the school because it was so muddy that there was a small sucking noise as your feet came out of the mud. The kitchen and the place where the teachers lived were leans-tos attached to the side of the house where some of the zinc sheeting had been extended to cover a few beds and a fireplace. The beds consisted of the same type of rough-hewn boards covered with sacks filled with straw. They had prepared a feast for me which consisted of a tough chicken, rice with onions and mustard greens, beans, and warm milk. They all watched me eat and seemed to enjoy the smacking noises I made to show how much I appreciated it. After my talks, I went and visited homes that had sick plants and gave prescriptions for each. We are going to try to build a new school, a house for the teacher, and stock medicines, especially anti-snake venom, so that the villagers can survive until the doctor comes. We will also be putting gardens at the homes and the schools, so some of the money you have sent will go here. I left with a feeling of accomplishment and remembering why I joined the Peace Corps in the first place. So I guess I'll stay for the remaining time until January.

I have to start filling seed bags now to go to a small village called Cañas (pronounce the *n* like a *y*) and work with the students in the school and have a 4-H meeting later on. I think I have just enough gasoline to make it there and back, so we'll see. There hasn't been any rain yet today, so I can probably cross the rivers okay. If it does rain and rain hard, I usually make a mad dash for the river, hoping that none of the four rivers between Cañas and Puerto Jimenez have risen too much to be able to cross them. You usually have about an hour to get to Jimenez and so I rush through whatever I am doing and try to leave so as to get to the river before it rises. I've mistimed the race a couple of times, and the river has risen a foot, becoming a torrent of swirling eddies and logs rushing down the riverbed. My motorcycle is a tank that has made it across the river with water completely covering the sparkplug. But once a log hit me and knocked me over, and it was a real struggle to get up, right the bike, and push it out of the river, avoiding other logs coming down the river. Have you ever tried to dry out a sparkplug in the rain when it has been underwater, and you don't have a dry stitch of clothing on? It's tough!

David Ives,
Voluntario de Cuerpo de Paz

Author's Note

Shortly after returning home from the Peace Corps, my sister Carol, who taught special education, invited me to speak to her class. It was a group composed of kids with special needs, so I thought it would be fun to talk about the most exciting experiences I had had while working as a Peace Corps volunteer. So I told them about the howler monkeys in the trees who made noises like tigers and scared me to death; riding my motorcycle through the mud, taking a spill, and getting all dirty; and teaching a class when an earthquake hit and shook the school building. The students said they thought I was the one shaking the building because I was so big! Finally, I talked about a big poisonous snake called a fer-de-lance which, if it bit you, would definitely kill you. In fact, the nickname for this critter was "the two-step snake" because after the bitten person took two steps he would surely die! A student raised his hand and asked, "Are you sure you would die two steps after it bit you?" I replied that this was what the people in my village told me. With the unbridled glee of a complete innocent, the boy shouted out, "Then you should only take one step!" I surpressed a grin and said with a straight face, "That is extremely logical." It remains one of my favorite stories.

Chapter Twenty-Three

DAVID AND THE SKIING HORSE

June 11

Well, here I am sitting in my office with my friend Jorge. It's raining again, and we're bored! We have been sitting around for an hour drawing ugly pictures of each other on the blackboard while waiting for the rain to stop. So far I have been losing, since Jorge can draw much better than I can.

I am looking for a new house here in Puerto Jimenez as I finally have had it with the people who I rent from. They let a whole lot of people stay in the house, but when one or two of my friends stay, they get annoyed. So since I want a place where anyone I want will be welcome, I am starting the process of looking for a house. Don't worry about my mail, because they all know me very well now as I pass by the Post Office everyday asking about it. The only reason I got mail today is that I went to Golfito yesterday and brought it over myself. I didn't get my mail yesterday because the bag was locked and they lost the key. Frustrating. I am reasonable about cockroaches in my bed crawling over me while sleeping, about no gas for a week, about lizards eating my gardens, about finding moving things in my rice and beans, about diarrhea every two or three weeks—but don't mess with my mail!

Last Monday I went to a place called La Balso and I thoroughly enjoyed myself. First, I traveled about a half-hour by cycle to a point by a river where someone was waiting for me with a horse. The horse he had for me looked sick and not at all enthusiastic about its impending work. Nevertheless, I mounted the horse, which looked around at me with an expression that said, "Who just backed a truck onto me?" Then it began to move in slow, plodding steps—wheezing like an old steam engine. We crossed a small creek and immediately began to ascend a cliff covered with mud. I felt like I would slide off the back of that poor horse. Finally, we got halfway up the hill, and the horse sank into a big mudhole. There was nothing else to do but to get off and drag him out. With great sucking noises, he finally emerged, and I finished climbing the hill on foot, literally two steps forward and one slide backward. When we got to the top of the hill, I remounted whereupon the horse turned his head around and looked at me as if to say, "Not again." So we continued down the hill. Halfway down it turned into a cliff again and the horse put on the brakes. His brakes consisted of kind of sitting down on his haunches with his front legs stiff and splayed and that's how we turned into the famous circus act: "David and the Skiing Horse." The brakes were not working very well that day, so we slid about fifty feet to the bottom, screeching to a halt in the middle of another mud puddle. The horse looking around at me once again and said, "*Now* look what you made me do!" I grinned sheepishly and got off and pulled him out. I'd like to say that I was extremely calm and professionally balanced myself on the horse as we slid down the hill. That would be a lie. I actually wrapped my legs tight around his ribs, and my arms around his neck—and hung on for dear life because the "ski trail" was an expert slope bordered by a steep cliff. Well, at least it had big trees on it which could have stopped the slide instantaneously had the horse and I gone over the edge. Thank goodness the rest of the trip was uneventful, although tiring for the poor horse! Up and down hills—but we did get to enjoy spectacular jungle views and colorful birds.

That school was one of the places which makes you wonder how anyone could learn; the roof leaks, the blackboard is cracked, the desks wobble, and the chairs fall through holes in the floorboards. But lots of learning goes on because the children really seem to want to learn, and in fact, several walk barefoot for over two hours on muddy, slippery, jungle trails to get there—sometimes dodging deadly snakes. And we complain about a thirty-five or forty-minute bus ride. While at this school, I had quite a thrill when they took me to an old Indian burial ground where we unearthed an entire, unbroken set of Indian bowls that seemed to me to be from a tribe related to the Mayans. The bowls were intricately painted and obviously very old and were lying alongside a complete skeleton. It was eerie to be looking at a skeleton and then looking at some of the people accompanying me who had Indian features. Such pots have not been made in the area for over two hundred years, as far as we can tell, and resemble others in the Costa Rican museum that are more than four-to-five hundred years old. Here in the middle of a jungle I encountered the remains of a civilization that had completely dominated the region, and I was standing in an area that would make an archeologist think Christmas had come—for, in addition to the bowls we found arrowheads, spearheads, and an old Indian corn grinder carved out of stone. It was a thrill of discovery that I will never forget.

Love,
David

| *Chapter Twenty-Four* |

PATRIOTISM vs. COMMUNISM

JUNE 17, 1982

Dear Dad,

I got your letter of June 3 when you seemed to get rather irate about my political beliefs. It seemed to me that you were blowing off some steam, and I even could imagine you doing it! Actually, the only part that got me was your closing, which was lovingly patriotic. To me, it implied that you don't think that my feelings are patriotic, so that was the only part that bothered me. What then, Dad, is your definition of *patriotism?* It sounds like it's along the lines of "America, love it or leave it." My definition of American patriotism is, "America, love it and improve it." I think it is dangerous to have the other kind of patriotism because it impinges on the freedoms that this country was founded on. In other words, when you have a difference of opinion with the government, all of a sudden you are not patriotic. I consider myself a rational patriot who sees America as a country to be proud of—as indeed I am. But there are many things that need to be improved on, and the United States has had many deleterious effects on many parts of the world—and I don't think many people even want to hear about them. Some of it is caused by our history books, which have glorified everything we ever have done without even implying that we have

ever done anything wrong. We also seem to think that God natu-
rally is smiling on us and that we are inherently better than anyone
else. So when we are criticized we assume a self-righteous attitude,
thinking—*how ungrateful, after all we've done*—or—*they're biting the
hand that feeds (or fed) them.* That reaction, consistent with a "love it or
leave it" patriotism, prevents a coolly objective examination of the facts
about a particular situation, because we are in a hurry to prove a point
instead of letting the point be proved. If we don't widen our myopic
vision of the world, I think we will eventually lose our independence
and become even more isolated in the world. To find the fault in many
of our relationships with other countries we only need to look in the
mirror and correct some blemishes. I think that is pretty patriotic.

I also have a larger vision of the world in which the United States is
only 6% of the population. I think that a world government would be
a good, if not idealistic, thing to come to—and given the interdepen-
dence that is developing, we are going to need the good will of other
countries to survive. We are losing that good will, and I propose to
understand the causes of that loss and do something about it. I think
that also is patriotic.

As far as the Falklands crisis goes, I hope you have received the
letter in which I enumerated my hesitations and disgust with the
Argentinean government. However, if the islands were Argentina's 149
years ago, I think they belong to Argentina now. If not, then I think
that England has a right to them. My understanding is still that an
Argentinean surrendered to an English captain 149 years ago although
I have not settled on anyone that I consider to be an authority on
the subject. I would also like to point out, historically speaking, the
economically exploitative relationship that England had with Latin
America, especially in the nineteenth and twentieth centuries. Some
people I know liken what England did to Argentina during this time
as rape. I would point out also that Venezuela offered arms and men
to Argentina, and Costa Rica wanted to change the capital of the

Organization of American States out of the United States to somewhere that had Latin American interests at heart. Peru is buying, or was trying to buy, weapons for them. As far as the Argentinean trick of firing on English soldiers after surrendering, I condemn it wholeheartedly. However, what about the historical atrocities committed by the British in India, China, Greece, the Balkans, Africa, and Latin America. But I will admit to having a tough time on this one because my distaste for Argentina runs very high.

I will have to stick to my guns about the knee-jerk reaction to communism. This knee-jerk, negative reaction to communism prevents serious thinking about its causes. If communism is negative, Dad, why did Russia go communist after two hundred-plus years of czarist rule and eight months of a democratic government. Why did China go communist in 1948? Why are communists in the government in Guatemala and El Salvador having problems with guerilla movements? What are also now the problems in Peru? Why did we intervene in the Dominican Republic in 1965? When you examine this issue, you may find a consistent pattern or characteristic of each situation, although the immediate circumstances particular to each situation are different. The characteristic is this: life was so bad that communism looked good! In Cuba, for example, the people were starving and illiterate before the revolution, and now they have unarguably one of the highest literacy rates and best health systems in the world, which has improved the lives of the vast majority of the population. Now that this has improved, I think the people there will want more freedom and Castro may have some problems. But the living standard has been raised for the majority of the people living in Cuba.

The ironic thing about this is that I have been an anticommunist for most of my life. I hope you will recall my letters from Los Chiles when I despaired about the direction the revolution was taking and the lack of freedom there. But a rational discussion about communism, an exploration of its causes, and indeed a plan to fight against it is impossible when the majority of the American population thinks, "Kill communists. That will solve the problem." That puts us in a position almost of animals. I think the way to beat communism is to is to kill them with kindness, visit them in prison, feed the hungry, cure the sick, help the poor people, and literally follow the Sermon on the Mount—not to mention the parts about loving your enemy and turning the other cheek. If you think of the purely Christian response to communism, Dad, I think you'd have to revise your thinking. And aren't the above things what you taught me?

I cannot stand what the Russians are doing to Poland. I have a great respect for the Polish people and their inherent greatness. I'm even going to stop telling Polish jokes! But I'd like you to compare what the United States is doing in El Salvador to what Russia is doing to Poland. I see very little difference between the two. I then would like you to compare what the United States did in Vietnam to what Russia is doing to Afghanistan. I also see very little difference in that. If you want me to talk about my perceptions of the similarities and differences in these situations, let me know, because I can go on for a long time on that.

I also don't view communism as the big monolith that you do, Dad. Read a book called *The Russians* by Hedrick Smith. He lived and worked in Russia for three or four years working as bureau chief for the New York Times. He describes in his book about five types of economic systems, only one of which is the official "socialism." He describes the main market in Moscow as being supplied from small private plots that the peasants work after they are done in their communal fields. And the private plots produce three to four times as much as the communally held plots, which is the reason many people in Moscow have fresh fruits and vegetables, despite that the official government system isn't able to supply enough. The Russians are hostile to the Chinese— Yugoslavia to both. Hungary reminds people of the west. Poland just had a remarkable tempestuous time, and Cuba said bad things about the Russian invasion of Afghanistan. In communism, are you talking about Marxism, Stalinism, Leninism, Trotskyism, Maoism, Titoism, or what? Where is the monolithic front? Dad, I agree that the communism should be shunned like the plague, but do you realize how bad things have to be for them to want "the plague"! [*My position has changed now. I don't think communism should be shunned.*]

No, you are not to be blamed for having a few extras in life. But is the man I know who chops sugarcane eight to ten hours a day for a pittance to be blamed if he, too, dreams of a few extras and gets resentful because he can't get it, then looks about for someone who will help him?

So, Dad, I'm very calm as I am writing this. The only part where I was perturbed was in the first paragraph about patriotism. I would like you to answer at least some of the questions I posed and I'll respond to them again. I really do think I'm reasonable!

I'd like to talk a little bit about some of the colorful characters around here. The first is Donia Ida, a Dutch woman who owns the land where I am endeavoring to have my garden. (I wish you would come down again, Dad, to shape up my garden as I am still adverse to weeding.) She is married and has two kids, with one in the oven. The one in the oven is due in September. She is married to a Dutch guy who sails looking for oil, doing work like Don did, only on a ship. He looks like a sailor, big and burly, and has a big handlebar mustache that sticks out about four inches on either side of his face. He's home for three weeks and sails for six weeks—and likes to laugh a lot and tease me. Ida reminds me of a frontier woman who makes her own bread, sews all her clothes and her family's, teaches her children, knows how to fix things, kills snakes, doesn't get upset about cockroaches, and is keeper of a small zoo. She has two of everything that has feathers: two geese, two turkeys, two ducks, two chickens, two roosters, and two parrots. Every now and then they set off a cacophony of sound, which is disconcerting. The geese also like to sneak up on people, so they are not only geese but goosers! She is a delight to be around and takes my kidding well and dishes it right back!

I'm going to go teach kindergarteners a few words of English today. I have to teach them the colors in English. I hope that it goes okay, because little kids have trouble with my accent, as do some others. But I think my Spanish is pretty good, and I hope that I never lose it and keep on practicing it siempre (always).

Looking forward to getting home!

Love,
David

JUNE 21, 1982

Dear Dad,

I have been finding out more and more about the history of the area and why part of the area was being more resistant than other parts of it to my promotion of 4-H clubs. On the map, if you go north along the bay from Puerto Jimenez, you find a place called Rincon. (At one point, I thought I was going to live there.) I have three schools in the area and I am also trying to promote 4-H Clubs there. The schools are going fairly well, but the 4-H clubs are going very slowly, to say the least. And over the last three weeks or so, I found out why. A gringo lumber company was in there from about 1960 to 1974 inclusive, and the people there almost hate us. As per usual, Latins aren't very direct because they don't want to hurt anyone's feelings. Unless they get angry. I began to realize that there was something else going on in the area through small comments like, "Are you from the company?" or "That's a tough area for you." I would just chalk things up to the gold mining and go ahead and work. But another Peace Corps volunteer down the road from me told me about a time when he gave a talk to a P.T.A. in one of the schools in the area and received a large and, to quote a phrase he used, overwhelming dose of hostility. He works with the care of the forest in the area, so the people got him mixed up with the lumber company and told him pretty angrily and directly where to put some trees. The company was called Osa Forestal, and I understand (but don't know for sure) that Milton Eisenhower was on the board. They paid for the rights to a large area of land for a tree farm to make lumber. The only problem was that the people living in the area were not informed, and all of a sudden, gringos were kicking them out of their houses and knocking some houses down. I have heard many stories about the atrocities committed by these gringos, including people being murdered in cold blood and burned out of their homes. I don't believe the majority of the stories that I hear from the Ticos in the area. (I started asking questions after I talked to the other Peace Corps volunteer.) Indeed, some people I know who are sympathetic to the company point to the jobs created by the company, the roads built in the area, the airstrip that was built, and the change of a stagnant area into a productive area. So, who's right? How do you evaluate a situation like that? You have to admit that the people in the area have a point because they didn't know anything about the impending change in their home area. You have to admit that the company made some physical improvements to the area, so the company certainly made some needed improvements. I can't find much good to say about the government deal here, as they made no effort, as far as I understand now, to communicate with the people in the area and to educate them as to what was going to happen. My more cynical side thinks that someone got paid off in the government to let the company in. But I have no proof of that. Anyway, the company did come in here and did expel the people from the land. They (the company) probably feel righteously indignant because they think they followed all the laws and improved the area. And to some extent, they would be right. But they should hold hearings in the area or make a strenuous effort to communicate with the people, however isolated they are. In the States, very few projects can begin without opportunities for the populace to fight them through the courts or through hearings. Here, there were none. Also, there was very little direct compensation for the land the company took. So instead of being perceived as a blessing to the area and a source of gratitude for the new roads, angry rumors and stories forced the company to leave, or perhaps they decided that it just wasn't worth it. And it affects me now, because they don't like gringos. I probably will just have gotten things going when the time comes to leave. Oh, well. I guess companies should realize that very few governments in the developing world communicate effectively with the people in an area to be affected, and that they should do it if the government doesn't—if only to protect their investment, not to mention any moral considerations.

Well, I have to get ready to go on a little trip to a school to work in the gardens, so I'll run along now.

Love,
David

July 15, 1982

Dear Dad,

I have moved to a different place, and I find this house to be much better for me. First of all, I am rid of the two obnoxious gringos who came down occasionally to live in the house which I rented from them. I was constantly trying to distance myself from them. The woman constantly wore ostentatious jewelry and liked to brag about it. This was hard to take after working with people who would have to work hard for years to get an equivalent amount of money to what she had on her finger. And the man was worse because he is the epitome of the "Ugly American." He went into a restaurant with me once and clapped his hands over his head and yelled for service fast. It was the last time I went anywhere with him.

My new living quarters are in a house that is infested by termites, leaving much of the wood something to be desired. I have one room about sixteen feet square, with the floor tilting to the door. There are two other guys who live in two different rooms, and another guy who rents a room to run a radio repair business out of. They are all nice and quiet and poor, and I am quite comfortable. The shower is outside the house and made of corrugated, rusted roofing—and is completed by a plastic bag over the shower head so that the water is directed downward as opposed to all over the place. There are a number of holes in the metal that surrounds the shower, making it easy to check if it is occupied. The "door" has a disconcerting habit of opening just when you have soap in your eyes, and there is no handle on it. I have to shower in a bent-over position, or my head would go through the roof, not to mention the difficulty I have in getting my head wet, since the showerhead hits me at about the sternum.

But I like it because I have the privacy I need and contact with other people to keep my Spanish sharp. Regarding my address, just change it to read: Á la par de la iglesia catolica instead of Á la par de los commandos, and the letters will get here. I pick up my mail at the post office, so there is no big deal about the address.

Love,
David

Chapter Twenty-Five

CHICO'S NEWS AND
JERRY'S DILEMMA

JULY 9, 1982

Dear Dad,

I recently saw Chico from Los Chiles, and he sends his regards. It was good to see him as it reminded me of how close I feel towards him and how much I appreciated his support while there—and how much I miss it now! In news from Los Chiles, Sobeda (the lady who did our wash and in whose home Dad put up shelves) was arrested and spent a week in jail in Nicaragua. After I left Los Chiles, she and her family started traveling to San Carlos, Nicaragua to buy and sell things she made. San Carlos is an hour away by boat, and people often went there to sell products from Costa Rica that are scarce over there, and vice versa. It seems that someone denounced her, that is, made a statement against her, alleging that she was a counterrevolutionary against the Sandinistas. On the basis of this statement alone, she was placed in jail for a week, as were Georgina and Jenny, her daughters. They took all her money, which amounted to some 20,000 colones, which would be equivalent to a quarter to a third of a year's salary. The Sandinistas would not give it back, so Sobeda loses big. The 20,000 colones were not free and clear because this was partly a loan from some friends and partly money that the family had earned. They had decided to pool these funds together to be able to buy things to sell and to pay off other debts. Needless to say, I was outraged at the inhumane treatment Sobeda received and, as Dad and Don well know, she is as far from a counterrevolutionary as Pluto is from the sun. She is just a struggling poor woman trying to make ends meet for her family and having a hard time doing it. I really feel bad for her and I know that the money will be hard to replace, if not impossible. It means a lot more hours of washing clothes by hand and ironing them if she can't find the work. Chico, too, joins the general condemnation of Nicaragua and its treatment of people and says he won't go back there until it changes. I hope it does.

After hearing that news, I left on my trip. I went to Cobano, Puntarenas to visit my friend Jerry, the one who was accused of being a communist. That controversy has died down, and I thoroughly enjoyed my visit there. Costa Rica is just full of these beautiful isolated beaches, and I keep on babbling about them. Jerry lives in lush green rolling hills at the tip of the Nicoya Peninsula which is about two hours west of Puntarenas on the map. He is an ideal volunteer and is doing a great job there. Then I went to visit my friend Eduardo Sawyer, who just moved to San Francisco de Coyote which is about thirty miles up the coast. It took me seventeen hours to get there! There is no direct bus between Cobano and San Francisco, and the roads were out, so the plan was that I would take a bus back east from Cobano to a place called Paqyero, another bus from Paquero to Playa Naranjo, and another bus from there to San Francisco. Problems began at Paquero when the bus that was to go to Playa Naranjo broke down, which caused me to take the ferry all the way back to Puntarenas and wait eight hours to catch another ferry to Playa Naranjo. It was quite an adventure—a boring adventure! Then, when my friend Eduardo picked me up, he dumped me in a river on the way to his house on his motorcycle.

Love,
David

Dear Dad,

I forgot to tell you about an incident on my recent trip to Cobano
to visit my friend Jerry, who almost got kicked out of the country for
having supposed communist sympathies. I met his landlord, who is
communist, or at least does have communist sympathies and voted for
the Communist Party in the last election. Now, for those of you who
have never met a communist and hate them anyway, let me describe
this man for you. He's about five-foot-seven and has a wife and two
daughters. He is a school teacher and is one of the few in the country
who teaches even when he doesn't have to—like on some holidays. He
is especially dangerous when he goes to work teaching illiterate adults
to read at night. He is especially provocative when he fights to open
two schools in two communities nearby that are very poor and have no
teacher. He is especially scary when he plays with his daughters and
allows them to climb all over him, laughing and tickling each other.
He is especially devious when he flirts with his wife, and they play
little jokes on each other and bask in each other's warmth. He is especially not to be trusted when the poor people ask him for advice, and
he always seems to have time to help them. I suppose he is especially
destructive when he helps get a dentist to visit the town every two
weeks. But he is an especially low-down, sneaky communist because
he is an active member of the Catholic Church and believes in God!
A Christian communist. For me, he drove another nail in the coffin of
monolithic communism. Thank God there are people, like this man,
who help to break down the stereotypes of what a particular belief is. I
asked why he is involved with communism, and he said: what or who

else works so extensively with the poor people because, at least in his village, no one else does besides my friend Jerry. Now that my sarcastic remarks are over, I want to say that I just think that if we are to beat communism as it is practiced today, we have to understand it and its attraction. And what I said before about knee-jerk negative reactions to communism is still very apropos for me. Hating communism causes the exact opposite things to be done that are necessary to beat it. Only when we have analyzed the different aspects of communism can we understand its weak points and undermine it. They certainly understand our weak points better than we understand theirs. [*I think that Jerry's landlord would not be a communist now, because he recognizes the lack of freedom involved in its application today.*] He does not like what's going on in Poland, for example. But for him, communism means justice for the poor. And if you spoke of him disparagingly or eliminated him as we are wanting to do, you would make a lot of enemies among the people he's helped and you would actually undermine your desire to prevent communism. That's what we do in the States so often in our foreign policy. We eliminate the leftists brutally in many situations, and whereas we think we have helped our cause by eliminating these "dangerous people," we cause more harm than good as we plant the seeds of hate for us among the people for whom the communists or leftists were their hope. Failure to understand this will increase our sense of isolation in the world and help us to lose friends, rather than gain new ones. Each communist movement is different and gives different interpretations to the myriad of communist theories that abound, and if we want to beat them, we should understand them and not react with hate. I say that we should be literally biblical with them—and love them and treat them in the way we would want to be treated. Well, that'll be all for now.

Love and kisses,

David

AUGUST 3, 1982

Dear Dad,

Well, —back in Puerto Jimenez after the annual mid-service conference and a two-day break in a place called Monteverdi here in
Costa Rica. Monteverdi is a Quaker community located right next to
a national park. The park protects one of the few remaining tropical
cloud forests in Central America. It is a type of jungle but is different
than the type of jungle I knew in Los Chiles and now know here in
Jimenez. It is different because it is in the highlands, very wet, and very
cloudy and misty. As you enter the forest, the forest kind of envelopes
you and the sky is suddenly gone. There is an awesome quiet there,
broken only by the soft drip of water from the trees. The trees are tall
and every growing thing is covered with vines and moss. You can't see
the bark on many of the trees because of this coverage. It gives the
jungle a mystical aura which, combined with the mist drifting through,
reminded me of scenes from Camelot when Wart was looking for
Merlin the Magician. It is like a wonderland—with all the shades of
green and all the soft colors. I had a great feeling of peace and con-
tentment while walking in there; in a sense it was like a womb. It was
great. The Quaker community was nice to see, although I didn't have
that much contact with them. They make the best cheese and have a
nice working relationship with the farmers around them, buying their
milk for making their cheese. I really do feel close to this aspect of
religion, especially the way they view each man as a minister capable
of determining his own relationship with God.

The other thing that is famous in Monteverdi is the Quetzals.
Quetzals are a variety of bird famous for their beauty and long tails. I
saw about ten of them—with their beautiful long tail feathers, brilliant
plumage, and grace while flying. The Native Americans attributed an
almost mystical sense to them and valued their feathers for making

decorative objects. In Guatemala the monetary unit is called a quetzal. There are two to three quetzals to the dollar.

sixty different varieties of birds a day. It was a paradise!

Well, back to the more mundane things in life. We have become a little more isolated here in Jimenez because the main launch that brings people back and forth from Golfito broke down and is out for a month of repairs. This means that it is going to be really hard to get in and out of here because the flights in have also stopped, and the road out is impassable. There is a shortage of sugar and rice here and a problem with the water system. The water may be bad, and they will have to fix it—but there is no money to repair the system with. So the people here don't have enough to eat, and their water is bad and could cause disease. There are no machines around to dig wells with as there is no money or way to get them here to dig more wells. Prices for anything you can get are doubling and tripling again in another round of inflation. A bottle of ketchup, once 2 or 3 colones, is now 21 or 22. Beans (their staple), once 200 colones for a hundred pounds, is now 1,400 colones. This morning there was a run on the seeds that I had in the office because people have gotten the word that my seeds grow, and they are free. (Actually, they are *your* seeds and gardens because many people back home have contributed toward getting them.) Over the last month, I have given a number of talks to teachers and people in the communities about gardens, and I have four 4-H clubs formed in ten communities, and 4-H clubs are well on their way to being formed in the others. I am not bothering to work with 4-H where there are gold mines because there are other interests that the men have there. I have helped to form an association for development in Puerto Jimenez to talk about what we can do for the long-range future of Jimenez, which is an important step toward receiving money from foundations and embassies. I'm also growing gardens in the churches here so that we could distribute food to the people who don't even have land to grow things on and live in shacks that blow down in a strong wind.

The garden I made for the nutrition center is now producing, and we have harvested melons, cucumbers, radishes, okra, mustard, Chinese cabbage, and beans to feed the kids in the breakfast and lunch programs that I'm working with. Originally intended to be a supplement to rice and beans, the garden is now the only source of food for this program, which would die without it—not to mention that it would eliminate meals for about forty kids and about ten pregnant mothers.

I keep my head above water in trying to emotionally deal with all the sadness around me. It is becoming overwhelming for me as inflation and the scarcity of basic goods gradually tighten the noose around many people's necks down here. There are more incidents of theft nationwide as people begin to steal food and leave radios and TVs alone. I have not lost my sense of humor yet and still enjoy many comical things that happen to me in my life here. But in response to those of you, in my family and out, who have said my letters are very serious and that I should write more stories, I would say that I have to maintain a balance between humor and the tragedy unfolding around me. I become sad many days and angry after that as I see our government and the International Monetary Fund, the World Bank, our government, and the Costa Rican government following policies that will increase the wealth of a few and increase the misery of many. I do have a hard time recapturing my humor when I see young girls driven to prostitution so that they can get money to buy food for themselves and their families, or when I see a young girl with thin legs and big eyes asking me for seeds or if there is an extra cucumber to take home today. I don't like to watch a woman of about forty looking like she is fifty or more spending all the money she earned last week washing clothes by hand to buy food for herself and her family that may last only four or five days if she stretches it. So I talk about the things that I think get in the way of people receiving the help they need—like knee-jerk anticommunism, like foreign aid programs that help the few instead of the many, like justice, like the arms race. I want to "close the window of vulnerability" that Reagan talks about—only not with missiles. Our vulnerability is hungry people, and our curse is that our policies increase hunger instead of helping it. It bothers me to get letters from good friends that mention nothing but good times, new sports cars, new jobs, more money, more beach time, more football games—when I am dealing with less of everything on a mere gut level. So I say things to make people think or react and ameliorate it, with some humor, because nobody could take all the heavy thoughts and angry feelings I have all at once.

Thanks for everything, and tell the people thanks for the $700.

Love to all,
David

AUGUST 24, 1982 (*excerpt*)

Dear Dad,

I am having mixed feelings about the impending end to my Peace Corps experience. I am really anxious to get home, but I'll be ending right in the middle of my work and before some projects are done. I am just now gaining the trust of the people here and know the power structure in town and know I can be really effective—at least in theory. Sometimes I think of staying for another year because I could do that, and the Peace Corps would pay for a trip home for a month. I doubt that I'll do that, but it is awfully tempting sometimes when I feel like I'm going to jump ship before the voyage is done.

Love,
David

SEPTEMBER 6, 1982

Here I am again, back in Jimenez after a short trip to San Isidro to attend a course there. Turned out to be worthless, so I am kind of sorry I left, except that I spent last night in a hotel that had a rusty air conditioner in the room. It actually worked well enough to make me cold, which is a sensation I haven't felt in a long time. It was great! I'm glad I'll be coming back in the middle of winter because I wouldn't want to miss the snow!

Things continue to go from bad to worse in Costa Rica, economically speaking. As you should remember from my letters, Costa Rica is in the process of painful belt-tightening in response to some onerous conditions set by the International Monetary Fund in order to receive more loans. One of these conditions is causing the price of food to go up exorbitantly and, as usual, the poor are the ones to suffer the most, since a large part of their income goes for food purchases. Now, in addition to these conditions, Costa Rica is facing a drought in its main rice-producing region of Guanacaste. That means in about three months Costa Rica will not have its regular large infusion of home-grown rice or, at the least, it will be considerably smaller. That will cause prices to spiral up again. They are also facing the prospect of drought conditions in the main frijol (bean) growing region, and that double blow to the two basic staples of Costa Rica could cause something to snap. There are already strikes and food storages, and the sanctions of the IMF have not even been fully implemented yet. The effect of the sanctions and the drought have the potential to be devastating. Even in my area, the rainfall has been below normal; I am still able to cross the rivers, and according to local lore, a horse wouldn't be able to cross now in normal times. I guess the old adage —when it rains it pours— is true. So I hope it does rain soon. Or else I don't want to think about what could happen.

Coming back the other day from visiting my favorite community, I did get caught in one of the few storms that we've had recently. The community's name is Rio Nuevo and I ride about a half-hour on the cycle and then about an hour-and-a-half by horse to get in. We saw the storm clouds gathering while I was giving a talk on nutrition and we thought it would be a small one. We were wrong. After we'd worked in the garden, a great windstorm came up and I had to high-tail it out of there—what with the wind blowing down trees and making the horses skittish. We also had to suffer through a driving rainstorm that turned the already bad road into a veritable sea of mud which the horses did their best to struggle through. It took two-and-a-half hours to make the trip to where my motorcycle was parked, and all the way there, I was afraid that a tree might have fallen on it. We got there and a tree had fallen in back of it, which we had to chop through with machetes to get the bike out. When we cutt through the tree we found that the area where I had parked had turned into a mudhole, and the bike had to be lifted out. I was tired from chopping through the tree and fell in the mud a couple of times. When the bike was out, it started right up and I took off. I turned to wave to my friends and heard a sharp crack as a big tree fell right where we had been. Scared me to death! The rivers hadn't risen too much yet, so I was able to cross them without falling over, although the currents were strong. I crossed the last river and accelerated the bike hard to get home and out of the rain, thinking I was home free. I rounded a bend, and there was another tree down. I was going too fast and I just barely stopped the bike before I hit it, going into a sideways slide but not falling over. I sat there for a minute and then got out my machete and started chopping again in order to get through. I was glad to get through and home!

Two days later I went to another school in the same area called La Balsa. It involves doing the same thing, riding the bike and then going in by horseback. The person who met me felt that I should not follow my usual practice of locking my helmet to the bike but should instead hide it in weeds so no one would see it to steal it. Since I had followed this practice for a number of months now without problems, I told the guy that it would be okay. But he was adamant, so I relented. On the return trip, I arrived at the bike without problems, pulled it out, and went to get my helmet. I was parting the grass and bushes with my hands when something hissed at me, causing me to beat a hasty retreat. I cautiously approached again, poked at the helmet with my machete, and found a snake had taken up residence in my helmet. It was small, and I don't know if it was poisonous, but I turned into a snake-chopping machine, and it "bought the farm." I put on my helmet and decided that having it stolen was better than having a snake in it when I got back.

A couple weeks ago, when I went to visit the same school, we experienced our first earthquake. I was in the school giving a talk and, as I am likely to do when I am talking, I walk around. That was when the earthquake hit. It was only a small one, and the building just shook a little bit, but the kids thought I was the cause of it! The nerve!! Actually, I also thought I'd done it since the school looks like a good wind could topple it over. So I stopped walking and the earthquake continued and then stopped. It is very disconcerting to have this happen, and I hope this doesn't mean that a big one is coming because it could destroy Costa Rica's economy.

Love,
David

Chapter Twenty-Six

DAD'S QUESTIONS

AUGUST 23, 1982

Dear Dad,

Your letter of Aug. 23 was waiting for me when I got back, and I am going to try to write more detailed descriptions, as you suggested. It will be good for at least three or four, more letters I think, so please continue asking questions as you did. I felt the tone of the questions was good, and I appreciated that.

First, I want to respond to your comments and questions about the man you talked to this summer who went into Los Chiles three years ago to talk to them about growing and buying cacao. He was right when he said that there was no way to get the cacao out conveniently because there were no roads, and I can see how he could read the people as being indifferent to the idea. Then I would have asked him why he thought that, and what are the reasons for those problems. Now knowing his responses, I will give you mine. First of all, I doubt if he was fluent in Spanish, and as I know from personal experience, this is a barrier to effective communication. Second, concentrating just on the indifference perception, most peasants (or campesinos) he would have met are shy, and it is easy to misread this shyness. Third, the culture here is often slow and unresponsive to gringos who come in and fly out in a short time period. The gringo is usually very forceful and wants things done right away and has little patience with the social amenities of the culture. Fourth, (and related to the third), a book called *Ten Keys to Latin America* by Frank Tannenbaum points to a basic cause of problems between Latinos and gringos. We think we are superior to whatever culture there is in the world, and the people from other countries we deal with pick it up. This comes across mainly in facial expressions and tone of voice, and is met by Latinos, especially by the humble people, with indifference. That man could have been the nicest guy in the world, but he is fighting 150 years of history. There have been many gringos through there, some bad and some good, but never staying. There have been many promises made and for every promise kept, three or four have been broken. Remember that it took me six months to begin to be effective in Los Chiles because the people took that much time to begin to trust me. That's why it was so hard for me to leave there and why I still think it was a bad decision to take me out of there. When they finally broke down and trusted me, a lot of the attitudes that I thought or judged to be indifference were anything but that.

This brings me to another point that made me mad. It is in relation to when I had to leave Los Chiles. About three weeks ago, Pepe (the Director of the Peace Corps in Costa Rica) came to visit me here in Puerto Jimenez. During the course of the visit, he asked me if I would consider going back to Los Chiles, and I said yes, and my initial reaction was to be very happy. I then asked him why. He said, because they are thinking about putting a number of Peace Corps volunteers along the Nicaraguan border to counteract the Sandinista influence that is spilling over into Costa Rica. I had a number of reactions then, the first of which was: "Well, if you're going to do that, why did you take me out in the first place?" I begin to lose the order of my reactions after that as they all became jumbled together, but they continued. One of them was: "If the reason you and the chiefs in D.C. took me out of Los

Chiles in the first place was to protect me from danger, what justification do you have for putting me back in now when it is, if anything, more dangerous?" Another was, "Do you expect to have me leave my work in Jimenez without it being done?" But my strongest reaction was sometime later, when I asked myself, "Is this a use to which Peace Corps should be put?" I have realized that Peace Corps is political, but this became too blatant for me because I, ever the idealist, joined Peace Corps to learn and to help hungry people—not to fight something that Reagan defines as bad. With all the abuses by the Sandinistas that I know about, I don't think it is all bad—and it should be understood, rather than attacked so vigorously. So often we have attacked a system that we don't like, only to have our attacks throw the baby out with the bath water. I'm afraid that this would happen again and *is* happening again. The Sandinistas should be understood in the context of the history of Nicaragua instead of trying to isolate them. It will strengthen them rather than weaken them.

Love to all,
David

SEPTEMBER 8, 1982

Hola Amigos,

Well, as promised, here is another installment in the continuing saga of the adventures of David—with this being a letter dedicated to answering the questions raised by Dad in his last letter. It's raining here in Puerto Jimenez, and the rain is very relaxing to listen to as it pounds on the tin roof that covers my head. I'm listening to the Voice of America's new broadcast right now and have heard about the eight Israeli soldiers captured by the PLO, and that Habib got some award for his work in Lebanon. After this letter, I am going to listen to a baseball game that will be broadcast on Armed Forces Radio to see how the sports world is going. I'd love to read a Sports III right now because I can't even tell you who is playing on what team, like I used to be able to.

In the last letter, I talked about the perceived indifference by that man who was in the Los Chiles area some years ago. Another aspect of his observations and Dad's were about the nature of the roads down here and the difficulty of getting products to market that are grown in a region that has bad roads. Dad said that the fact that there are no roads to an area means that the government is ignoring that particular area, but I don't think that this is necessarily true. It is, however, very true that the roads are abominable in many places down here, and Los Chiles is a typical example of the bad roads that predominate in rural areas of Latin America.

Once again, I think a historical perspective is beneficial to considering the problems of Latin America and where to fix the blame for many of these problems. It is also beneficial to consider history when deciding what to do to combat the problems of underdevelopment. Traditionally, roads have been built in Latin America to serve— not the countries themselves, but countries in the developed world. During colonial times roads were built to carry out Spanish gold from the Incas and Aztecs. Those roads may have gone from the capital to the port and were nothing compared to the network of roads developing in what were to become the States. Why was that? Because in our development, we started along an eastern seaboard and spread inexorably out towards the west, following and creating roads as we went. Most people that went West had some family back East that they kept in touch with, or friends that might follow them later. Communities developed along the way to service the travelers or settlers, and people expected the government to protect them from Indians. This required a string of forts along the ever-changing frontier and roads to get there. On the other hand, Latin America had about four or five major centers spread out among Latin America— centers in Mexico, Venezuela,

Peru, and Argentina—and some might consider Rio de Janeiro a historical center. Each of these centers was oriented back towards Spain or Portugal through the export of gold and silver. There was very little attempt to move into the interior of the country because the Spanish were not there to colonize or settle in the English and French style in North America. Rather, they came to take out as much gold and silver as possible and return it to Spain. Also inhibiting in the development of roads were the great natural barriers of rivers like the Amazon and the Orinoco in Venezuela—and rugged and impassable mountains like the Andes. And there were thick jungles, wild beasts, snakes, hordes of biting insects that caused lots of different diseases—and intense tropical heat, rain, and mud. Most historians and geographers would agree that the natural barriers to road construction in Latin America were and are much more formidable then that which was and is encountered in North America. Therefore, in the beginning there was no push in Latin America to have an extensive road system—and indeed, building one would have been impossible because of natural barriers.

As Latin America progressed, the roads and railroad systems that were built followed the development of businesses for export. In Brazil, sugar cane; in Bolivia, silver; in Peru, gold and silver; in Chile, nitrates for fertilizer; and in many places—coffee, bananas, meat, and cacao. Usually, this meant a road or a rail line to get the product from a central place of collection to a port and did not mean that a very extensive system of transport was being provided. Most of the minerals and agricultural products of Latin America were developed and exported for use in Europe, and then in the States, and were not responses to the demands of the local populace. So economic development in Latin America did not foster the growth and spread of transport systems, especially in comparison with the development of North America.

Costa Rica didn't even come into the world economically speaking until the 1860s or so, when they discovered that coffee could grow very well here. Then some roads here developed to get the coffee to Limon to export mainly to Europe. With the advent of the banana, a railroad system was constructed by the banana companies to get their product to port. But the foreign-owned businesses and the country or in other words, to the majority of the country. The elite in Costa Rica had the systems they needed to maintain their income, as did the banana and coffee growers and exporters. It was not until the 1960s and 70s that Costa Rica began to earn enough money to embark on a nationwide road building program, which was only about thirty to forty years behind our major efforts to improve our roads in the States. The interstate system we have now in the US was begun in the 1950s, so Costa Rica was not that far behind us and far ahead of most countries in the region and in Latin America. So I don't think that they are doing too badly. It is also difficult to get the equipment needed to build roads since it is constructed outside of Costa Rica and the prices that Costa Rica gets for its products are way down, making it difficult to do some of the things necessary to develop. And when the control of export earnings is in the hands of foreign businesses and 1% or less of the native population, it is difficult to get what is needed to develop effectively. The blame is really about: natural barriers, foreign businesses, the elite in the countries themselves, and the attitude historically that Third World countries are there to be exploited toward maintaining our standard of living. So there ends as short an explanation as I can give about roads. I even cut out some things I could have expanded on so I wouldn't bore too many of you. It is not a simple exercise, and books have been written about this. I'm afraid what I said just scrapes the surface.

You asked about what things can be done in Puerto Jimenez to help the economy here. I think the thing most necessary here is to blow up the gold mines and end the gold rush fever. I find that anything I do here, or anybody else does, has to compete against this so much that it wouldn't be worth it to start another company here. Also, the road needs to get in here from the outside and it is in the process of arriving. I am also helping a community development association look at the feasibility of improving the airport service and boat transportation service so that we can get products in and out of here once this gold rush stops or slows down. I think that there are things that could be done to help the economy here, but the transportation system has to be improved.

Please remember that, when I criticize the States for their contribution to problems here, I acknowledge the responsibility that Costa Ricans should uphold toward addressing this mess. European nations, especially England, have to share the blame for what has gone on in the developing world. I do want you to realize that we have historically sided with the rich elite to maintain the status quo. In our inordinate fear of communism, we have forgotten our pro-democracy and justice commitments that make us appear hypocritical when our Declaration of Independence is compared with our actions in other countries, especially here. We must take a good hard look at ourselves and what we can change in order to help these countries reap and share the bounty. More on this in the next letter.

Love to all,
David

Chapter Twenty-Seven

A DAY IN THE LIFE
OF PUERTO JIMENEZ

SEPTEMBER 12, 1982

Dear Dad,

Hi there! It is Sunday afternoon and I have spent the day very lazily. Some friends were down for the weekend, and when they got up at 3:00 a.m. this morning to catch the launch to Golfito, I, of course, was awakened. They bustled and rattled about until about 3:35 when it was time to walk to the launch and it was time for me to go to bed again. Having felt tired, I thought that it would be no problem to go to sleep again. But some of the dog packs that roam around at night gathered for a howl-fest right outside my house around 4:15 a.m. This necessitated the launching of several projectiles also known as rocks in the general direction of the choir. However, I think that woke up the roosters, who then commenced to howl or sing or crow or whatever. This was around 5:00 a.m. Since most roosters around here are under the house next door, it is tough to hit them with a rock without raising the ire of your neighbors. When the din finally died down, with a sigh I settled down to sleep and was on the brink of slipping away when I heard these faint crackling noises emanating from the corner of the room. I turned the light on and caught two mice in the act of breaking into a tinfoil-wrapped piece of cake that one of my friends had left me. They scampered into a hole that I had not noticed before, so I tried to cover it up with a book and a rock and went back to bed. After about two minutes of blissful rest, I then noticed a sliding, scraping noise as the two mice endeavored to either eat the book or move it. I waited until their heads appeared and then I threw another book at them, missing of course. By this time, I was annoyed, so I got up to find a board to put over the hole and hung the cake up in a bag from a nail on the wall. I went back to bed. A little later: Crackle—crackle—crackle! The little rapscallions had climbed into my house through another hole, climbed up a chair, up a hanging T-shirt—had jumped from the shirt to the bag, and were eating (or starting to). I know this because when I turned on the light again I saw their escape route, which was the reverse of the above. So, I covered up the other hole and did the only thing left to do. I ate the cake, thereby removing the temptation from the premises. Impudent rodents anyway.

Well, it's rained for two or three days off and on, breaking the mini-drought that we were having here. It was too late to save some gardens, but the majority should be okay. Those of you who saw the movies while I was home know that I build raised beds for drainage purposes in order to allow for the high rainfall. Well, when there is no rain, the sun just bakes the ground, killing the seeds and turning fertile earth into a veritable desert of hardpan. It's tough to grow a garden down here!

Dad asked me to be more descriptive—and this I will try to be—by describing the life around a bar here in town called La Endja. It is rapidly becoming a town institution and will probably remain so for as long as there is gold in the area—for La Endja is the local hooker hangout (or whorehouse). Every Friday the launch from Golfito arrives with its cargo of human flesh and inebriating liquids so that the miners that do find something will have someplace to waste their money and squander their dreams. The women are all sizes, shapes, and ages—ranging from thin to fat, teenagers to forty to fifty-year-old women, and none very attractive. They come bursting into town decked out in tight, tight shorts or jeans that look as if they've been spray-painted on, high-heeled sandals or shoes, their breasts and fat almost spilling out of tube tops or halters. I am always struck by their forced gaiety as they walk into town and when groups of them cluster together during the weekend. They are always leering at men who they know from before, making lewd suggestions, much like the ones on 42nd Street in New York, except not quite as aggressive. They always say something to foreigners because they are sure they have money. I get propositioned at least once a weekend by a new one who hasn't been in town before, but she usually doesn't do it again because they have a grapevine on who isn't a "good trick." It is especially painful for me to observe the young ones who obviously are not as hardened as the more experienced or older ones. Knowing that many young women are being economically squeezed into that kind of existence is painful, and each weekend there seem to be more young ones around. Their eyes usually show the hurt of being forced to grow up too soon, but they also have the most bravado and are the most rowdy. I always wonder about the individual forces that led them to this work as I watch them strut, looking for some action. They can make 400–600 colones for only three lays in a day, which is two to five times as much as they can make in most other jobs. The economic crisis is inexorably beating down the country.

As I said, most of the action takes place at La Endja. When I first came here it was a seedy looking dump with rotted boards all around. They have since replaced the worst of the boards and constructed little rooms in the back where the whores can "service their clients." The place is painted a garish blue and has western style swinging doors in the doorway. It is dimly lit, with bare light bulbs and a bar in the corner dispensing expensive shots of the local alcohol made from sugar cane, called guaro. The girls are clustered around four or five tables, talking and all dolled up. Men congregate around the bar and about ten other tables, fortifying themselves with liquid courage in order, I think, to make the whores look better. Eventually, individually or in groups, they start approaching the girls and ask about prices,. It is about 200–400 for a "lay," which usually lasts about fifteen minutes. It costs about 1,000 colones for an hour's worth of pleasure during which you can do it as many times as you want. The price depends a lot on a white card that the whores are supposed to have which is issued by a doctor saying she is free from venereal disease and the date of the exam. Only about a third of them have these cards, so those that don't usually have to charge less. After the fifteen minutes or hour is up, both parties emerge from the back rooms to the shouts of the other customers or companions, asking how it was and, "Does it itch yet?" (This, of course, is kidding about the chances of VD.) Occasionally, a whore comes off the street with her client if he doesn't have a place to take her, because some from the Endja look for action on the streets. It's like a hub of the wheel. Occasionally, the police come looking for the ones who don't have their white cards because it is illegal to not have one. Usually, the whore just serves the policeman for free, and there is no problem. A more cheapening experience I cannot imagine, and the pervasive influence it has on Puerto Jimenez is eating away at the core of the town. It's disgusting and very sad.

That's all for today, folks. I am now going off to supper.

Love,
David

Chapter Twenty-Eight

A PAINFUL STORY
ON A JOYFUL DAY

SEPTEMBER 17, 1982

Dear Dad,

This past Tuesday, the fifteenth, was Costa Rica's Independence Day. I was invited to go to a small school and give a short talk to the assembled multitude of about twenty-five to thirty people, half of them kids. The school is called El Sandelo and is in one of my favorite communities. The school's best feature is its cement floor. From there on, the school looks like it could blow away in a small breeze. The walls are holey and termite trails run throughout the building. Sometimes I'm not sure that the walls will hold up the cracked blackboards. The leaky roof is made of corrugated zinc, and two students are hard at work attempting to prevent the floor from turning into a lake while the rest study. Soon someone else takes over and it goes on like that for as long as the rain lasts. The rain comes often now, so it is kind of hard to learn or teach. But it is better than nothing.

When I arrived at the school, I got there on time, and nobody was there yet! Typical. But the school had been gaily decorated with some small paper Costa Rican flags and there were homemade streamers all over. There was a raggedy full-sized Costa Rican flag hanging from

a bamboo flag pole. I had brought another flag with me and someone, when they got there, went into the woods and cut another pole.
Another guy had his fishing line there, and we used that to rig a way
to raise this new flag. Finally, an hour and a half later, we began the
ceremony with the singing of the Costa Rican national anthem and
the raising of the flag. The children were lined up in military forma-
tion in front of the flag while the adults and guests sat in chairs in a
semi-circle in the back. It was cloudy, and I kept eyeing an especially
dark cloud heading for us. The ceremony continued with a number of
songs, including one for Independence Day and one or two for other
things. Then the teacher gave a short history of the independence
from Spain in 1821. Essentially, Costa Rica didn't have to do much
to get it, because Spain, as a result of declining power and influence
in the world, ceded what is now Honduras, Nicaragua, Costa Rica,
Guatemala, Mexico, and El Salvador without a fight. Then it was time
for me to speak. I talked about the importance of liberty and justice in
this world and that their country was very important because they are
free. I said, "Coming from a country where liberty and justice is valued,
I appreciate being here and being asked to speak." I said I hoped that
they would always continue their pattern of liberty and would be forever free. The ceremony ended and we were treated to watching folk-
loric dances by the school children and drinking lemonade (or something similar). The dancers were very colorfully dressed, especially the
women. They had on skirts with wide horizontal stripes in red, green,
and blue with white blouses, while the boys wore colorful bandanas
around their necks and sombreros. It was a most enjoyable time and I
appreciated being there in the middle of nowhere celebrating liberty
with a bunch of campesinos. A good feeling!

A couple hours later, the teacher and I were sitting around talking.
He said to me that this was a special day for him besides being
Independence Day. I asked why. And he told me that his first child
had died two years ago on this day. I waited for him to continue, and

with tears in his eyes, he told me this story. Two years ago he had been working in a place called Rio Oro, which is about seven hours from here by horse. It is accessible only two or three months of the year by a wheeled vehicle other than a tractor. It has a landing strip but no regular service. His wife was pregnant with their first child, and they were very excited about it. He had arranged for a plane to come in the day after Independence Day to take his wife to San José so she could have the baby there. The doctor had visited Rio Oro a week before and had told them there were no problems. On Independence Day, at about 2:00 a.m. his wife began to have severe labor pains. It was a month early. An hour later a huge storm hit, knocking out the radio and turning the grass strip into a quagmire. They both were very scared because they knew nothing about birthing procedures, nor could they get out. There was an old woman in the village who was a kind of midwife, and that was all. They made such provisions as they could and waited. At about ten in the morning, the pains increased and it became obvious that she would have the baby. There were no cars in town, no radio, and no doctor. Only he and the midwife. They were already scared and then saw the baby coming out feet first! The baby came out okay and was kicking, but its head got stuck in the vagina and they couldn't get it free. Blood was flowing freely from his wife, and he was afraid he would lose them both. No matter what they tried, the baby wouldn't come out. The mother passed out and the baby slowly stopped kicking. Finally the baby popped free, but it was too late. It had suffocated. His wife didn't regain consciousness for hours, and when she did, she asked for the child. My friend could say nothing, but she read his face. She got up from the bed and went to where he had laid the baby and she held it, and he held her, and they cried and cried and cried. Finally, he took the baby to the mountain and buried the child. But instead of making him bitter, it made him want to work harder and help his people more. Two weeks ago, his wife had a baby girl in San José and on this Independence Day he was both happy and sad. I was moved at this man's story and his dedication to his job. He willingly goes out to the most God-forsaken corners of the country and tries to help. He is not bitter but is now renewed in spirit to prevent this from happening to others. It shows the fragility of life, the importance of giving it your best shot while here, and the comforting power of a simple faith in God. I am honored to know a man as dedicated as he is.

Love,
David

Chapter Twenty-Nine

THE CIA DELUSION

SEPTEMBER 22, 1982

Dear Dad,

I have spent today touring the gold mining areas with some members of Costa Rica's congress. They are investigating the rumors and destruction that are occurring here. They want to know where all the gold is going—and that's a good question! It seems that the amount of gold the companies are reporting would barely pay for about 80% or so of its operation. People (who work for the company) have told me that some of the gold goes to Panama, where they can receive dollars for it. I, too, wonder what is happening because there are as many stories as there are people mining. Hopefully, something will come of this. I feel like I have to be careful about what I say around here because tension is building between the town and the mines.

I want to continue along the lines of my last letter with some of the things that happened to me after my Independence Day speech. There were two teachers whom I work with in the audience, and the next day they were visiting Puerto Jimenez. They came by my house at separate times, and I spent two hours talking with each of them. They both gave me compliments on my speech and asked me questions before finally coming to the point, which I knew they were leading up to. The first asked me if black people and Latin Americans in the US have the freedom I was talking about. The second teacher asked me how I could talk about liberty or say that the US supports liberty when we have an agency like the CIA? Both questions are very hard to answer, and I'll take them one at a time.

The first teacher had heard a number of things both true and untrue about American race relations. He enumerated things he'd heard about the lynchings and economic exploitation of black people and wanted to know how he would be accepted as a brown-skinned Latin back in the States. I had to admit that there had been numerous lynchings of black people in the US, and there still is a high degree of exploitation of black people, economically speaking, in many parts of the country. I did point out that most of the lynchings have stopped and that black people can now vote in most places. He was surprised that there was a time only seventeen years ago when they couldn't vote due to the toll taxes and educational requirements in many areas. I then had to tell him that in the States he would now find prejudice and racism against Latins. He said, "I know that. I've heard from other Latins who have been there." A friend of his had been bullied in Texas a couple of years ago and another friend had been punched out by a group of toughs in Florida. I guess in working in a university environment before I joined Peace Corps had made me forget about the issue of race, or maybe it was just not at the forefront of my thoughts—where it should always be. But this conversation and others, along with a book I have read, entitled *Ten Keys to Latin America*, brought home the importance of race in the perceptions of many of the "persons of color" in the world. Although whites are in the minority worldwide by a wide margin, a person of color coming to our shores always wonders how we will receive him or her. It is a scary feeling to be judged by the color of your skin, and the idea that many people have in other countries does not help our image when we talk about freedom and justice for all. It makes us look like hypocrites.

The other teacher's question (about the CIA) was even more painful as I had just had a long talk with another teacher about whether or not I was a CIA agent. And as you will recall, I received many questions when I left Los Chiles and while I was there, asking me whether or not I was CIA. It is a topic that makes me shudder involuntarily to think that I might be associated with this odious and noxious organization. If anyone wants or needs more evidence of the dirty tricks we have played, read any part of the Congressional Record on the Church Committee hearings, or the book *Inside the Company: CIA Diary* by Philip Agee, or *The CIA and the Cult of Intelligence* by Victor Marchetti and John Marks. Read about the CIA in Vietnam in *The Best and the Brightest* by David Halberstam, or Michael Maclear's *The Ten Thousand Day War*. You will find involvement of the US in some of the most brutal, inhuman, scurrilous schemes that can be imagined. We have murdered and tortured people, funded clandestine wars, faked and planted incriminating documents on innocent people whom we didn't want to come to power in a particular nation, funded and encouraged riots, and otherwise lied and cheated to preserve "American interests." Those interests were usually to maintain the status quo, which means maintain the power of the wealthy minority, often associated with American business interests or in the name of "anticommunism," while leaving the majority of the people in extreme penury. This is why I shudder when I am associated with the CIA.

The same teacher wanted to know if the seeds I had were treated in any way to cause sterility in the people who ate the vegetables grown from them. He wanted to know how many reports I did a month to forward to Washington and the CIA. He wanted to know if the CIA is active in the ongoing attempt to isolate Nicaragua, considering the increasing amount of bellicose actions and statements emanating from Honduras, Costa Rica, and Washington. He wanted to know if the projects I am trying to push through AID (the Association for International Development) help my standing with the CIA. He felt that each project request I was able to have the people make would be indicative of me gaining the trust of the people, which would mean that I could turn to my real mission—importing arms. But the topper of all was this: I had read a letter that this teacher had written to his government in which he complained about an eminent purchase of arms from the US. He felt that Costa Rica didn't need arms because they wanted to live in peace. I asked him for a copy of the letter which I was going to translate and send to a senator I worked for from Delaware. He didn't want to give me the letter because he was afraid that the CIA would try *to kill him*! I swear that this is true. I asked him to repeat it. He did. I sat in stunned silence. How could anyone think that I could be involved with a project like that? Or to sterilize people? Or to import arms? I wanted to cry! I vehemently denied everything and swore to him that I would never do any of that. While in the garden with the kids, I made a point of eating some mustard leaves and Chinese cabbage leaves. After returning home, I thought about this again and I could see how the teacher could think that, based on the *facts* of what the US *has done* in many Third World countries. When the facts are combined with the many rumors flying around, the result is a dangerous and insidious poison that gradually permeates the fabric of our relationships with developing countries. While this may appear ludicrous, I find that most educated people I meet might even wonder if I'm with the CIA, or did wonder it at some point. I am distressed that people have to wonder about our motives in helping people, but on the basis of the facts, I can see why they do. You can see why the teacher that heard me talk on Independence Day also wondered why I could talk about liberty and justice for all and our tradition of liberty in the States. He felt that we say it when it's convenient. I agree with him. We need to return the CIA to the purpose of its charter of just collecting intelligence and try not to involve ourselves in reprehensible conduct in the internal affairs of sovereign nations.

Love,

David

September 27, 1982

Dear Dad,

Had an interesting week last week! Six legislators from Costa Rica arrived in Puerto Jimenez the other day to investigate the rumors about the gold mines here. Their trip was sponsored by a group of concerned citizens that I am working with called the Puerto Jimenez Association for Development. This is a group that I helped organize to do various projects around the community that need to be done—like improve the roads, build bridges, improve the water system, build a dock, and other needed measures. They are also trying to do something about the fact that the gold mined here leaves with Puerto Jimenez not receiving any money or benefit from it in the form of taxes or anything else. So, the legislators came from San José to hold hearings on this subject, and we took them on a tour of the gold mines so they could see for themselves what is happening and could pass legislation enabling us to get a little money for Jimenez. Anyway, the legislators listened to everything anybody had to say on the subject and saw everything they wanted and that anybody wanted them to see. I felt good about my work after they'd left. It is quite a process to pull something like this off. This visit has shown the people that I work with that it is possible to do something constructive. Their expectations are high that the legislators will do something, but I hope that the association learned that they don't have to be passive recipients of what life gives them. I also hope they don't bite off more than they can chew as they gradually find and understand power. But for the moment, I think we had an educational experience.

To let you know more about what I am doing—specifically, now that I can see better, I have gardens that have produced food for the students in each of the schools. In the process of preparing the gardens and planting them, each kid has learned something about agriculture. I have lectured at least five times in each school about nutrition and agriculture. I have about five 4-H clubs formed and working. I have between fifty and sixty home gardens for sure—maybe more. I am helping communities in various ways. One is trying to build a bridge, two are trying to build a road connecting them with the outside world, and the Association for Development is working with the gold question and the dock. We are also going to establish an agricultural committee in the region to promote planting. And I'm doing a garden for the Catholic Church in town to use to distribute food to the poor people. In addition, I have my own garden which I experiment in and grow food for the nutrition center lunch program. So I keep pretty busy when it's not raining. It's going to be so hard to leave here!

Love,
David

OCTOBER 7, 1982

Well, I've just got back from a week of meetings and the like in San José and San Isidro del General. After the meetings, I had eight tons of errands to run: There were several rolls of barbed and chicken wire that finally arrived at the Ministry of Education. I needed to get parts for my motorcycle. I had to do soil tests for some schools and find out about a class on pigs I am arranging with a veterinarian—and many other things. But the most important thing is that, on November 10, Miguel Angel Robiero will receive his hearing aid. He and his mother are coming in from Los Chiles on the ninth and returning on the eleventh, after getting the hearing aid and visiting the school. The hearing aid seems to be a good device, as it is powered by batteries readily available in Los Chiles and will be specially fitted to his ear. After that, I will go to Cuidad Quesada to make arrangements for his stay there for the school next year. According to the doctor, we got him on time!

While in San José, I went to see a movie called *Missing*.[1] I found it to be very powerful in many respects and would highly recommend it. I went to it twice in two days so I could get it all into my head. It is the story of an idealistic young reporter who disappears during the coup d'état in Chile in 1973. In the process of detailing the reasons for the young man's disappearance, the involvement and hypocrisy of the US position in Chile becomes apparent. It chronicles the reasons for the growing perceptions and cynicism that Third World countries have towards the States. When and if you see the movie, please think of the rhetoric that the US puts out. We all talk about freedom and human rights and the importance of democracy. Please remember that we say these things a lot. And then look at our involvement in the affairs of another country in which we helped to kill thousands of people (as portrayed graphically in the movie) and you will see why there is a strong difference between what we say and what we do. I think every word of this movie is true. Go and see it.

Love,
David

OCTOBER 14, 1982

Dear Dad,

I've gotten real busy lately. The rains have halted enough so that I've been able to leave and be able to cross the rivers, although the crossings are a little hairy. There are a couple of rivers I have to cross

---

[1] Film: *Missing*, released February 12, 1982. Produced by Edward Lewis. Directed and screenplay written by Costa-Gavras, based on the book, *Missing*, by Thomas Hauser, starring Jack Lemmon and Sissy Spacek.

that are now up to the seat of my motorcycle—with a strong current in some places. The motorcycle will keep going for about five or six seconds before the water drowns the spark plug out—and that's about the time it takes for me to cross the deep part. So, the only thing to do is to hit that spot going as fast as you can in first gear—which is pretty fast. It causes a big splash and is great fun if you don't hit a rock. I make it across about three quarters of the time, and the rest of the time I stop and have to push the moto out of the river. It is very important to stay upright because the motorcycle usually starts right up once out of the river. However, if you fall, that means you have to dry the motorcycle out for about an hour. I feel like Evel Knievel as I wind up the motorcycle, pop the clutch, and splash into the river—usually emerging on the other side—but sometimes stopping, and always wet. A friend who saw me do this says it looks like a giant water bug, especially when I put my legs out and try to propel myself when I think I might stop. It's fun!

Ten days from now, the development association that I am working with and I are holding a peninsula-wide meeting to form an alliance to promote agriculture in the region. I was quite flattered that they asked me to moderate the meeting. I am nervous about it because the meeting is being called by the association as the next step toward combatting the gold fever in the region. I don't know exactly if I'm to moderate the meeting because they know I'm neutral between the various political and personality clashes in the town—or because I'm perceived as fair—or because if the thing fails, they can blame it on the gringo. Anyhow, you can imagine what one feels like before a big meeting or session where you have to be on your toes to handle anything that might come up and keep the meeting on track in front of a couple of hundred people—and then have some guy get up, start talking at 85 mph and leave me standing there not understanding, looking like a dope. But if this thing comes off well, it could do some long-lasting things for the region. I also have to learn the Costa Rican law on cooperatives and associations so I can answer points of order and other questions. So I will be preparing myself this week for this meeting. After this, I'll bow out, and Costa Ricans will run all the succeeding meetings.

Love,
David

Chapter Thirty

PONDERING THE
LAST TWO YEARS

NOVEMBER 10, 1982

Dear Dad,

I'll be home for in time for Christmas! My work will be done by December 15. On December 12, I'm going to Nicaragua, then returning to Costa Rica via Los Chiles to go to the wedding of Georgina (daughter of my laundress) on the eighteenth, returning to San José on the twenty-first, and leaving for the States on the twenty-third.

Love,
David

NOVEMBER 17, 1982

Dear Dad,

Well, today I got hit by another truck. But this time there was no real damage to the motorcycle, just to me. Yes, ladies and gentlemen, I am scraped up again. As I was preparing to turn into my office, a truck with no brakes that was going too fast came up beside me and somehow caught me across my back just before I turned. Whatever hit me scraped me pretty good, but I'm going to be okay. Cheated death again.

I have been trying to put my thoughts together to evaluate my last two years and answer the question: what did I accomplish here? Did I have any long-lasting effect that could be construed as positive? In most of my thoughts I think that the results are mixed. I am saddened and angered that I was taken out of Los Chiles because I think I would have been happier and would have accomplished more—especially when the decision to take me out turned out to be so political. I still have a great deal of resentment toward that decision. I had a number of things started there, but I'm not sure now about their final status. The nursery for growing coco plants for chocolate has had some problems since I left. The daycare center I was working on has not been built, and now there are not as many gardens as there were when I was there. But there are more gardens than were there before I came, and some people have gotten coco trees, and some people have learned how to raise funds for the daycare center. I understand from other volunteers and embassy officials who have had contact with people from Los Chiles, that there are many there who talk about me favorably. Maybe people were quite impressed with my brother and father when they were there. There were some kids in the schools who ate better than they would have and learned about agriculture. But I was unable to complete the things I started in Los Chiles, so it is a mixed evaluation.

Here in Puerto Jimenez, it was a constant struggle to get things moving in the community, but I was more successful with the school gardens. It was hard to get 4-H clubs going, but the ones that are going will stay going. Eventually, a development association was formed here along with another association to promote agriculture. Through these and other activities we were able to influence the Ministry of Agriculture to approve the construction of an extension agency in Puerto Jimenez. I think these associations will have a long-lasting affect if they don't get discouraged. So once again, the result is mixed because some things were done but some things weren't completed. I'll also never really know what my effect was on the people here in Jimenez. In Los Chiles I was the only gringo in town and I know that people are still talking about me up there. But here, I had too much to compete with to have a very strong impression.

As for me, I'll return to the States with a wealth of new experiences that have affected me immeasurably. I am still the same man, but at the same time, I am totally different. Being in jail put a scar on me that I'll never get over. Seeing the innumerable poor people I had to deal with has a special niche in my memory. A lady I met from El Salvador when I was in the Honduras who had to watch her husband tortured is a particularly searing memory. The amount of mud I've fallen in, the number of times I've been soaked to the skin, the number of seeds I've put in the ground, the number of problems with my motorcycle, and the good feelings I have received from the majority of the people—seem uncountable. The idyllic beaches I have lunched on, the teeming vibrant jungles I have enjoyed, the mountain views that have taken my breath away are also going to be hard to forget. I, like most Peace Corps volunteers, am leaving here with more than I came with. The friends I've made, the Ticos and the other PCVs, are good friendships—and it's painful to approach the time of saying goodbye.

However much I did or did not accomplish, I am inspired by the words that comforted a young Dr. Tom Dooley when he was forced to leave the hospitals he founded in Laos because of cancer. The words, written by Kahlil Gibran, were spoken to Dr. Dooley by Albert Schweitzer when Dooley visited the great missionary doctor in French Equatorial Africa. Dr. Schweitzer said, "The significance of a man, Tom, is not in what he attains but rather what he longs to attain." I longed to attain many dreams here but only attained some of them. But I have many years ahead of me and I will continue longing to attain things.

Love to all,
David

Author's Note

*Before I left the Peace Corps, I had become interested in another vol-
unteer named Barbara Kay Gustafson who was in a program for the
prevention of blindness and deafness, and to gather data for the World
Health Organization. Only, she had a boyfriend who knew I was interested in her—and the only one to not realize this in all of Peace Corps
was Barbara herself. I managed to make sure I was seated within con-
versational distance of her when a group of PCVs went out to dinner or
dancing, when we were in town. We happened to be on the green bean
crew together, preparing green beans for the annual Thanksgiving Day
dinner at the US Ambassador's residence in San José. After a group of
us finished the task of preparing the beans, we somehow found several
bottles of wine, which we demolished and were quite loopy when they
came to pick us up to go from the green bean preparation station to the
place where the beans would be cooked. On the way there, I found out
that Barbara has the loudest wolf whistle I have ever heard as she and
other female PCVs turned the tables on the men of Costa Rica by returning all types of unwanted catcalls and whistles that they had to endure
during their tenure in Costa Rica. I fell in love with her at that very
moment—a smart, somewhat rowdy woman.*

| IV |

BEYOND COSTA RICA: DREAMS OF STATESMEN

Search and see if there is not some place
where you may invest your humanity
—Albert Schweitzer

Chapter Thirty-One

BECOMING A GLOBAL CITIZEN

*O*n *May* 7, 1983, just before I began my new position of Associate Dean of Students at Colorado College, Barb and I were married. One of the most enjoyable things we ever did together during our years in Colorado was to travel to the Philippines and escort four boys under the age of three and a young girl of about fourteen to the US to be adopted by their new families. As we left Manila without incident, bound for San Francisco via Tokyo, we were ready for any eventuality—with enough diapers and whatnot to get us to Denver where their new families were waiting. But as it happened, the only airport open on the whole West Coast was San Francisco, and all the flights coming across the Pacific were being routed there. This meant that we circled the San Francisco airport for at least an hour before we could land. Then it took another hour to find a gate open so we could disembark, another hour to get our luggage, another hour to get through customs and another hour to recheck our baggage and sprint off to where our connecting flight to Denver was just leaving. But we missed it. I had one kid on my back, one in my arms—and my wife had the other kid on her back. I reeked of urine because I had taken one little boy to the bathroom, got him all lined up to urinate—and just then the plane hit an air pocket and his aim was thrown off. So there was urine on me, the kid, and everything except the toilet. and when we got to our gate for the Denver flight, we saw the plane backing away.

Barb and I started yelling at each other, each blaming the other for being slow and missing the plane. The kids were looking up at us like we were the escorts from hell, and then we started laughing. We had been up for close to twenty-four hours, and by then were famished. There was enough money left to buy chicken sandwiches and some French fries, but we did not know that the boys had not been taught how to eat and were unfamiliar with chicken. So they would grab some of the food and it would land on the floor and anywhere but in their mouths. Finally, we finished and went to our gate and got on the plane to Denver. The stewardesses and most of the passengers found out that we were escorting kids to their new families, so an entire planeload of people tried to be helpful, and it became an adoption flight. When we landed we were the last to get off and found the passengers and crew (including the pilots) waiting for us. And as we put each child into the arms of each new family, there wasn't a dry eye in the house. When I put the kid I was carrying into the arms of his new mother, I would have left right then for the Philippines and done it all over again. It was a wonderful feeling to be a stork, especially right around Christmastime, and this trip was one of the highlights of my life.

Speaking of adoption, one of the main reasons I am so high on it is that our two children, Taylor and Kelsey, were born in the Philippines and came to us when they were twelve and thirteen months old through Barbara's efforts in international adoption. Although not biological siblings, they quickly learned to squabble like any other siblings and have brought boundless joy to our lives.

As a boy, I had occasionally heard my father speak out against homosexuality from the pulpit. Like many others at that time, he considered homosexuality an abomination. However, I was confused. Despite my deep respect for Dad, I did not understand why seemingly decent people would want to punish someone who was perceived as effeminate—or as we said in those days, queer—or even just *different* than we were?

Later on, when (as a student at OSU) I was working as a lifeguard, I had my first experience of being hit on by a guy. My reaction was toxic. I told him to shove off or I would beat the crap out of him. Eventually, I was compelled to ask myself why I had such a violent reaction toward someone whose orientation was simply different than mine? The answer to this question became another journey for me. Much later on, as Associate Dean of Students at Colorado College I was in charge of mentoring student organizations and helping them plan programs. One of the most rewarding challenges I undertook was as volunteer advisor for the Gay Student Union. Through that work I became convinced that homosexuality was a "new normal" and indeed should be celebrated by country and culture when an LGBT individual has the courage to accept who they are and speak out with pride. At that point I knew that, along with the N-word, which I hate, I also hated the F-word (faggot).

I also often worked with the Air Force Academy professors on issues related to peace. We cosponsored a talk by former President Ford, and I met President Carter at a speech at the academy. I have been deeply impressed with Carter, both as a president and during his post-presidency. Many people do not realize that he got more bills/ laws through congress than the next three presidents combined. He has been a very effective leader and was the only recent president to not be involved in a war.

Carter was, of course, the one who suffered the most from the CIA-led coup that ousted a freely elected prime minister named Mossadegh from Iran. This proceeded to wreck democracy in Iran for decades by installing the corrupt government of the Shah so that England could benefit from controlling Iranian oil. Teddy Roosevelt's grandson, Kermit Alexander, coordinated the activities in Iran that led to the coup, providing money to create large mobs that took over the streets. This was accomplished with the compliance and assistance of the Dulles brothers, who held the positions of Secretary of State and Director of the CIA and (coincidentally!) were also board members of the United Fruit Company. Talk about a major conflict of interest. My friend, the 2003 Nobel Peace Prize Laureate, Shirin Ebadi is the first Muslim woman to ever win the Nobel Peace Prize and the first female Islamic judge in a Muslim country. She currently lives in exile in London, and I think she is constantly under the threat of death from her enemies. Her story is a prime example of how the loss of female leadership can be traced back to the 1953 that undercut all aspects of democracy in Iran. She is active and working hard on gender issues not only in the Islamic world, but on a worldwide basis as well—a very courageous woman. Yet the loss of her judicial position can also be traced back to the coup that started the ball rolling in undermining democracy that was sprouting in the developing world and Carter, as a result, was dealt a devastatingly bad hand in Iran.

While at Colorado College I also had the opportunity to meet doña Hortensia Bussi de Allende, whose husband Salvador was president of Chile from 1970 until he was ousted with the help of our CIA in 1973. He was murdered in the course of the coup d'état by someone in the Chilean military, but no one is exactly sure who did it. Once again, our CIA was instrumental in overthrowing a freely elected government because it enacted policies that were against the interests of our government, especially those of Secretary of State Kissinger. Each time we have done this ourselves or supported proxies to do our dirty work, we have been viewed by the rest of the world as hypocrites. The coup d'état in Chile was a clear case of the chickens coming home to roost, and I am not sure that peace will ever come to that region of the world again.

Yet if we had merely applied the values expressed in our Declaration of Independence outside of our borders in case after case, on problem after problem—our reputation would have been salvaged.

Chapter Thirty-Two

UNITED IN SERVICE AND
DEDICATED TO PEACE

I was proud to have been Executive Director of the Rotary International Peace Forum in 1987 when RI president, Charles Keller, created the slogan: *Rotarians: United in Service and Dedicated to Peace*, which remains to this day a distinguished hallmark of Keller's time in office.

My position required me to travel internationally, implementing conferences dedicated to world peace sponsored by Rotary International. Under my leadership, we established a global series of peace forums in countries troubled with humanitarian issues and regions affected by the aftermath of war. Anecdotally, these conferences seemed effective and were motivational for the participants—at least for a time.

Our first forum was in Costa Rica just after President Oscar Arias (who, by the way, is a Rotarian) won the Nobel Peace Prize in 1987. Arias' dream was to establish a museum in San José that celebrates institutions, individuals, and peace treaties that have led to a resolution of conflict and could lay the groundwork for achieving a harmonious relationship between the many sides of a conflict or war. Can we not have at least one museum that emphasizes efforts toward peace rather than war? Why not celebrate endeavors such as: the decision by

South Africa to eliminate their nuclear weapons program; Woodrow Wilson's dream of a League of Nations which, despite its failures, is the foundation of the current United Nations; and the Camp David Accords negotiated by President Carter to end the conflict between Egypt and Israel—a treaty that is still holding now, some forty years later, and a stellar example of what can happen through negotiation. Of course, there is also Dr. Arias' negotiated peace treaty, Esquipulas, which brought about peace in Central America.

In 1988 we decided to hold a forum in the Ivory Coast, despite the fact that the president of the country, Félix Houphouët-Boigny was a brutal dictator. This was because the Ivory Coast would admit Rotarians from South Africa, and almost no other country in Africa would do so at the time. The result of taking this risk was that African and European Rotarians were able to mingle with South African Rotarians to discuss the future of Africa in general, and South Africa in particular. All sides knew apartheid was doomed, so it was mainly a matter of how violent the transition would become. It is my understanding that Rotarians from all over South Africa who went to the peace forum played a small, but significant, role in ending apartheid. It was a behind-the-scenes instance of Rotarians working in the interest of peace—for which we could and should do more.

While in Côte d'Ivoire to run a peace forum with the Rotary Foundation, I spent a day helping give hundreds of people, especially children, freedom from the fear of that crippling disease, polio, by getting them vaccinated. For me, this was the thrill of a lifetime. This personal experience also made me proud to be a Rotarian because, among other things, Rotary began the Polio Plus program, which has protected literally millions of people around the world with polio vaccine, way before Bill Gates entered into this fight. (I would note that I had to shave my beard in order to gain the permission of the president of Côte d'Ivoire to hold the forum there because he thought that anyone with a beard was a communist! The only other time I shaved my beard since high school was for a bribe of fifty dollars from my grandmother, who wanted a picture of me without the beard. (I needed beer money.)

In a conference in Hiroshima, the evils of nuclear weapons were discussed, and the people and the Rotarians of Japan sent a message to the world saying that they did not blame anyone for the atomic attack on Hiroshima and Nagasaki but felt strongly that an atomic attack should never happen again. It may be time for another peace forum laying out a plan or plans for combating the use of atomic bombs in any situation. I remain haunted by the carbon shadow cast by the human who was standing in line outside the Hiroshima mayor's office at the time of the atomic explosion who was a living human one second and in the next millisecond was vaporized. The only thing left was an amorphous black stain on the steps of the town hall. This man or woman didn't literally know what hit him or her. I stood in front of this carbon shadow, mesmerized, as I contemplated what humankind could do to itself.

In Melbourne we discussed the needs of aboriginal peoples. And for a time after our peace forum occurred, Rotary clubs in Australia were among world leaders in resolving differences between aboriginal peoples and the white majority. We also discussed the problems between New Zealand, the United States, and Australia when New Zealand would not let US warships into their harbors if they contained nuclear weapons—and the US would not reveal which of our warships and/or submarines were carrying nuclear weapons. We discussed the *Law of the Sea Treaty* and how to divide vast oceanic resources, as well. On the floor of some of the deepest areas of the ocean in international waters there are nodules of pure manganese. The question became, who do these nodules belong to—to the people of the world, or to the company or governments that have the technical ability to mine them? This is controversial even today, although there is a mechanism to decide called the International Seabed Authority. I like to think that we started the conversation.

In Nice, France we discussed the problems of the Maghreb region and the middle east and failed to come to any helpful conclusions, although some Palestinians and Israelis did attend and speak civilly to each other. I guess that was a major accomplishment!

Chapter Thirty-Three

TEENS TAKE ON CONFLICT

*W**hen international travel became** problematic for a father with a young family, for the next eleven years (beginning in 1989) I served as Executive Director of the Louis August Jonas Foundation. The Jonas foundation ran a program called Camp Rising Sun, near Rhinebeck, New York, which brought bright teenagers together from all over the world for eight weeks of leadership training and learning to resolve conflicts without violence. During this time, Barbara worked as a nurse at the Astor Home for Children, located in the Rhinebeck area. It was and still is a residential treatment facility for children with histories of psychiatric and emotional problems. What Barb was especially concerned about was what could happen to these children when they aged out of the system—in other words, when they are too old to remain in a wonderful facility like the Astor Home for Children and consequently might end up on the street. What would happen to them and, indeed, what would happen to our society is that a ticking time bomb has been released with no one there to help. In my opinion, Barbara made a huge difference in the lives of many children who suffered prior to receiving appropriate mental health treatment.

Indeed, at one point when I was over in the Philippines recruiting teenagers for Camp Rising Sun, I was appalled at the terrible opportunities to exploit children that seemed to abound on every street corner. Once, because I probably looked like a typical American out for a good time, a cab driver took one look at me and asked if I wanted a virgin that night. A store I went into that was like a Seven-Eleven in a park in downtown Manila literally had young girls stored in cupboards ready to be used by sick pedophiles for sexual purposes. I wonder what will happen to many of these young girls. I also wonder about the houses of prostitution that have popped up around our military bases. It shames me and should shame all of us that some of our military bases may support the "careers" of child prostitutes.

Yet while in the Philippines I also had time to take a speedboat out to visit Corregidor, where General MacArthur escaped the advancing Japanese army in World War II. And I visited the Bataan peninsula where surrender to the Japanese resulted in the infamous Bataan death march in which hundreds of American soldiers died while marching to the prison camp where they were to be incarcerated for the duration of the war. My Dad had flown over these islands on bombing runs, and it made me feel close to him because, in a sense, we were at the same place—me on the ground quite aware of its history—and my Dad in the air some fifty years before. I suddenly felt tremendously impressed by the bravery of all the men and women who have fought for our freedom during WW II and beyond.

As director of Camp Rising Sun, I made sure we accepted kids from countries with histories of conflict, such as: Greeks and Turks; Chinese, Japanese, and South Koreans; Israelis, Palestinians, and Egyptians; Ecuadorians and Peruvians; Catholics and Protestants from Northern Ireland; and as many different cultures and races that we could get from around the US. This included Mormons from Utah and Navajos from Arizona—and young people from Mississippi, Georgia, Texas, Minnesota, California, and the five boroughs of New York City. We had many kids from at least twenty European countries which not that long ago had suffered two world wars. We had separate facilities and camp sites for boys and for girls. (This was especially necessary because some countries would not send their girls to a coed camp.)

The students essentially ran the camp program using the term *sachem*, the Native American word for wise leader. The sachems, leading teams of six to eight campers for a week at a time, were in charge of cleaning up the kitchen, scrubbing the willy (bathroom), and many other tasks—so everyone got to be a sachem for one week. On their teams they could find a kid from Japan and another from Barbados—so you can imagine the cultural divide between a student with a relaxed Caribbean attitude towards getting the work done and a German or Japanese camper with a compulsion to complete the job in a precise and timely fashion. (As a result, there were many such teachable moments throughout our program.) We had intellectual discussion groups in the morning and service projects in the afternoon. We also put on a play in both camps to which the other camp and the general public were invited. It was the highlight of the summer.

There have been many such camp programs that tried to bridge the gaps between countries and cultures with histories of conflict. Ours was unique because we did not single out one culture or political entity in conflict with one other; rather, we had several cultures and/or countries with histories of conflict with each other in our program. At the time there were also several programs that tried to encourage peace between the Israelis and the Palestinians. But too often the Palestinians felt as if gaining peace meant accepting the status of second-class citizens, in other words, peace would be gained if the Palestinians did not make waves, but accepted peace on Israel's terms. Our program did not do that; all representatives from countries with histories of conflict were treated equally in terms of the history of conflict in their homeland. In every country where I tried to recruit students for Camp Rising Sun, or where I tried to organize a peace conference, I needed to know the background of each side of a dispute—and there normally were multiple sides. For example, if you want to do anything in Latin America, you need to know the history of Spain and Portugal to understand that Spain was not a democracy until the middle of the twentieth century, and that they had brought a royalist system of government along with a mercantilist economic system to Latin America, instead of anything like a capitalist economic system rooted in democracy.

One of the stories I like to tell had to do with our drama production and the fact that we had an observant Jew in our girls' camp, which meant that she could not ride in a vehicle on the sabbath to go see the production at the boys' camp, which was located seven or eight miles away. It looked like the play would go on without her, but the girl campers would have none of it. And it was the girl from Palestine, who had developed a strong friendship with our Israeli camper, who badgered me with her idea. That was to have all sixty girl campers walk together to the boys' camp to watch the play that night. I relented, and it turned out to be a very special occasion, with everyone feeling proud that this march of solidarity had engendered such good feelings. I drove up alongside them and noticed that the Palestinian girl was holding hands with the Israeli camper, and they were skipping down this bucolic country lane singing "We Shall Overcome" at the top of their lungs! I was extremely proud of this and told this story many times while running this program.

However, when I visited Palestine three or four years later, I had a chance to talk with the Palestinian girl who had skipped down that country lane. By then, she practically hated all Israelis because some of her family members and friends had been incarcerated or shot, and at least one had been killed. She felt that we were in too much of a bubble at the camp and that we needed to do a better job of supporting campers after they returned home. It was almost worse to have raised expectations for a peaceful world and then have the hopes and prayers for a more peaceable future dashed. A few years later, while running the Albert Schweitzer Institute I made another trip to Israel and Palestine with Sean Duffy and Erin Sobeda to see if there was any way to have some sort of conference that would help take even a few small steps towards peace. Our friend Anat Biletzki set up several meetings with political and educational leaders of Israel, and we spent several days discussing the prospects for peace in the Middle East. One individual who had held a high-ranking position in a previous Israeli government took me by surprise when I asked him if he was optimistic about the prospects for peace in the Middle East, given the fact that he criticized every effort for peace that anyone even mentioned in passing. He said he was optimistic, and I said, how could that be? He replied that he did not want to die a pessimist. That is not much of a basis for achieving peace, and I fear that this will not change.

In Haifa on a trip to recruit students to attend Camp Rising Sun, I was interviewing candidates from a local high school. When I was finished, the guidance counselor asked me where I was going next. I said, "Ramallah." She said, "Where's that?" I said, "In Palestine." And she said, "Where's that?" She smiled, or rather kind of smirked, and I finally realized that she was telling me in her own way that, to her, Palestine didn't exist. No wonder I thought at the time that the chances for peace are virtually nil. I would note, as I write this, that not much is mentioned in the general media about Palestine nowadays.

The same thing happened to our campers from Northern Ireland. The male camper got his butt kicked when he tried to visit one of our female campers in her Catholic neighborhood.

I never got a chance to implement the change I saw as necessary—and that was to plan for support groups for anyone returning to their own cultures. This would have helped prevent feelings of isolation upon their return from an idealistic experience by which they had dealt with the reality of conflict in their homelands. There are many different ways to do this, but historical divisiveness and lack of trust make such work difficult.

When I first took this position, I had to go to Japan and repair some of political damage caused by something my predecessor had done. I had to meet with all the senior Japanese alumni and explain that I was new and sensitive to their concerns and make sure that I had their interests in mind in the future. I must have made a good impression because I was invited to a formal Japanese dinner the night before I left for home. I did not realize that each Japanese alumnus would make a toast and then knock back a shot of sake. After the third one toasted me (and there was beer in between) the room was starting to spin, and I knew that if I drank anything else I might embarrass myself. Thereafter I pretended to drink the shot, and there were at least seven more shots that I had to survive, plus the glasses of beer. I promised myself that I would make it through the dinner without regurgitating anything and I would eat anything they put in front of me. I understood later that I did just fine, but I did eat some flowers that were supposed to be decorative.

Chapter Thirty-Four

ROUND TWO:
GUILLAIN-BARRÉ SYNDROME

*A*fter the camp season a couple of years into my tenure at the Louis August Jonas Foundation, I noticed some tingling in my feet and that I was gradually having trouble climbing the stairs to my office. The tingling progressed up my legs, which were also starting to feel numb. So, I went to my local doctor and he sent me home telling me I might have multiple sclerosis but didn't think so because my onset was very rapid, much more so than MS or muscular dystrophy! I decided to call my brother Don, who was in medical school and doing a neurology rotation at the time. He consulted with a neurologist and then called me, saying, "You have Guillain-Barré syndrome and you need to get to a hospital that can treat Guillain-Barré by ambulance—with someone on board who can do a tracheostomy in case you stop breathing." My brother Don, as I have told him many times, saved my life with those words.

So began six months of hell. Guillain-Barré syndrome, also known as French polio, is very rare and means that I have had all the possible polios in this world. Sometimes there is a trigger event, such as the swine flu vaccine in 1976, but often there is none, and neurologists are left scratching their heads as to the cause.

I was taken by ambulance from my home in Hyde Park to Albany

Medical Center, which is about an hour and a half away, but was the closest place that had the medical equipment I needed. When the ambulance arrived, I refused to be put on a stretcher in front of my kids, Taylor and Kelsey. I struggled to walk normally out of the house, but as soon as I was out of sight I collapsed onto the gurney. Barbara stayed home with the kids because we had no ready-made baby sitter, and the kids still felt and knew that something was seriously wrong with their father. A big EMT rode shotgun with me, ready to cut my throat if necessary to keep me alive! I kept trying to breathe loudly so he wouldn't feel obligated to use the scalpel he held unholstered in his hand—ready to roll.

When I arrived at the hospital I was taken to the emergency room and immediately had to urinate and I was able to walk the few steps to the bathroom and relieve myself. Three hours later, I tried the same thing and I immediately collapsed of the floor of the Emergency Room. If I wasn't getting the attention that I thought I needed, there is nothing like a patient collapsing on the floor of the ER that gets the attention a patient may need! I was admitted to the hospital and immediately began treatment of what had been officially diagnosed as Guillain-Barré syndrome. My symptoms were classic GB—tingling and numbness that began in my feet and progressed towards the core of my body and then started in my hands and progressed slowly up my arms towards my chest. The doctors were afraid that the progression would eventually compromise my breathing and necessitate intubating me. I remember being pretty scared that I would die, but I tried to fight it with all my might—which wasn't much, given my physical limitations and the progression towards paralysis I was experiencing. The treatment I began was plasmapheresis, which involved sticking big needles in both arms and taking the blood from one arm to some sort of centrifuge. Then the centrifuge spun out the virus or whatever it was that was attacking my nerves and compromising the myelin sheath. The myelin sheath needed to grow back so the nerves could properly deliver the impulse to direct my various body parts to move on command.

I had about eight of these treatments and was making some good progress towards regaining my ability to function. Then I was transferred to Sunnyview Rehabilitation Hospital which had strong expertise in physical and occupational therapy. For the first few days I continued to improve, then I soon began to experience a gradual loss of strength and control. I couldn't even muster the strength to open a packet of ketchup. The doctor assigned to me kept telling me not to worry—she had never seen loss of control happen once improvement started. But it did. They had to pin my call button to my pillow because, now completely quadriplegic, all I could move to push the button was my head. Suddenly, I recognized that I was losing my ability to breathe and I tried to hit the call button but knocked it off my bed and onto the floor. My voice was just a whisper, so I couldn't get anyone's attention. Luckily, the respiration therapist came into check on me and leaned over to listen. I told her that she needed to move quickly to get me into an ambulance back to Albany Medical Center to see if more plasmapheresis would save my life. In remarkably a short amount of time we made a red-light run from Sunnyview back to Albany Medical Center. We arrived in record time, and the lady (Kate) who ran the plasmapheresis machine took one look at me and hustled to get the machine connected and functioning. Later on, she told me that she did not think I would make it through the night! But as soon as I was hooked up, I felt a little better, and soon my voice returned. After ten more treatments I was making enough progress that the doctors thought I could return home for Thanksgiving and continue with home-based physical therapy. But after a few days, the weakness began to return again, and this time I was really upset. Was I ever going to recover totally and be able to function in society again? I don't remember who took me to Albany Medical Center, but I arrived and was immediately taken to the floor I was on during previous visits. The nurses, who had taken excellent care of me, were almost as upset as I was to see me back.

This time, I had to be lifted out of my bed on a daily basis and placed in a folding chair where the nurses would then beat on my chest with cupped hands to loosen the mucus around my lungs to help prevent pneumonia. It usually took four nurses to transfer me from bed to chair in the morning and then again at night. They called me "the load." One night, they forgot to lock down the bed and it began to move while I was betwixt and between. If a patient is dropped on the floor, there is hell to pay, so all four nurses somehow dove onto the bed while hanging onto me. It worked, but I landed with my head somehow on the chest of a rather buxom nurse, with one of my hands on another nurse in a place on her body where it shouldn't be and with my other hand similarly situated on yet another nurse where it also shouldn't be. We had a great laugh about it and I told my nurses to take their time as we disentangled ourselves from each other, Later, I told Barbara that it was the first time I had ever been in bed with four nurses, but unfortunately I was quadriplegic and couldn't move anything except my head. I definitely needed to laugh because at that point we did not know how much of a life I would regain.

But this time the doctors had a new weapon to fight Guillain-Barré: Gamma Globulin. It worked! After four or five bags of gamma globulin, I made a remarkable recovery and was able to attend the annual Christmas Party of the Louis August Jonas Foundation. When I walked in unaided I was met with the best standing ovation I have ever received.

All this brings to mind the need for health insurance and the ability to get care anywhere in the world. Each bag of Gamma Globulin cost $3,000, and the total of my medical and hospital bills was around $160,000, which is way out of reach for most people. In terms of our own debate in the US, I fail to undersand the opposition to government financing of health care, which to some is *socialized* medicine, an apparently dirty word. I am not doctrinaire in my beliefs; rather, more pragmatic: If all children and adults get the care they need, I am for it and I don't care who provides the financing, whether it be the government, churches, synagogues, the private sector, or some combination thereof. I agree with Albert Schweitzer's ideas regarding the basis for funding treatment for everyone.

Chapter Thirty-Five

THE BEST MEDICINE:
LAUGHTER *AND CHILDREN*

My son and daughter, Taylor and Kelsey, were instrumental in my recovery from Guillain-Barré syndrome. They were respectively in second grade and kindergarten, and it was hard on them to see their father lying immobile in a hospital bed far from home and unable to hug them. Kelsey would insist on climbing up on the bed and hugging me even if I could not hug her back. Taylor would stand beside my bed with his hand on my shoulder for sometimes the whole visit as if he was transferring his young and healing energy into me. I felt a bond with both my children that is unbreakable to this day, and it helped me fight hard when there were down days in the healing process.

Kelsey was always jealous of her older brother because he was able to do things before she could, such as go to school, get a visit from the tooth fairy, and read books by herself. Barbara worked one night a week caring for an ailing older woman. Wouldn't you know it, but that was the night Kelsey lost her first tooth—and was this little girl excited about the impending visit from the tooth fairy. Dad, whose job it became to be the tooth fairy, was not as excited about his new role. Bedtime was 8:00 p.m., and Kelsey carefully made sure that the tooth was wrapped up in toilet paper and placed underneath her pillow. Dad (the tooth fairy) checked on Kelsey at 8:30, 9:15, 9:45 and 10:30—each time hoping Kelsey had fallen asleep. Each time, the tooth fairy encountered a young girl ever so wide awake and asking Dad if he had seen the tooth fairy. A very sleepy Dad finally found Kelsey apparently asleep at around 11:15, but as he lifted the pillow to take the tooth from underneath the pillow, she sat straight up in bed and asked if the tooth fairy had come yet. A very tired Dad went back downstairs but rallied at 11:45 and found his daughter finally asleep. As I took the tooth and left a quarter under her pillow, I found a hand-written note that said: "Dear Tooth Fairy, please draw a picture of yourself so I know what you look like, love Kelsey."

Now anyone who knows me knows I cannot draw to save my life—and all the women in the neighborhood were asleep—and I could not disappoint my daughter, so I made six or seven attempts to draw a tooth fairy, all of them pretty bad. (What the hell does a damn tooth fairy look like, anyway?) Finally, Dad had to go to bed, so he tucked the least bad example of a tooth fairy under her pillow and turned in at around one in the morning. Barbara got home at about seven or eight, and Kelsey woke up and was all excited to find the money and the picture I had drawn. She seemed happy about the drawing of the tooth fairy, but said the tooth fairy was pretty ugly.

My favorite story about Taylor is that he noticed when he was four or five that his skin color was different than mine. Out of the blue he asked me, "Dad when I grow up am I going to be white like you?" (I said to myself, *do not blow this*). Taylor, who has beautiful brown skin befitting his Filipino heritage (as does Kelsey), was just curious—but his father blathered on for ten minutes about the fact that he was born in the Philippines, which had been a crossroads for many different cultures—and in fact many white people sun bathed, trying to get skin that looked like his. All Taylor wanted was a yes or no answer, so I said no and finally shut up—and Taylor went off to play. Five minutes later, he was back and he asked, "Did you leave me out in the sun too long?"

I cracked up, but said no, and he seemed cool with his skin color after that. He would color himself in any color when he made drawings that included him, except white.

At this point in my life, I began to seriously question the Christian beliefs I was brought up with. Actually, it started much earlier—in the Peace Corps when I learned about all the children around the world who died needlessly on a daily basis and I thought that no one really cared about these children. But as I lay there on the hospital bed, unable to move, I really had serious doubts about the Bible verse "All things work together for good for those who love the Lord and are called according to His purpose." I became increasingly mad at God and questioned his/her existence, and that it was more good luck and/or good genes and/or where you were born as to the future success in one's life. When I had GB, I received thoughts and prayers and get-well cards galore and visits from people from many different faiths, all praying for me. These included Catholics and Protestants, Islamic and Buddhist friends, agnostics and atheists, Jews and Gentiles, Native Americans and Hindus—all convinced of the efficacy of their petitions to some sort of Allmighty. I am not sure which of their petitions worked. My Dad, whom I loved so much, prayed in his traditional way and was sure God answered his prayers. Others were not so sure, so I participated fully and gratefully in prayers of all kinds and thanked everyone for their caring and support. A friend of mine who is an MD thinks that the number of deaths and recoveries from disease for those who get prayed over is equal to the corresponding number for those who don't receive any prayers. I would note that the young boys' soccer team recently rescued from the depths of a water-filled cave in Thailand were Buddhists, and thanked the Buddha for their rescue. Could be the Buddha, or could be luck. Or it could be the well-trained members of the Thai military and the expertise of the divers who came in from around the world to help out—all very brave. As a result of all this, I think I am a Schweitzerian agnostic and polytheist with special feelings towards Jesus' *Sermon on the Mount* and his concern for poor people.

My mother was the definition of virtue and dedication to others and to the good of mankind. Yet she died early and before she had accomplished all of that which she was capable. I thought that a caring God would not allow that, but he/she did. When one is reminded about the abuse of women, child mortality, hunger, lack of medical care, and many other afflictions—all things did not and do not work together for the good for those who love the Lord and are called according to his purposes.

To be honest, I think my Dad was mad at God, which was also something he could never admit publicly in his role as a man of God. One time, I did see him in a prayerful position in the sanctuary of our church mouthing the word *why*. He went there on the night of Mom's death and said he prayed and asked *why* all night. I don't think he got an answer.

Chapter Thirty-Six

REVERENCE FOR LIFE

*F*or fifteen years—*together* with the post of Adjunct Professor of Philosophy, Latin American History, and Political Science—I held perhaps the most important position of my career: Executive Director of the Albert Schweitzer Institute at Quinnipiac University. I retain the honor of Executive Director Emeritus to this day. In many ways, this has been the culmination of my life's work. Over the years, I have been reading as much as I can on all aspects of the fascinating life, deeply-compassionate work, and profound philosophy of the 1952 Nobel Peace Prize Laureate, Dr. Albert Schweitzer. I have been communicating with those who knew him and with scholars who have chronicled his thoughts and achievements—and I have really never stopped.

The visionary leader and president of Quinnipiac University, Dr. John Lahey, was the person who brought the Albert Schweitzer Institute to campus and had the good grace to hire me. In the spirit of Schweitzer, I too tried to make my life my argument. I arrived in January 2002, welcomed by a most gracious VP for Academic Affairs, Kathleen McCourt, and we worked together to overcome some of the problems of the past and get the Schweitzer Institute on the right track. The board of directors, chaired by Dr. Lahey, gave me my marching orders, which were to promote the values of Dr. Schweitzer on a worldwide basis with special emphasis on peace, health, and human-itarian values.

It was the vision of the Albert Schweitzer Institute to play a dynamic role in introducing Dr. Schweitzer's philosophy of Reverence for Life to a global audience in order to bring about a more civil and ethical human society characterized by respect, responsibility, compas-sion, and service. This is the overriding theme by which I measured the validity of every idea and action of ASI. It is also consistent with the ideals of Quinnipiac University and behind the mutual decision to absorb the Institute into Quinnipiac.

Representing a Nobel Laureate in Albert Schweitzer gave me entree into the world of Nobel Peace Prize Laureates, especially my good friend Dr. Oscar Arias and his Executive Director (and a good friend of mine), Luis Alberto Cordero. Don Luis invited me to become involved in promoting and developing something called the Arms Trade Treaty, which was designed to take guns out of the hands of criminals and track where and to whom each shipment of arms was directed. For example—if a police department in X country employs of force of only twenty and yet has more than two hundred M-16s—where do you think those extra guns went? They fell into the hands of criminal gangs and other nefarious persons.

In 2004 don Luis invited me to attend a meeting/workshop in Costa Rica to which all Spanish-speaking Latin American countries sent high-level diplomats. The subject matter of the conference was a discussion regarding the role that Latin American governments should play in supporting or not supporting a treaty called *The Responsibility to Protect*. This treaty would come into play if and when a country could not, or would not, protect its citizens. At first, I was proud to be the only North American in attendance, but what followed turned out to be quite painful.

At one point all of the diplomats were asked to comment. One by one, they did, and the discussion took a different turn. To a person, each diplomat turned to me and said something like, *I am sorry to hurt your feelings, but what I am worried about is whether the United States would honor this treaty, given its inappropriate intervention in my country over the years.* There were many examples. This included military interventions in the Dominican Republic, Guatemala, Cuba, Mexico, and Nicaragua—and CIA interventions in almost every other country in Latin America (usually in the name of fighting communism). I knew about a lot of this history but these remarks were not coming from crazed radicals; rather, from seasoned diplomats who had checked out the facts. It flew in the face of our ideal of promoting democracy, and it seemed that each Spanish-speaking country in Latin America had a terrible story to tell. I have been critical of US foreign policy in many cases—but to have to sit there and listen to the litany of awful things the US had done contrary to our values expressed in the Declaration of Independence was deeply troubling. Some may view me as unpatriotic, but I believe that sometimes it is patriotic to criticize your country. It is not *America—love it, or leave it*, but *America—love it, and fix it*.

Back home at Quinnipiac, I decided that to just give speeches about the life and accomplishments of Albert Schweitzer would leave students and others positively bored by hearing me talk ad nauseum! And it would do little to further our mission. So I decided to create a series of profound experiences for delegations of Quinnipiac students in the developing world, as I had had in the Peace Corps—only within a much shorter time period for maximum impact. I visited León, Nicaragua through the New Haven/León Sister Cities Program and made the connections that got us in the door and into La Villa, a neighborhood where, over the years, local residents had already been housing students from North America. This proved to be an essential element of the trips that were to occur in coming years. All in all, we sent hundreds of Quinnipiac University and Rhinebeck High School students to the impoverished communities around León to build (alongside the students from Nicaragua) classrooms, cafeterias, a science lab, and other projects that the communities wanted. (We normally sent a team of leaders six months ahead of the actual construction delegations to ask the communities what kind of project they wanted us to do.) In the beginning, we called ourselves the "sweat brigades," and sweat they did—digging ditches, mixing cement, hauling lumber, and much more—under the watchful eye of Nicaraguan foremen who knew their way around construction.

Barbara contributed significantly to the success of these alterative spring-break trips due to her proficiency as an RN and EMT, her fluency in Spanish, and her background as a nurse at the Astor Home. She was a lifesaver, and when the students' parents heard of Barbara's talents, they were a lot more likely to approve of a trip to Nicaragua for a son or daughter. Our kids Taylor and Kelsey were also instrumental in the program's process, having participated several times as quasi-leaders, helping provide the continuity necessary for delegations and projects to go smoothly. They both learned Spanish quickly and were able to solve problems and misunderstandings that might occur with the host families with whom our delegations stayed. It was a real privilege for me to be able to enjoy my children throughout their college years because they were students at the university where I worked and advocates for my chosen journey. This program that Barbara, Taylor, and Kelsey helped build in Nicaragua flourished for ten years until recent political problems and the return of a dictatorship made Nicaragua unsafe again and possibly on the verge of civil war.

We also developed projects in Nicaragua for our nursing, occupational and physical therapy programs—training Nicaraguan teachers and small-business men and women. In one survey of our students we found that 91 percent of the participants in our programs felt that they had a life-changing experience. One of the main reasons for our program's success was the efforts of Oscar and Eira Aragon. With the help of the Schweitzer Institute, Oscar (a medical doctor) and Eira (a lawyer) established an English language school called Alianza

Americana, which had been one of their dreams. Alianza Americana has become one of the leading educational schools in all of Nicaragua and has helped ASI to run and organize the programs affiliated with Quinnipiac University mentioned above.

For several years we had a bus driver in Nicaragua named Sergio, who quickly became a part of the Quinnipiac family. He was a wonderful person and an even better driver—and our students loved him! While providing transportation for another QU humanitarian trip, Sergio had an accident as he was fixing the motor on his bus. He had his hands inside the motor when it accidently started up and caught his middle finger, nearly ripping it totally off. My understanding is that his finger was literally hanging by its skin. He was rushed to the hospital in León, where the surgeon told him that there were two options: to cut off Sergio's severely damaged finger and repair the area around the injury, which would be very expensive; or to cut his whole hand off just above his wrist, which would be lot cheaper. Sergio realized with horror that, if he chose the less expensive option two, he would have to give up his bus and therefore his income because he would not be able to drive or continue to fix his dilapidated bus. If he chose the first option, he would have to borrow money from a local loan shark and would be in debt forever because their interest rates are exorbitant— and Sergio only earned enough to pay the monthly interest charges, which meant that he would be in debt for the rest of his life. Two days after the accident, I heard about Sergio's problem and was appalled at the terrible choices he would have to make. With infection starting to set into Sergio's hand, I let them know I would find the money, so Sergio took out a loan ($2,000, I think). Our second-year leaders for the upcoming humanitarian trip caught wind of this and loved Sergio so much that they quickly set up a fundraising campaign. To make a long story short, my student leaders raised about $2,500 in two weeks, and I didn't have to do anything. It was a deeply moving experience for everyone when we were able to give him the money to pay off his loan, and he burst into tears. So did everyone else. But this is the way it is in most Third World countries. The rich can get appropriate health care and the poor get scraps of what they need. And even in the US, families have to make awful choices. And not that many people in the world care about about people like Sergio, I am sorry to say.

We also began programs in Guatemala through the 1992 Nobel Peace Prize Laureate, Rigoberta Menchú. She was the first indigenous person to win this prize, and she deserved it. For many years a K'iche' human rights activist, she is reviving the traditions and practices of the Mayan indigenous people, who had a more sophisticated educational system than the Europeans who conquered them.

From 1960 into the 1990s, Guatemala was afflicted by a seemingly endless civil war in which the Guatemalan army, under the leadership of brutal dictatorships, did their best to eliminate indigenous people from their native lands. In my opinion, it was genocide and thousands of people were killed for no good reason. During that period the US generally supported a sessional of dictators until a peace treaty was signed in 1996. In 1954, the CIA had intervened and overthrown a freely elected government in Guatemala once again led by the brothers Dulles, whose United Fruit holdings were threatened by the Guatemalan government, which wanted to redistribute the land to ensure that all Guatemalans had access to farmland. The land had long belonged to the oligarchy (read white people) that had controlled the area since the time of the Spanish conquistadors

Rigoberta Menchú, herself, lost her entire family in the bloodbath of the Guatamalan Civil War. After her mother and brother were kidnapped, tortured, and murdered—her father was shot and killed in the notorious burning of the Spanish Embassy. He was one of a group of indigenous leaders, the Committee for Peasant Unity, who had decided to occupy the embassy for a protest. Instead of negotiations to free these brave men, the Guatemalan army set the embassy on fire and shot them one by one as they fled the burning building.

One nearly survived but was beaten to death by the surrounding mob. Rigoberta Manchú also had other relatives massacred by the army during their purges of indigenous villages. I think she is still in danger, and I pray for her every day.

The ruins of Tikal are a must-see in Guatemala, and a feeling of peace that came over me on the central plaza as I sat contemplating the marvelous temples and structures made by indigenous people using more sophisticated building techniques than was available in Europe at the time. The Mayans invented the mathematical concept of zero and built huge pyramids with large stones, making the tolerances between stones so small that one could not get a piece of paper between them. Their Mayan calendar is quite detailed and advanced, and I am sure there are even more discoveries to be made in the years to come. But for now, I think the world lost a lot of knowledge when the Europeans eliminated a great majority of the indigenous population through disease and conflicts in the colonial era. I eagerly support Rigoberta in her efforts to revive the Mayan culture. The Mayans died off in great numbers, as did the Aztecs and the Incas—not from battle, but from the virulent diseases that the conquistadors brought with them.

In one of the most poignant moments of working in Guatemala came in the village called Flor de las Rosas, which was the home to Rigoberta Menchú's personal assistant, Aury Cuxe, perhaps the most friendly and dedicated person whom I knew in Latin America. We were in her village to set up some clinics for our occupational and physical therapy students and were about to examine patients as they came in. Two potential patients entered our classroom. One was a paraplegic who could not move his legs. He was hoping against hope that we would have a magic cure for him, but we didn't, because his spine had been severed. We gave him some exercises to strengthen his upper body, but that was all we could do.

The second boy was named Pablo, and he walked into the little clinic with the support of his aunt on one side and a cousin on the other. It was obvious that he had severe drop-foot in both feet because he had to lift his feet very high, even with the support of his relatives. Remember now, that I am the only bilingual person in the room, and I am listening to the family describe his affliction and how it occurred, and I am trying to help my OT and PT students think of what therapy could help this kid. It seems that Pablo had fallen in his bedroom and hit his head, and since that time he had trouble walking. He was eleven when he fell and he was fourteen or fifteen when we were seeing him. He had spent three weeks in the hospital, which had completely depleted the family funds—and then some! Toward the end of his examination to determine the strength of his legs and arms and body, Pablo's aunt said that one of the neurologists in the hospital thought that Pablo had Guillain-Barré syndrome. I sat in front of Pablo, stunned. I couldn't speak. He had the same disease I had had many years before. Guillain-Barré syndrome is very rare, and to have a person from the US meet a young person from a remote section of Guatemala with the exact same diagnosis was some sort of a miracle. Tears flowed freely from my eyes, which upset my students, so I told them what had happened—and *they* started crying. The Guatemalans noticed that all the gringos were crying and wanted to know what was going on, so I explained it to them—and then *they* started crying, and it turned into a big blubbery mess.

So my students went to work and designed some exercises for him and taught him how to use a walker. For the next three years or so, delegations of OTs and PTs from Quinnipiac checked on him when they came to visit and scolded him if he was not doing his exercises and gave him a cane and crutches. They made little exercise books in terms of his legs and their ability to strengthen and function as he progressed.

Finally, three years later, the same group of OTs and PTs who initially encountered Pablo came back to Guatemala to do their capstone project. As they approached Pablo, he surprised and shocked my students as he walked unaided to greet them with almost no foot-drop!

Once again everyone started crying because it doesn't get any better than this—to give the gift of walking to a young man with his life in front of him who now feels much better about himself. He told us he was back at school and sheepishly admitted that he had a girlfriend. For me, with thirty-plus years in a variety of accomplishments—it doesn't get any better than this.

I did learn that disabled people in the developing world often face discrimination and they are often confined to their homes because able-bodied persons think that the disabled person's handicap is contagious. Pablo, for example, had not left his house much, except to go to the doctor. He was made fun of at school, so he didn't want to leave home to be treated poorly by his so-called friends and neighbors.

I think that the Declaration of Human Rights should have an article on the rights of the disabled to the kind of physical and/or occupational therapy that they might need. I walk because I got the therapy I needed when I had first polio, then Guillain-Barré syndrome, and these types of therapy should be available for every disabled person no matter what problem they have, be it a loss of hearing, sight, or bodily function.

Chapter Thirty-Seven

ROUND THREE: PARKINSON'S DISEASE– CHUMBAWAMBA!

I *am facing this* now even more directly than a few years ago; I was diagnosed with Parkinson's disease. Now I try not to show it, but I was mad at God, if there is one, because I am gradually beginning to drool and lose my fine motor skills—and sometimes it is difficult to pull my zipper down to go to the bathroom or button shirt cuffs or clean myself after going to the bathroom. None of these diseases will kill you by itself, but as I grow older I may gradually lose my voice and may tremble a little more. I cannot eat soups with a spoon. Rather, I must use a mug to lift the concoction to my lips. I have had polio, post-polio syndrome (which is a return of symptoms fifteen to twenty years after my original bout), Guillain-Barré syndrome, carpel tunnel surgery, Type 2 diabetes, and now Parkinson's. Why do I have to have several major diseases, when most people get only one or two. But according to the rock group, Chumbawamba, if I get knocked down, I get up again. You are never going to keep me down. A friend of mine overheard me complaining about Parkinson's and he told me to shut up and that I could now stick a spoon into some hot cocoa and my hands would shake so much that the hot chocolate would mix itself!! I had become a *mixologist*—a very fine mixer of hot chocolate, alcoholic drinks, and other delectable potions—and could offer my services for free for anyone with a mixing problem! I had to laugh.

This why I put humorous stories in this book—so I can laugh along with the crying. Robin Williams committed suicide after being diagnosed with Parkinson's, so I know how psychologically debilitating it can be. I won't let that happen. *You are never going to keep me down…*

AFTERWORD

*A*s a high school student in the late sixties, I remember seeing the first Peace Corps volunteers come to my hometown (San Ramón) in Costa Rica. We received them with joy during some very turbulent political and historical moments in the world.

Fidel Castro and Ché Guevara had recently won the revolution in Cuba, and we celebrated their victory as they liberated Cuba from a dictator who abused of the poor in that country. Very soon we saw the shift of Cuba towards communism and an alliance with the Soviet Union. Then the Cuba missile crisis supported by Soviet Union leader Krushchev prompted President Kennedy to threaten to bomb Cuba if the Soviet missiles were not removed. I—as well as the whole world, I am sure—was never so concerned about a total disaster should an atomic war actually happen. I have never been so afraid of the destruction of the world as at that time. Now, with the danger of what we are doing to the planet, I am again as concerned as I was then.

In his book, so well remembered and narrated from his life experience in the poorest areas of Costa Rica, David Ives makes us reflect on the real causes of our conflicts and divisiveness as human beings. In many passages he makes constructive criticism about the way we handle politics, war, and self-interest. David shows us the real meaning of life and how far away from justice and fairness our society has strayed. He greatly admires his father, who was a pastor and a naval aviator during World War II. However, despite the influence of his father's patriotic beliefs, through his experience in the jungles of Costa Rica David came to realize that violence, war, and communism were not simply contagious evils; rather, they were the consequences of unfairness toward the most needy, corporate greed, and the inhumane legacy of colonization. Equally responsible were the political and private business interests of his own country, the United States, and its interference in the affairs of the so-called developing countries of Latin America. With great respect for his father, David questions US interventions in many of these countries and criticizes how disrespectful American policies and and politicians were of the United States Constitution written by the forefathers of their nation. From his own letters to his father from the Peace Corps in Costa Rica in the 1980s, to his interspersed author's notes written today—David examines the past and present role of the US in Latin America, elsewhere, and at home. He proudly explains that he loves his country but challenges everyone who says, "love America, or leave it." Instead he says "love America, and fix it."

David's memoir brings alive the remote places where he did his work as a Peace Corps volunteer in Costa Rica. He lived among the poorest of the poor. What is most remarkable in reading his letters and accounts is that he became one of them. The gringo who people in the village thought was CIA was actually the greatest ally of their poor and weak. He endured the toughest living conditions in the rural communities of Costa Rica. David's passion for living and his strength in enduring all kinds of difficult health problems in his youth and later in life came from his mother. As a young child he had polio, and the doctors told his mother he would never be able to walk without crutches or braces. His mother didn't tell him, but kept exercising him and never gave up. Not only was he eventually able to walk on his own, but he was also able to play American football and become a wrestling champion in high school. He acknowledges his total recuperation to his mother. Sadly, she was later killed in an accident with a drunk driver. As you read the book, you will understand how much he suffered and still does by the unexpected early loss of the person he loved most and who meant so much in his life.

While a Peace Corps volunteer David performed his job with great professionalism. He understood that the reason he came to Costa Rica was to help the people and learn from them. He also recognized the contradiction in the reality that some of the help the US claims was actually in favor of the people to be helped—yet some of it was simply a way to conquer and benefit from the assisted country and its people. His dedication and understanding of the challenges of the people he lived with is clearly shown by the letters he writes to his family and his personal reflections in this book. His experience in Costa Rica helped him better understand what is important in life and how unfair the world can be to those who have little. He also learned that happiness is not about how much you have, but how well you are able to cope with the difficulties life presents to you. He saw what pain is, how hungry people can be, how unfortunate some people are without medical care, how difficult it is to survive without studies—and at the same time how happy you can be with very little if you are surrounded by love.

After his service as a Peace Corps volunteer, David worked with organizations like the Rotary International and the Albert Schweitzer Institute, for which he has been closely involved with the peace process in many countries. He has been nominated for the Nobel Peace Prize, and for many years his life has been dedicated to bringing peace to the world in almost all continents. He is currently an active member of the Nobel Peace Prize organization.

In later years, David was diagnosed with Guillain-Barré syndrome, which almost took his life, and more recently he was diagnosed with Parkinson's disease. In spite of these illnesses, he has never given up his cheerful way of looking at life. Most amazing is how he continues to advocate for uniting the world through love and understanding and fighting the injustices we continue to encounter in our society today. This book is a critically important attempt to deliver his message and teachings on how we can learn to live together in harmony and respect.

I am sure that if President Kennedy were alive today, this story about David Ives as a Peace Corps volunteer would make him proud and would probably make him say that everything he dreamed about the Peace Corps Program was worth it. This book is a must-read for all. If we follow David's life example and his commitment to make a difference in the world, that world will be a much better one.

Jose Zaglul, PhD
Founding President of EARTH University/Costa Rica,
Member of the Board of Directors of the American University
of Beirut, Lebanon, Member of the Board of Directors of
Ad Astra Rocket Company

A DAY OF UNITY, PEACE AND PRAYER

L *ast year I was* asked by the human rights organization, Unity Peace Prayer, to be one of their keynote speakers at their annual global peace and unity rally in Washington, DC, co-sponsored by the Albert Schweitzer Institute. Standing before the Lincoln Memorial on the National Mall on September 2, 2018, I gave the following speech:

I am greatly honored to be one of the keynote speakers at this wonderful event. I have been asked to explore thoughts and ideas to help move this country—and indeed this world—toward peace when we are so divided in so many important ways.

I need to give you a word of warning. I am in the midst of a battle with Parkinson's disease. Sometimes I slur some words. I assure you I have not been drinking. Rather, in my passion for peace and understanding my tongue does not always keep up with my brain. But the good side is that when I put my spoon in a cup of hot chocolate, my hand mixes the drink itself. I am a "mixologist," and I am available to mix drinks at any party that needs my professional services.

I have wanted to talk about some important thoughts and stories before I literally lose the ability to speak, which is a possible consequence for anyone with Parkinson's. But, hopefully, that will occur somewhere farther down the line. I am privileged to live in the Hudson Valley, near the home of Franklin and Eleanor Roosevelt. During the Second World War, Eleanor Roosevelt spoke or wrote many times about a variety of issues. However, the quote from Eleanor Roosevelt that I find helps me enormously when I get discouraged—and perhaps will help you is the following: "Surely, in the light of history, it is more intelligent to hope, rather than to fear, to try better, than not to try. For one thing we know beyond all doubt: Nothing has ever been achieved by the person who says, 'It can't be done.'"[1]

So now let's try together.

Albert Schweitzer was someone who agreed with Eleanor Roosevelt. He won the 1952 Nobel Peace Prize. It has been my honor to promote his values and ideas on a worldwide basis for the past sixteen years as Executive Director of the Albert Schweitzer Institute at Quinnipiac University, and as an Adjunct Professor of Latin American Culture, Political Science, and International Relations.

Schweitzer was regarded by most people around the world as one of the greatest persons of the twentieth century. He took an unusual path to fame, becoming world famous for his humanity by caring for—and about—others.

Dr. Schweitzer was one of the first—if not the first—European to go to Africa with the intent of alleviating suffering, not exploiting its vast resources or making slaves of its people.

Although he went under the auspices of a French society of missionaries, he did not go to proselytize, or convert Africans to a Christian perspective. He went to alleviate suffering. I find this very unusual for our times, and even more so for the times he lived in.

Dr. Schweitzer continued examining new ideas and philosophies throughout his life. He became interested in many different religions

---

[1] Eleanor Roosevelt, *You Learn by Living: Eleven Keys to a More Fulfilling Life* (New York: Harper Brothers, 1960), 168.

and he wrote about the Eastern religions in a comparative fashion. He, nevertheless, maintained throughout his life a strong affinity for Christianity and its philosophy of love.

He also showed great concern for the environment, often writing on the interconnection between all living things. Indeed, the first book that took a really serious look at the degradation of the environment—*Silent Spring*, by Rachel Carson—was dedicated to Schweitzer.

Nevertheless, Schweitzer felt that his greatest contribution to the world was not his work as a doctor, a theologian, a humanitarian, or a musician—but his philosophy of *Ehrfurcht vor dem Leben* or *Reverence for Life*. He wrote: "The most immediate fact of man's consciousness is the assertion *I am life that wills to live in the midst of life that wills to live*."[2]

What he wrote included plant and animal life. He felt that all options should be carefully considered before any life--of any kind-- was taken. If this philosophy were applied to the world today, it would result in different decisions being made about how people and the environment are treated. He was not, however, a complete Pacifist. He recognized there was such a thing as evil in the world and sometimes that evil had to be stopped and/or eliminated. He also knew that people had to eat, and that involved plants and animals and their deaths.

I was on the Navajo reservation some years ago, and a medicine-woman invited me to her house for lunch. We went to her garden to get some lettuce for a salad. As she bent to cut each lettuce leaf, she prayed to the plant people and apologized for taking its life in order to sustain her own. It's that kind of reverence that Schweitzer is talking about.

I understand that the word *ehrfurcht*, in German, is translated as the word *awe* in English. The word awesome is overused by many who speak in English, using awesome to talk about anything that they feel is the least bit remarkable. But I think Schweitzer meant for us to dig a little deeper and look at each other with a sense of awe *and*

---

[2] Albert Schweitzer, *Reverence for Life: The Words of Albert Schweitzer* (San Francisco: Harper, 1993) 105.

wonder—so that when we behold another person for the first time, we will have a feeling of amazement that this person standing in front of us actually exists.

Schweitzer wanted us to have a sensation towards another person that would be like the feeling of exhilaration we all get when we are on top of a mountain contemplating and drinking in the incredible view in front of us.

Or the feeling of astonishment we get when we watch a powerful thunderstorm in the distance. Listening to the lightning. Hearing the rolling thunder, I think we all become awestruck.

Schweitzer thought that each person you may interact with for any reason should be regarded as a miracle and one who deserves all the love and help you can give to this phenomenal being with whom you are interacting.

To have this perspective, this sense of astonishment, should make it very hard to kill or hurt or hate anyone. It should make it very hard to separate children at our border from their parents. It should make it very hard to ignore the poverty that people live in around the world that causes the violence that inevitably occurs when people cannot find a job or feed and clothe their families. It should make it easy to understand that refugees do not leave their homes or their countries unless there is a threat to their existence that is dire.

If each and every person in the world is viewed as a miracle, then the first thing to do is to hug them and to tell them they are safe now. And to ask them "How can I help you?" Young people in this country, and indeed around the world, are hurting because too many of them have not been treated as if they were a miracle, either.

So steps one, two and three: To treat everyone as if they are a miracle.

In my own country, I am embarrassed by the wall that is slowly being built along our border with Mexico—the wall from San Diego (in the west) to Brownsville, Texas—in order to make certain that our neighbors in the south will remain in their place in poverty. And by the way, Mexico is not going to finance any part of the wall.

We should take one-third of this money and use it to build schools and medical clinics. And also use it to train teachers and doctors and nurses! Then we should use the ideas of Nobel Peace Prize Laureate Muhammad Yunus and of the Grameen Bank to fund small-business loans and to fund them most specifically to women, since they are often more responsible in using their money wisely and benefitting their families. Small-business loans given to a group of women have historically had over a 95% repayment rate, and it is well documented that Dr. Yunus' ideas work.

Several years ago I made two visits to Central America. One trip was to Guatemala during the summer to work with the Rigoberta Menchú Foundation. We went to build classrooms for her Mayan people. Then we went to Nicaragua to work on building classrooms there, as well.

This incredible fence the US is building will keep out many of the people whom we met in both countries. Think of it. These people who are working for a dollar a day, if that. Some of them are reduced to making hamburgers out of a combination of clay and soil to eat in their tortillas.

One of the teachers we worked with asked me, plaintively, if I could help her find a job in the United States, as she only made four dollars a day, even with her university degree. This meant that she had to choose whether to buy black plastic to cover the holes in her walls and roof, or to feed her children.

Right now, laborers in our country and many others in the so-called "First World" countries are often exploited and disposable because they are poor. But even more so because they are viewed as different, or as the dangerous other.

I am sad about what happened to the young woman from Iowa recently. She was killed by a so-called illegal Mexican immigrant with emphasis on the word illegal. First of all, there is no such thing as an illegal human being, and I would point out that North Americans have committed many crimes while visiting countries in Central America.

However, a strong belief in Schweitzer's system of ethics would prevent people from being perceived as disposable. Instead, they would be *welcomed* into the United States. Or they would be helped to live in their own country with dignity. Instead of building the wall along our border, we should tear down that wall! Let us use the money, instead, to work together with our Latin American brothers and sisters to provide roads, schools, clinics, and anything else that can provide everyone with a way of life full of pride and honor in oneself. We can create customers for our businesses instead of refugees.

In Guatemala, I came face-to-face with the second-class citizenship that many Mayans endure in their indigenous communities. As my students and I entered the village where we were to build a classroom for their school, we first had to go to a town meeting to which every resident was invited. We had to assure them, with the help of representatives from the Rigoberta Menchú Foundation, that we were not there to kidnap their children, nor were we there to take minerals from their sacred mountains. Only then were we allowed to live and work in their community.

The Mayan people have had too many negative and exploitive interactions with North Americans who looked like me, who had taken advantage of them to the detriment of their way of life, their pride, and their self-esteem.

Our students lived with Mayan families, many of whom had never before had intimate contact with North Americans. At first, my students were treated with suspicion. But within a day both the Mayan families and my students—some of whom are in this audience—were sharing with each other as equals! The Mayans taught my students their language, and my students taught them English, using rudimentary Spanish. There was a celebration of sorts occurring in a dimly lit,

mud-brick home that transcended boundaries and enabled us to connect as equals through some magic of shared experiences and the wonder of a different culture. Hence, the students began to understand the
causes of poverty—*not* by spending their time on a big tourist bus that
drives by people in their shacks; rather, by engaging people as equals.

What I have learned is that many people do not give a damn about
the poverty in the world. How can they make a difference if they do
not care. It is a lack of political will to change what causes the poverty
I have seen throughout my life in around fifty-plus countries. There
was and is no excuse for it.

Do any of you remember any candidate for public office anywhere
in this country who spoke about the needs of poor people anywhere
in the world in the last election. I do not care whether the poverty to
combat is here or abroad. Poor people need our attention. Otherwise
expect violence and/or more caravans of refugees.

And we should become activists and keep on keeping on—bringing these conditions to the attention of governments, churches and
synagogues, nonprofit organizations, and many more. One can argue
that it is hard to tear down these walls between cultures, religions, and
ethnic groups. Many times, it is. But often, if one can learn to celebrate
differences instead of letting our differences divide us, these walls can
melt away. If we have reverence and awe for one another, as Schweitzer
suggested, perhaps some of these walls can be torn down.

I have been lucky enough to have met and worked with several
Nobel Peace Prize Laureates. If you are looking for people who are
performing miracles with limited resources, take a look at some of the
women who are Nobel Peace Prize Laureates.

One is Iranian. Her name is Shirin Ebadi. She was the first female
judge in Iran. She co-founded the Defenders of Human Rights Center
in Iran in 2001. She has defended journalists who have been arrested
and imprisoned for what they wrote. She has also been a leader in

promoting gender issues. She lives under death threat. Helping her would help a lot of women to survive.

Another very engaged female Laureate is from Yemen. Her name is Tawakkol Karman. She is a journalist. She won the Nobel Peace Prize for her non-violent struggle for the safety of women, for women's rights, for democracy in her country, and for peace-building work. She founded Women Journalists Without Chains, which reports on violations of freedom of the press.

Yet another dynamic Nobel Peace Prize Laureate is Leymah Gbowee from Liberia. She and a group of Christian and Muslim women were instrumental in overthrowing a brutal dictator named Charles Taylor. You should check her out on *Ted Talks*. She is a dynamic leader and one that we all should recognize as a very talented person. She runs a camp every summer to which she invites young people from different ethnic groups in Liberia—most with a history of enmity between them—and teaches them to live in peace. The camp costs between forty and fifty thousand dollars to run annually. Each year Leymah struggles to raise the money to open it. Investing in this camp could help save a country. It is a model to be used throughout the world to support diversity and to heal our wounds.

There is Betty Williams, who won the Nobel Peace Prize in 1976 (awarded in 1977) along with Mairead Corrigan. Betty has a special place in her heart for children. She has been working in Italy, to build homes for all those refugees and their families who are coming across the Mediterranean to escape death at home in the Middle East and Africa. She could use some help to create apartments so the refugees can live in dignity, so they can live without fear of reprisal from death squads, and so that they can have an education.

One of the finest moments in my life occurred when Betty invited me to Athens, Greece for a fundraising concert with famed Greek tenor Mario Frangoulis for Betty's work providing homes for refugee families fleeing from violence in their home countries in the Middle

East and North Africa. The concert was held in an ancient Greek amphitheater that seated three thousand people, which had perfect acoustics without a sound system. The theater oozed Greek history and culture. Mario gave a tremendous concert and then asked Betty to come onstage and describe her work to the audience. Then, to my surprise Betty invited me onstage to desribe my work and my support for Betty's work. When I came out onstage I was struck by the vision I had of the Pantheon off to my right about a half-mile away on some sort of bluff bathed in the light of several search lights. It was beautiful, and I almost couldn't speak in this magnificent setting—and how the hell could someone from a small town in Ohio actually be in this stunning place with a Nobel Peace Prize Laureate, a great singer, and little old me. I did speak and was coherent, I think, but the feeling of absolute wonder gave me goose pimples at the time, as I basked in the historical ambience of the Pantheon and the amphitheater.

And Jody Williams. She is as dynamic as they come. She won the Nobel Peace Prize for her work to eliminate land mines. With five other women Laureates she cofounded a group called the Nobel Women's Initiative, which coordinates efforts among the Laureates to increase the visibility of women working for peace. Why, in the current negotiations between North Korea and the United States, are women not included in the negotiating team? They certainly should be.

Oscar Arias, the two-time former president of Costa Rica and Nobel Prize Laureate, wants to build a museum—a museum filled with the people who worked tirelessly, without stopping, for peace. Too often, our museums are about who wins a war and the battles that lead up to it. Our museums chronicle something awful that happened, like the atomic bomb explosions in Hiroshima and Nagasaki, or places like Auschwitz, battlefields like Verdun—all deserving of the attention they get for the horrific events that happened at these spots and many more. Why can we not have at least one museum that emphasizes efforts towards peace?

Rigoberta Menchú has run for president of Guatemala twice, and has founded her own political party. She runs in order to be a part of her Mayan people. She hopes that, down the line, the Mayan people can celebrate their heritage and that more Mayans will run for political positions. And when they are in the majority they will take back their country.

Many people do not realize that Jimmy Carter, through the Carter Center, has been instrumental in eliminating two dread diseases in the world. One disease is river blindness (caused by black flies), which if not controlled causes permanent blindness. The second (Drancunculiasis—GWD) is caused by the Guinea-worm. It rests inside one's body for several months and then a worm that has grown exits through skin and is very painful. Most people do not know of President Carter's efforts to eradicate disease, but these two diseases are well on their way to eradication.

The Carter Center is also heavily involved in promoting democracy around the world. It often provides election monitors to observe elections in order to prevent corruption, to avoid stuffing ballot boxes, and to clarify intimidation of voters of any party involved in an election. President Carter is one of my heroes. He is a remarkable man.

I am inspired by the Dalai Lama. He feels that his most important concern is meeting with the public. That is because his primary commitment, his major interest, is the promotion of human value, human affection, compassion, and religious harmony. As he says so often, his philosophy is his kindness.

Michelle Obama has said that right now, when we're hearing so much disturbing and hateful rhetoric, it is so important to remember that our diversity has been—and always will be—our greatest source of strength and pride here in the United States.

Miracles don't have to be big. In a small village in Guatemala called Joya de Las Flores, I helped our occupational therapy and physical therapy students set up a clinic for people with disabilities in our school's classroom. One particular boy, Pablo, caught my eye as he arrived at the clinic. He was being helped by his mother on one side and by his aunt on the other. It was obvious that he had severe drop-foot in both feet, and it turned out that three years before, when he was only eleven years old, he had gotten out of bed and fallen on the floor.

We thought he had hurt his head, but it turned out after much discussion that he was diagnosed with a disease called Guillain-Barré syndrome. GB was the same disease I had gotten over twenty years before—a disease that had turned me into a temporary quadriplegic. This disease is very rare. So here I was, in a small town in Guatemala, and I had made contact with the only person for miles around, perhaps in the whole country, who had the same disease that I had had. I had tears in my eyes and I could hardly speak. Finally, I told my students why. And we all cried. I then had to tell Pablo's family why all the gringos were crying, and then *they* started crying too. We were able to get him some crutches and a walker. Our students made him an exercise book. We checked on him over the next three years. Of course, we scolded him if he wasn't doing his exercises. After three years were up, we saw him again. He walked out of his house without any support and greeted us. We had given him the gift of walking—and now Pablo was back in school, had a girl friend, and was a member of society again. This small miracle doesn't get any better than that!

However, any discussion of poverty and Schweitzer had to mention the threat of nuclear weapons, which was very important to him, and will take a major miracle to solve. Now the US is actually thinking about modernizing our nuclear bombs so they explode better! We already have enough to destroy the world. Why do we need more? The money for this expenditure will come directly from the poor, from global warming efforts, from education, and from health care.

With the inflammatory rhetoric that characterizes the current impasse over the possible development of nuclear weapons in Iran, most people seem to have forgotten the lessons of Dr. Schweitzer—and, for that matter, Schweitzer's friend and contemporary, Albert Einstein, the father of the atomic bomb. Both men believed that an explosion of nuclear weapons anywhere in the world would be an unmitigated physical and moral catastrophe.

It would therefore be of immense importance if the United States in this hour of destiny could decide in favor of renouncing atomic weapons, to remove the possibility of an eventual outbreak of atomic war. The theory of peace through terrifying an opponent by a greater armament can only heighten the danger of war.

Schweitzer's words still resonate. "The awareness that we are all human beings together has become lost in war and through politics. We have reached the point of regarding each other only as members of people either allied with us or against us and our approach—prejudice, sympathy, or antipathy—are all conditioned by that. Now we must rediscover the fact that we altogether are human beings, and that we must strive to concede to each other what moral capacity we have. Only in this way can we begin to believe that in other peoples as well as in ourselves there will arise the need for a new spirit which can be the beginning of a feeling of mutual trustworthiness toward each other." We ignore Schweitzer's warnings at our own peril.

Therefore I call for a gradual reduction of nuclear weapons on all sides until we have none left.

For the men and women who hold the fate of nations in their hands and avoid with anxious care any actions that may worsen the situation in which we find ourselves, and by so doing make it even more dangerous, we should tell them this: please, may they take to heart the words of the Apostle Paul, "So far as it lies in your power, be at peace with all men."

And now I will close with the words of Martin Luther King Jr.: "Our lives begin to end the day we become silent about things that matter!" And *I repeat*—"I say that our lives begin to end the day we become silent about the things that matter!"[3]

So let us not be silent. Let us believe and make miracles large and small—and may we be in awe of all people, may we forgive each other, and may we truly celebrate the richness of difference.

---

[3] Martin Luther King Jr., *I Have a Dream: Writings and Speeches that Changed the World,* ed. James Melvin Washington, (New York: HarperOne, 2003).

Appendix 2

SUGGESTED READING

Agee, Philip. *Inside the Company, A CIA Diary.* New York: Farrar Straus & Giroux, 1975.

Carson, Rachel. *Silent Spring.* New York: Houghton Mifflin, 1962.

Galeano, Eduardo. *Open Veins of Latin America: Five Centuries of the Pillage of a Continent.* Translated by Cedric Belgrage. New York: Monthly Review/English language edition, 1973.

Halberstam, David. *The Best and the Brightest.* New York: Ballantine Books, 1993.

King, Martin Luther, Jr. *I Have a Dream: Writings and Speeches that Changed the World.* Edited by James Melvin Washington. New York: HarperOne, 2003.

Kinzer, Stephen. *The Brothers: John Foster Dulles, Allen Dulles, and Their Secret World War* New York: Times Books/Macmillan, 2013.

Maclear, Michael. *The Ten Thousand Day War: Vietnam 1945–1975.* New York: St. Martin's Press, 1981.

Mandela, Nelson. *Long Walk to Freedom: The Autobiography of Nelson Mandela.* New York: Little, Brown, 2008.

Mao Tse-Tung. *Quotations from Chairman Mao Tse-Tung.* Independently published, 2018.

Marchetti, Victor and John D. Marks. *The CIA and the Cult of Intelligence.* New York: Dell, 1980.

Smith, Hedrick. *The Russians.* New York: Ballantine Books, 1984.

de Soto, Hernando. *The Other Path: The Economic Answer to Terrorism.* New York: Harper & Row, 1989.

Tannenbaum, Frank. *Ten Keys to Latin America.* New York: Vintage, 1966.

Timerman, Jacobo. *Prisoner Without a Name, Cell Without a Number.* Translated by Toby

Talbot. Madison, WI: University of Wisconsin Press, 2002.

ACKNOWLEDGMENTS

I am deeply grateful for my wife Barbara's many wise comments and sharp perspectives during my process of writing this book. She, too, was a Peace Corps volunteer and was the first to suggest that I remember my experiences in print.

To one of my best friends in the world, Brian McAree, who inspires me and many others with his personal fight against spinal muscular atrophy—never giving up.

To the people of Pierpont, Ohio and my father Reverend Lee Ives, who ministered to them for some thirty years.

To Ruth Anne Hoover, my Dad's longtime church secretary, who typed up a mimeograph of all of my letters home from the Peace Corps and sent them to my friends.

I am very pleased and most grateful for the work of editor Dory Mayo and the efforts, encouragement and support of publisher Paul Cohen of Epigraph Publishing Service (Rhinebeck, NY.) Without the vast experience and knowledge of these two professionals, this book would never have happened. I appreciate their patience with me as a first-time author, which helped immensely toward developing this work.

I also want to thank Roselee Blooston for her expert initial assistance, which helped me find the promise that this endeavor held for a unique book and story.

Special thanks also go to the following, for their encouragement and editorial assistance:

Larry Adamkiewicz, Oscar and Eira Aragon, Carolyn Bernitt, Anat Biletzki, Damian Brennan, Crystal Brian, Michael Chapin, Luis Alberto Cordero, Aury Cuxe, Viktoria Devdariani, Monica Deignan, Mario Doreste, Maria Dosso, Sean Duffy, Michael Eilbaum, Michael Frazier, Maureen Gates, Jerry Goldstein, Steve Gustafson, Rebecca Holt, Carol Hughes, Cathy Ives, Don Ives, Marcia Ives, Peter Ives, Julie Linton, Rob Linton, Livia Malcangio, Jill Martin, Jay and Nancy McCleary, Signian McGeary, Connie McKay, David McKay, Lois Wright Merton, Ivania Montero, Jeff Newman, Benjamin Page, David Ping, Greg Rakow, Constantino Reyes, Jeff Scales, Bill Schaefer, David Steward, John Thomas, Lou Trapani, Cristopher Tsagaris, Louis Turpin, Renee Tursi, Celeste Valentino, Louis Venturelli, Sujata Gadkar Wilcox, and Ekatarina Zagladina.

CPSIA information can be obtained
at www.ICGtesting.com
Printed in the USA
LVHW040805040820
662297LV00002B/82